/PARENT COLLECTION/

OCT 30 2015
Ø 9:23

Telling the Truth to Your Adopted or Foster Child

Telling the Truth to Your Adopted or Foster Child

Making Sense of the Past

Second Edition

Betsy Keefer Smalley and Jayne E. Schooler

An Imprint of ABC-CLIO, LLC
Santa Barbara, California • Denver, Colorado

Copyright © 2015 by Betsy Keefer Smalley and Jayne E. Schooler

All rights reserved. No part of this publication may be reproduced, stored in a retrieval system, or transmitted, in any form or by any means, electronic, mechanical, photocopying, recording, or otherwise, except for the inclusion of brief quotations in a review, without prior permission in writing from the publisher.

Library of Congress Cataloging-in-Publication Data

Smalley, Betsy Keefer, 1949–
Telling the truth to your adopted or foster child : making sense of the past / Betsy Keefer Smalley and Jayne E. Schooler. — Second edition.
pages cm
Includes bibliographical references.
ISBN 978-1-4408-3404-2 (print : alk. paper) — ISBN 978-1-4408-3405-9 (e-book) —
ISBN 978-1-4408-4281-8 (paperback) 1. Adoption—United States—Psychological aspects. 2. Adopted children—United States—Psychology. 3. Foster children—United States—Psychology. 4. Secrecy—Psychological aspects. 5. Communication in families—United States. 6. Disclosure of information—United States. I. Schooler, Jayne E. II. Title.
HV875.55.K45 2015
649'.145—dc23 2015022619

ISBN: 978-1-4408-3404-2
EISBN: 978-1-4408-3405-9
Paperback ISBN: 978-1-4408-4281-8

19 18 17 16 15 1 2 3 4 5

This book is also available on the World Wide Web as an eBook.
Visit www.abc-clio.com for details.

Praeger
An Imprint of ABC-CLIO, LLC

ABC-CLIO, LLC
130 Cremona Drive, P.O. Box 1911
Santa Barbara, California 93116-1911

This book is printed on acid-free paper ∞
Manufactured in the United States of America

This second edition of
Telling the Truth to Your Adopted or Foster Child: Making Sense of the Past
is dedicated to our favorite truth tellers,
our grandchildren.

Betsy's grandchildren:
William Matyas, Griffin Keefer, and Evelyn Keefer

Jayne's grandchildren:
Micah, Annalise, and Aaron Matheson
and Lacey Jayne Schooler

Contents

Preface ix

Acknowledgments xiii

1 The Power of Secrets on Family Relationships 1

2 Truth or Consequences: A Great Debate 15

3 Just the Facts, Ma'am: Why Do Children Need Them? 29

4 Learning about Your Child: A Fact-Finding Mission 43

5 Adoption Through a Child's Eyes: Developmental Stage 59

6 Through a Parent's Eyes: The Challenges in Creating an Environment of Ongoing Adoption Communication 81

7 Principles of Talking about Adoption 97

8 Sharing the Hard Stuff: The Adoptive Parent's Challenge 111

9 Twelve Tools of Parent/Child Communication 131

10 Transracial or Transcultural Adoption: Talking about Adoption and Race 155

11 Kinship Foster Care and Adoption: Telling the Truth When It's "All in the Family" 177

12 Adolescence: Parents Matter—Keeping Lines of Communication Open 191

13 Managing Communication with Openness in Adoption: Questions Most Asked by Parents 211

14 Communication about Adoption Outside the Family 233

Appendix A: Information Needed to Prepare a Case for Adoption 251

Appendix B: Triggers for Adoption Issues 255

Appendix C: Lifebooks—They Are Effective for Children in Understanding Their Story 257

Notes 263

Index 275

Preface

You shall know the truth, and the truth shall make you free!

What would it be like if you were Laurie? Laurie, now 17, was adopted at age three. One afternoon at a family reunion, she sat dumbfounded as her cousin told her what really happened in her past: her birth father killed her birth mother, and he was in prison. The problem was that everyone in the family knew it except Laurie. Why wasn't she told the truth?

What would it be like if you were Sarah? Sarah, age 11, often drew pictures of the house where she imagined her birth mother lived. It was a large house, encircled with beautiful trees and flowers. One day she announced to her adoptive parents, "Someday, I am going to visit my birth mother in her big house." The problem with that picture was that Sarah's mother did live in a "big" house: she lived in a prison. She was convicted of drug possession and assault and would be incarcerated for a very long time. Why wasn't Sarah told the truth?

What would it be like if you were Jason? Jason, age 8, knew he was "given up" for adoption, but he didn't know why. The truth was, his birth mother loved him very much, but as a young teen she was unequipped to raise Jason to adulthood. Jason's adoptive parents knew the whole story, but they assumed that the less said, the better—for everyone. The only problem was that Jason was left believing there was something "wrong" with him, that he had been unlovable from birth. Why didn't his adoptive parents realize the complex feelings their son was battling?

From a historical perspective, adoption loomed under the cloak of secrecy for decades. Adoption practitioners believed it would be best to create a new world for all those involved in the adoption circumstance. This world would be a place in which adoptees were told to forget the past, as though it did not exist. Adoptive parents were told to create a new reality, given freedom to exist in total anonymity. And birth parents were shoved aside and told to erase the grief and loss of their birth children from their memories. Many individuals who grew up as adopted or foster children during those decades felt that they were reared under the shadow of secrecy, silence, and shame. It proved difficult for them to build their identities and feel secure when key aspects of their pasts were unknown, unimaginable, and even frightening. Many felt like walking time bombs because no one gave them words to explain the traumatic events that had happened to them.

One of the most important tasks for a competent, compassionate adoptive/foster parent is to help a child grow in understanding of his life narrative. Although some adoptions occur because the birth parents were simply not emotionally or financially able to care for their child, a much larger majority happen because of traumatic or difficult life circumstances. Because of that connection to troublesome experiences, adoptive and foster parents have a crucial responsibility to communicate the circumstances of their child's past in a manner that will lead to understanding, resolution, and healing. Many parents feel they lack the knowledge and skill to deal with this unique parenting challenge.

Telling the Truth to Your Adopted or Foster Child was originally published in 2000. Our desire then was to equip parents with the knowledge and tools they will need for a lifetime as they communicate with their adopted or foster child about the complex, troubling, and often painful aspects of the past. Since that time, our commitment to help families with this challenging task has intensified. We have grown in our understanding of the depth of traumatic wounding. We recognize at a far deeper level what happens to a child who is never given the opportunity to process those horrific circumstances. Without the opportunity to bring those aspects of a fragmented past to light, a child is sentenced to journeying alone. It is for this reason we have undertaken the update of *Telling the Truth to Your Adopted or Foster Child*. No child should journey alone carrying a painful past into an uncertain future.

Telling the Truth is designed to meet the informational and practical needs of the following groups:

1. Adoptive parents of infants, adopted domestically and internationally
2. Adoptive parents of special needs/older children

3. Foster parents
4. Adoption professionals who work with and educate adoptive or foster parents
5. Mental health professionals who work with adopted or foster children
6. School teachers and counselors who have adopted or foster children within their population (which is in every school, in every city, in every state in the United States)

Telling the Truth to Your Adopted or Foster Child can be used as a topic resource for foster and/or adoptive parent pre-adoption groups or post-adoption support groups.

Adopted persons who are now adults have taught us important things:

- Secret-keeping is damaging and divisive.
- Deception creates family mistrust and shame.
- Hiding the truth destroys family intimacy and security.
- Open, honest, sensitive communication about adoption and the past builds the gateway to healthy individual adjustment and family life.

Acknowledgments

It takes a team to write a book. We were fortunate to receive a great deal of help and support in compiling the information contained in this book. We would like to thank ABC-CLIO and editor Debbie Carvalko for this opportunity to update this book. It is a desire we both have had for quite a while, and we so appreciate the opportunity to do it.

We would also like to extend thanks to Corinne K. Matyas for her capable and professional editing through the rough draft stages of the original manuscript.

Many individuals paved the way for this work by their leadership in the areas of child welfare and adoption. Authors and experts we wish to thank include Dr. Ronald C. Hughes and Dr. Judith S. Rycus (authors of the *Field Guide to Child Welfare*), Sharon Kaplan Roszia (co-author of *The Open Adoption Experience*), the late Greg Keck (author of *Adopting the Hurt Child*), Vera Fahlberg (author of *A Child's Journey Through Placement*), Dr. Susan Smith (author of *Promoting Successful Adoptions: Practice with Troubled Families),* and Beth Hall and Gail Steinberg (authors of *An Insider's Guide to Transracial Adoption*).

Other experts whose work informed this manuscript include Dr. Denise Goodman, Dee Paddock, Susan Cox, Beth Brindo, Jane Nast, and Susan Peleg, and Dr. Randolph Severson.

We would like to call particular attention to the outstanding work of PACT Press (publisher of *An Insider's Guide to Transracial Adoption*) and the Parenthesis Post Adoption Program in pioneering many of the materials and concepts used in this book.

Several exceptional adoptive families or adopted individuals shared their stories with us so that other families might benefit from their wisdom. Norma and Anne Ginther, the Erickson family, the Taggart family, and Dan and Theresa Balsbaugh, the Barr family, and Kevin Hoffman were especially helpful in lending their time and years of experience to inform a new generation of adoptive families.

When we needed some aspects of this project illustrated for us, good friends, Jack A. Kammer and his daughter, Kristi Kammer Reese, offered their time and talents.

We also wish to thank our colleagues and curriculum writers in the Ohio Child Welfare Training Program. Their assistance greatly enhanced the quality of the information presented in this book.

Finally, we wish to thank our families for their support, encouragement, and perseverance as this project was completed.

CHAPTER 1

The Power of Secrets on Family Relationships

I know that sometimes a lie is used in kindness. I don't believe that it ever works kindly. The quick pain of truth can pass away, but the slow, eating agony of a lie is never lost. It becomes a running sore.

from *East of Eden* by John Steinbeck

Laurie, a tall, beautiful adolescent with a gregarious personality, dark curly hair, and a winsome smile, always celebrated her birthday at the family reunion. This year, now her fifteenth birthday, would be no different. The entire clan was there. However, right after the usual rite of birthday songs and presents, a casual conversation with a cousin forever changed Laurie's perception of who she was and how she came to be with her family.

Laurie had always known she was adopted. She knew the story inside and out. When she was barely two years old, Laurie came to her family as a foster child. She had been told that her mother died of natural causes; her distraught father could not care for her, left her with a friend, and took off. They didn't even know his name.

That afternoon after the celebration had quieted down, she and her cousin went to the pool. Laurie sat dumbfounded as her cousin told her what her mother had just told her—the truth about Laurie's birth family.

Her mother had not died of natural causes. Her father hadn't just disappeared. What really happened in her past? Both her parents had abused drugs and alcohol. Her mother died of a drug overdose. Her father was still alive but imprisoned for a long time due to a murder conviction. They knew who and where he was. The problem was that everyone in the family knew it . . . everyone except Laurie.

After Laurie and her family returned home from the reunion, Laurie began to change. She distanced herself from her parents. She challenged their every word. Her parents called it her rebellious stage. Laurie had always had a lot of friends, and her school performance had been excellent. Both began to deteriorate. She started cutting classes and running with the wrong crowd. When she was at home she was increasingly moody and sullen. Her angry outbursts frustrated her parents. Were her parents the problem? Was school the problem? Were her friends the problem? No—the keeping of a powerful secret did the damage. Why wasn't she told the truth? Family secrets . . . haunting words that evoke unsettling memories, disturbing thoughts and uncomfortable feelings. A family secret . . . something that hides in almost every family cedar chest . . . information that is banished to a darkened attic, buried under dust and cobwebs, hoping to remain forever under lock and key. What do family members keep from one another? Why do families keep secrets? What impact does secrecy have on family relationships and the person from whom the secret was kept? Why has secrecy shadowed adopted children and their families?

WHAT DO FAMILIES KEEP FROM EACH OTHER?

"To keep a secret from someone is to block information or evidence from reaching that person and to do so intentionally. It is a purposeful act. To keep a secret is to make a value judgment, for whatever reason, that it is not that person's right to possess the secret. To keep a secret requires a complicated maze of family communication manipulated by concealment, disguises, camouflage, whispers, silence, or lies."[1]

Most families have secret keepers. Secret keepers cloud positive husband and wife relationships, block healthy communication between a parent and a child, and impede supportive extended family connections. Families keep secrets from one another around potentially embarrassing, shameful, humiliating, or painful events. A teenage love relationship, an untimely pregnancy, an adoption plan, financial mismanagement, serious mental or emotional illness, a criminal history, drug use—all fill the compartments of that darkened cedar chest.

When Robert was 23 years old, his father died suddenly. He had a tremendous relationship with the man he called his hero. His world shattered one afternoon as he and his mother took a walk through a neighborhood park. On that bright, sunny day, clouds overshadowed the memories Robert nurtured of his father. On that day, his mother told him of a relationship that she had had earlier in life. At 19, she had fallen in love with a man who loved her and left her. After his departure, she discovered she was pregnant with Robert. When Robert was eight months old, she met David, the man Robert knew as dad. He never formally adopted him. "We intended to tell you all along, son," she related in a trembling voice. "I kept putting it off."

WHY DO WE KEEP SECRETS? SECRECY AS A TOOL

To Keep Control

When Jennifer was 17 years old, she experienced an unplanned pregnancy. Feeling overwhelmed and inadequate to parent, she made an adoption plan. That was 21 years ago. She has told no one of her secret, not even her husband and family. Why? Control. As long as she kept her secret, she alone would have absolute control over it. In her book *Family Secrets*, Harriet Webster notes that "secrecy is a tool we use to adapt what has happened to us (or our children). Through the conscious, deliberate concealment or disclosure of information, we take some control of our life and exercise a degree of power over those with whom we interact."[2] We use the tool of secrecy to keep control. Why else do we keep secrets?

To Protect

Individuals and families keep secrets from one another to keep a blanket of secure protection over them. The less other family members know about a particular past circumstance or event, the less vulnerable that person is to pain. The less others know, the less chance that the family member will be placed under the microscope and subjected to unhealthy commiseration, unconscious criticism, judgment, or blame. One rainy afternoon, Carla, age 15, and her older adopted sister, Rachel, age 17, were cleaning out the attic. They stumbled onto a shoebox full of old newspaper clippings. The articles told the grisly details of Rachel's birth mother's death at the hands of her father. The articles related the aspects of a very messy trial and his subsequent imprisonment. Rachel sat stunned. She knew she was adopted, but always thought her mother died of cancer and her father just couldn't care for her. When confronted with the information, her mother said, "We just wanted you to be shielded from such a hurtful history." We use the tool of secrecy to feel protected or to protect. There are still more reasons families keep secrets from each other and from those outside the family who could provide love and support.

To Hide Shame

Joyce and Kelly had been close friends for nearly six years. They shared hurts, joys, hopes, and dreams. Yet, there was still something that Joyce had never shared. While they were finishing their usual Thursday afternoon lunch together, Joyce opened up. "I need to tell you something that I have told no one since we moved here. I need to tell you that I am adopted." Kelly responded, "Why didn't you ever tell me? There wasn't any reason to keep that from me."

"I just couldn't," Joyce said. "I have always been ashamed of the fact that I was adopted. I have always thought of myself as not worth much because someone got rid of me. I thought if you knew, you wouldn't want to be my friend anymore." We use the tool of secrecy because of our sense of shame. It is a shame that leaves us feeling defective and without power.

To keep control, to protect or be protected, to hide shame, all these are reasons why families keep secrets. Another reason people keep secrets is to protect their public persona—their image. If others knew about their adoption plan or their adoptive status, would life be different?

To Maintain a Public Image

Masking one's secret of childlessness through an adoption by never talking about it, either inside or outside the family, used to be a routine mode of family communication. Living as if an adoption plan never happened used to be a familiar route taken through life by birth parents years ago. Not telling a child about his or her adoptive status also was a means of quietly handling a child's placement in the family as well as the image of the family itself. What does that type of secrecy do to a child who discovers the secret?

Parents are forceful people in the lives of their children, Ken Watson says. They occasionally, through the strength of their authority, press a child into silence (if the secret is found out) in order to protect their public image. A child who feels that mentioning adoption in any way outside the family is a threat to the family's image begins to wonder what is really important—appearances or reality. "Are reputation and image so sacred that they must be preserved at any cost?"[3]

Questions begin to fill the mind of this silent child. "If my parents choose to protect the image of the family and if I am a sacrifice that has to be made in the process, the child wonders, how can I be worth anything?"[4] We use the tool of secrecy to guard our public image and reputation. There is yet one more reason why families use the tool of secrecy.

To Forget

Fourteen-year-old Michael joined his adoptive family at two years of age. Michael had been severely neglected, often left an entire day by himself. The condition in which he was eventually found by social workers was beyond deplorable. It was beyond disgusting. Both of Michael's adoptive parents feel that the less said about Michael's past the better. If it is not talked about, it will be forgotten. The entire family maintained the attitude that bad things belong buried in the past. We use the tool of secrecy to forget about the past.

WHAT'S PRIVATE? WHAT'S CONFIDENTIAL? WHAT'S A SECRET?

What about privacy? Aren't there things that should be kept quiet? Of course, says Michael Mask. But there is a difference. "What sets a family secret apart from a matter that is appropriately kept confidential within the family is the effect it has on the family."[5] Is the issue discussed freely and openly within the family? Or if the issue is raised, does a look or a word squelch it?

Secrets damage the family. Secrets have power over family members because nobody talks about them and yet a few influential ones know about them. A little lie is told. A little bit of a cover-up is relayed. A secret is born. It gains more power, Mask says, as it passes from one generation to another.

Confidentiality, however, does not damage the family. "Confidentiality," stresses Mask, "protects and strengthens the family."[6] It teaches families to deal with issues openly and honestly. Confidential matters allow for appropriate communication within healthy boundaries by those directly touched by the event or circumstances or with those who can act within the arena of support.

THE HIGH COST OF KEEPING SECRETS WITHIN THE FAMILY

Secrets are powerful things. Secrets within any family can distort reality, undermine trust, and destroy intimacy. Secrets create exclusion, destroy

3 1326 00514 8319

authenticity, produce fantasies, evoke fear, and kindle shame. The discovery of a life-altering secret can also freeze development at crucial points in life.[7] Each one of these deserves further examination from the perspective of adoption.

Secrets Distort Reality

Lois Roberts, now in her early fifties, grew up as an only child, loved and almost worshipped by her parents. Occasionally, her mother would say to her, "We couldn't have any children, and then you came along." The phrase had no real meaning to Lois.

Following the sudden death of her mother and during the subsequent resident nursing home care needed by her father, a family secret emerged. As Lois visited with her father, each time she entered the room he would ask the same question, "Are you adopted?" Puzzled, Lois contacted family members, who confirmed the truth. All the other relatives knew. Everyone knew but Lois.

"I have a lot of questions," Lois stated. "I feel a sense of abandonment. I feel like the whole world is on the inside of a glass and I am on the outside. My prevailing emotional feeling is that everybody marches along to a family rhythm, and I don't know what mine is. And now it is too late. I don't know what my reality is. I should have counted somewhere enough to be told the truth."[8]

"While some secrets can bring people together by giving them a sense of intimacy and sharing," says Betty Jean Lifton, "secrets can be destructive if they cause shame and guilt, prevent change, render one powerless or hamper one's sense of reality."[9]

Secrets Undermine Trust and Intimacy

In 2009, Helen Riley explored what happens to adults who discover the secret of their adoption later in life. She describes these individuals as "last discoverers." One of the most significant impacts for these "late discoverers" revolves loss of trust at a very deep level.

> Intrinsic trust lies at the core of parenting and parent/child relationships. Trauma responses in children whose parental figures have betrayed intrinsic trust through acts of incest, violence or abandonment are well documented. Research on trauma and post traumatic stress responses defines intrinsic trust as "our fundamental assumption about the world and our safety in it." It is this type of trust that

> is violated in traumatic situations such as torture, terrorist acts, and brutal assaults. Feminist philosopher Dr. Susan Brison identifies some of the harms encountered through a violation of this type of trust as including "cognitive and emotional paralysis," a loss of "one's memories of an earlier life," an "[in]ability to envision a future," leaving one with "no bearings by which to navigate" (1997 p. 14–21). The significance and weight late discoverers place on trust supports a view that the late discovery experience can also involve the betrayal of a much deeper and more significant level of trust—intrinsic trust.[10]

When Karla found out that she was adopted, it impacted her relationship with her mother.

> I felt profoundly betrayed. My mother and I had always been close. I felt I could tell her everything. When I was seventeen, she told me the truth. What keeping this family secret did to our relationship was subtle and gradual. I found myself sharing less and less with her, guarding what I did tell and always wondering in the back of my mind what else she hasn't told me.[11]

Secrets Create Exclusion and Division

Keeping a secret puts family members into exclusive clubs: those who know the secret and those who do not. Secrecy impacts many arenas in the secret keeper's life. To keep the secret, the secret keeper must carefully guard all communication with others close to him. This defense mode often leads to distance, anxiety, and awkwardness in relationships with intimate others.[12] Where there is exclusion and division from one another based on secrecy, the probability of mutual caring, mutual understanding, and mutual honesty is seriously diminished.

Secrets Destroy Authenticity

In families where secrets are kept, another problem emerges: the creation of the family mask. What the family members seem to be on the outside to one another is not what is truly on the inside. In secret-keeping families, the sense of authenticity is lost.[13]

Living with secrets, Mask offers, means remaining entangled in a web of deception, even if the motive is pure and protective. Deception is so destructive that it breaks trust and breeds confusion. When the truth is kept secret, then corresponding emotions are denied or repressed, and defense mechanisms rise to take their place. When children are told, "Don't think, don't ask, don't see, don't feel," they lose their sense of what is real.[14]

Secrets Produce Fantasies

Lynn, age 12, was quite imaginative. She often would sit and tell her friends stories about her birth mother. The stories always included the same basic facts. Her birth mother lived in a beautiful home in a city near the ocean. In fact, she could see the ocean from her house. Her home had a pool and was surrounded by beautiful gardens and trees.

The problem with Lynn's story was it was nowhere near the truth. Lynn's mother had been involved in selling drugs and was in prison. She would be in prison until well into Lynn's twenties. Because Lynn never knew the truth, she created one for herself. It was a "truth" that would only serve her for a season—until the "real" story comes crashing in.

Secrets Evoke Fear

"I grew up never knowing anything about my past. No one would ever answer my questions so I stopped asking them," Kim Kelly related. "Because of that, I also was never able to share an overwhelming fear I had with my parents. I grew up with the fear that some day I was going to wake up and nobody would be there. The house would be empty. They would have all disappeared. I just wonder . . . maybe that is what really happened to me in the very beginning."

When secrets are kept, there is a vacuum that must be filled. That vacuum is filled with a preoccupation with the secret. That preoccupation then leads to anxiety and fear. "Secrecy . . . creates a condition (a feeling) of chronic vulnerability," says Jim Gritter. "Fear alters our ability to gather and interpret information, decisions are often based on fantasy—enhanced speculation rather than the fact. Secrecy can accentuate the distressing feeling of being different from others."[15] And when one feels different and doesn't know why, fear is a constant companion.

Secrets Kindle Shame

Drew, age 12, knew he was "given up" for adoption, but he didn't know why. The truth was, his birth mother loved him very much, but as a young teen she was unequipped to raise Drew to adulthood. Drew's adoptive parents knew the whole story, but they assumed that the less said, the better for everyone. The only problem was that Drew was left believing there was something "wrong" with him, that he had been unlovable from birth. A feeling of shame haunted his thoughts and impacted his relationships. Drew wasn't alone.

"I could never talk about adoption in our house. It was like the family's secret word. If I brought it up, you would have thought I'd said a dirty word," commented Jackie. "I grew up thinking that, because adoption was never talked about, it was a horrible secret. If there was something wrong with adoption, there must be something terribly wrong about me."

Secrets Can Impact Development

> Every family experiences developmental stages. These are most evident when someone enters the family by marriage or other committed relationship, birth, or adoption, and when someone exits the family by leaving home or through separation, divorce, or death. Such entrances and exits require that a family reinvent itself in order to accommodate new roles. The stages of development are not discrete events, but rather processes that take place over time. When that process goes well, complex adjustments occur in every corner of the family. When a secret is made in the midst of this process, adjustment screeches to a halt.[16]

Jennifer was 19 years old when she experienced an unintended pregnancy. Shipped off to a relative for the duration of the pregnancy, she returned home only with the promise that she must keep this secret from everyone. That secrecy froze Jennifer emotionally at nineteen in many ways. She was never allowed to process grief and to have support through the reorganization of her life after the loss. Secrecy also froze relationships with her parents, who never again visited the subject of the child placed for adoption.[17]

All types of families keep secrets for a number of reasons. The effect of secret keeping on family members can be harmful to healthy family growth, intimacy, and communication. It is important for foster, adoptive, and kinship families to understand the power of secrets as well as to understand the origins of secrecy in adoption.

THE ORIGIN OF SECRETS IN ADOPTION

From history's earliest days until the present, the practice of adoption has served a variety of functions, according to Ken Watson, internationally known adoption expert. It has spanned a continuum of needs, from "providing a royal family with an heir, to adding 'indentured' hands, to making a family financially self-sufficient, to emptying orphanages to save community dollars."[18]

In recent decades, adoption has served two additional functions: (1) to meet the needs of couples whose dreams of a family were shattered by infertility, and (2) to provide a solution for birth parents who found themselves facing an unintended and untimely pregnancy. What emerged from the latter two functions of adoption during the middle decades of the past century was an idealist picture, one that characterized a perfect solution to a societal problem. As Miriam Reitz and Ken Watson state:

> Adoptive families and adoption agencies collaborated to present adoption as what it can never really be—a chance for birth parents to go on happily with their lives, for children to grow up in trouble-free families, and for adoptive parents to fulfill themselves and find immortality through children to whom they have sole claim by virtue of adoption.[19]

"Years ago," according to Sharon Kaplan Roszia, "myths were perpetuated through the adoption community. One myth taught those whose lives were touched by adoption that the most healthy attitude for all members of the triad was to make a clean break."[20] That break meant no looking back, no information passed on, a story left untold.

Ken Watson remarked that "the implications of the adoption on the subsequent development of the child or family [were] either viewed as inconsequential or denied altogether." These perceptions—"we are just like a biological family, adoption has no reference to the future, and things are best kept a secret"—further established a precedent on how children were told about their adoption and what they were told, if they were told at all.[21] Little thought was given to the impact the lack of information would have on an adopted child, including the child's relationship with the adoptive family and eventually birth parents if a reunion occurred. Adoption practitioners of the day followed a prescribed course—create a new world. It would be a world in which adoptees were told to forget the past, as though it did not exist. Adoptive parents were told to create a new reality and given freedom to exist in total anonymity with no pressure for disclosure. Birth parents were insensitively shoved aside and told to erase the present events from their memories.

Those who advised secrecy in adoption practice had good intentions. It was assumed that if the anonymity of all individuals involved was protected, then the following goals would be met.

- The birthmother could more easily resolve her feelings about the placement.

- The birthmother would be protected from the label of "fallen woman."
- The child would be protected from the label of "illegitimate."
- The child would be more easily integrated into the family.
- The family could portray their structure as that of a biological family.
- No one would have to look back.[22]

However, for all the efforts made to serve "the best interest" of adopted children by denying the past and relegating it to the sacred halls of secrecy, those efforts have not served them well.

SECRECY HAS NOT SERVED THE ADOPTED PERSON

Many adoptees experienced the "disquieting loneliness" that Alex Haley, the author of *Roots* (a television series about six generations of an American family descended from an African slave), described.[23] Devastating feelings of abandonment, rejection, shame, and guilt grew out of a lack of knowledge about their heritage and the reasons they were placed in an adoptive family. Adopted youngsters were plagued by questions about who their birth parents were, why they couldn't care for their children, and whether they would ever meet. Concerns about their genetic past or their medical history left them wondering if something devastating would surface later in life. The need for such knowledge frequently nudged adoptees into a consuming and never-ending search for the truth, sometimes impairing their ability to lead productive lives.

"Adoptees can feel frustrated at their inability to connect with their roots," says Marshall Schecter, a psychiatrist at the University of Pennsylvania School of Medicine. "Some have trouble forming an identity when they reach adolescence because they have been told little to nothing about their past. Others may develop fantasies—both positive and negative—about their birth families. Some adoptees spend a lifetime never finding answers to their questions. For others, this black hole which exists where their past should be becomes too much of an emotional burden for them to bear, leaving deep psychological scars."[24]

Adoption scholar David Brodzinsky of Rutgers University says, "For adoptees, part of them is hurt at having once been relinquished. That part remains vulnerable for the rest of their lives as they grieve at various predictable points for the unknown parents who gave them away" and for the code of silence and secrecy that prevented them from finding out.[25]

Jim Gritter feels that secrecy has created a deeper issue within the heart and mind of the adopted person. "That greater issue is shame: Secrecy is symptomatic of a much deeper issue—namely shame. Adoption flounders as an institution because it is built on a foundation of shame. For decades, adoption has functioned essentially as a two-step program of disowning and owning. In that form, it is an almost perfect script for shame, for there is great shame in disowning and owning; and obviously, there is great shame in being disowned and owned. Shame is a matter of defect, powerlessness, and rejection—familiar themes in adoption . . . . I believe shame is at the heart of adoption, as we have known it in our lifetime. It is the DNA of closed adoption."[26]

Secrecy has not served the adopted person well.

WHAT ABOUT TODAY? IS ADOPTION COMMUNICATION IN THE FAMILY IMPROVING?

According to author and researcher Susan Livingston Smith, LCSW, parents are more aware of the needs to communicate about adoption than there were years ago. There is so much more emphasis on this topic. However, she commented, "We still have a long way to go."[27]

"Even though we are doing a better job, there are still challenges. In our research we found that parents often underestimate the difficulty their children have in talking about adoption as well as the reality that the level of communicative openness can vary between a child and each parent as well as across different adopted children in the family," she said.[28]

So, which process—secrecy or honesty and transparency—works best for children? The research provides evidence to guide us to the answer.

> Communicative openness, which is defined as the free expression of feelings and discussion within the adoptive family is a key factor in the adjustment of the adopted children, regardless of the level of structural openness. Adopted children experiencing more open communication in the household talk of higher self-esteem and their parents report lower behavioral issues.
>
> Adopted teens who grew up in families where adoption conversation was the norm talk of more trust for their parents, fewer feelings of alienation and better overall functioning.[29]

SUMMARY

Secrecy in adoption has not served anyone touched by adoption well. There is an expression that has meaning at a very deep emotional, psychological, and spiritual level: "The truth shall set you free." How very true this is for adopted persons who have grown up in an environment of honesty, transparency, and love.

QUESTIONS

1. Have you ever found out a "family secret" that directly affected you? How did you feel? How did you respond in the short term? Over time?
2. What are five reasons we keep secrets? Can you think of any more?
3. In small groups, discuss each reason as it relates to adoption.
4. What is the difference between confidentiality and secret keeping as you understand it?
5. What are the consequences of secret keeping in the family? Discuss each as it relates to healthy adoptive family living.

CHAPTER 2

Truth or Consequences: A Great Debate

Children are afraid of the dark. Adults are afraid of the light.

If I tell my child about his birth father, he will be hurt and angry. It is best that he doesn't know the truth.

The layers of their stories should be respected, not erased.

Jennifer, age 15, was adopted shortly after birth into a family with two birth children, both several years older than she. At the time of the adoption, the social workers told her parents that Jennifer's birth mother was a patient in a psychiatric hospital. The mother claimed to have been impregnated following a rape by an African American man, also a patient at the hospital. Because Jennifer did not appear to be biracial, her adoptive parents never told her the birth mother's story about her birth father. Their older children overheard their discussions and learned some of the information shared by the social worker. When Jennifer began struggling with her identity, the parents asked a therapist if they had been right to withhold this information from Jennifer, citing as an excuse the mother's lack of credibility. After some exploratory discussion with Jennifer, the therapist discovered that the older siblings had told her years before that she was biracial. She had been struggling alone for many years, with no parental support or guidance, with this information (or, potentially, misinformation) about her racial or ethnic heritage. It was small wonder that she experienced a crisis of identity formation as a young adolescent.

The wrestling match between the pros and cons of telling children the truth about their birth family and birth circumstances plays out regularly in foster and adoptive families. Should we tell? How much should we tell? And what's the right timing?

Research regarding the consequences of open versus closed adoption communication supports an open approach. H. David Kirk, a psychologist and adoptive parent, felt that a lack of communication about adoption-related issues would serve to disrupt children's growth and maturation.[1] Additionally, open communication about adoption-related issues meets adolescents' information needs for information about themselves and their families on which to build a cohesive identity. In addition, such communication allows teens to feel comfortable with their adoptive status.[2]

Most adoptive and foster parents are loving and concerned. Of course, they want to protect their children from pain and unhappiness. When adoptive parents consider the impact of separation from the birth family on their child, or less-than-ideal circumstances surrounding that separation, they sometimes imagine that they will "protect" the child from pain or difficulty in adjustment by:

- Not telling the child at all about the adoption
- Not telling the "whole" truth by telling a "hole" (partial) truth
- Avoiding conversation that might be upsetting to the child

In reality, parents who attempt to "protect" their child in this manner are creating a scenario in which the child lacks trust in and attachment to the adoptive or foster family. When a child, adolescent, or young adult finds information that has been known to the adoptive parents but withheld, the adoptee wonders what other lies or half-truths have been perpetrated by the adoptive family. The outrage felt by someone who has not experienced honesty from the people committed to one's protection and welfare can be intense, leaving no room for trust or attachment.

A foster or adopted child, lacking a life story that makes sense, is forced to make one up. The imagined history is often either extremely positive or extremely negative. When the fantasy history is very positive, the adopted child may yearn for the fantasy parent who will never punish, will always be patient, will be famous, rich, and beautiful, and will lavish attention, gifts, and love on the child. When the fantasy history is very negative, the child may feel like a "low-life" who does not deserve a loving, stable adoptive family. The child may strive to be like the negative image of his birth family, an image that might be far from reality.

Often, the adopted child's self-esteem is more damaged by silence or deceit than by reality. The silence or deceit communicates the truth is shameful, something to hide. The greatest generator of shame in adoption is secrecy. The adoptee feels shame and believes the information is withheld or distorted because of the parent's desire to shield him from knowing that he springs from "bad" seed.

When parents are not willing to talk openly about the situation that led to adoption or foster care, the child is forced to cope with overwhelming questions with little or no parental support. It is hard enough for adults to make sense of difficult circumstances. Children and adolescents, without help, are not able to integrate information about innumerable social ills: war and political unrest, cultural beliefs that make it impossible for some single birth mothers to raise their children, alcoholism and substance abuse, discrimination that sometimes accompanies minority group membership, mental illness, and developmental delay, to name only a few.

Many adoptions today have varying levels of openness. Parents in open adoptions have the advantage of access to information unavailable to families whose adoptions are confidential or closed. However, an open adoption relationship certainly does not preclude the need for open adoption communication within the family. In fact, parents with a great deal of information also have a great deal of responsibility in deciding how and when to share it with the child. "Regardless of the level of openness and the circumstances that surrounded the adoptive placement, all adoptive families are faced with the unique normative task of discussing the role of adoption in the family."[3]

Challenging realities for parents today are the Internet and social media resources. Many young people are finding birth family members on such sites as Facebook, learning information previously unknown to them. Some adopted persons are reuniting with members of their birth families. This opens uncontrolled access to information given to them by the person who has lived it. Many times that information has been "rewritten" to remove personal responsibilities or make the information more palatable to the "giver" and is not necessarily historically correct.

Adopted persons who find out their adoption status later in life often call themselves an LDA (for Late Discovery Adoptee). Responses may include anger directed toward the adoptive parents, depression, and issues with trust in other close relationships. In a small study of late discovery adoptees, the following were significant findings:[4]

- Forty-one percent of the sample was told of their adoption by someone other than the adoptive family, relatives, or birth family.
- Sixty-two percent of the sample never suspected they were adopted, but many felt that it made sense of their family relationships, as they always felt different from everyone else.
- Sixty-two percent of the sample went on to have contact with their birth family after the discovery of their adoption.

> I had the best of parents, however at the end of the day, I still don't know, fully, who I am, and I do not know at all where I came from. Earlier acknowledgement, explanation and acceptance of my origins could have celebrated rather than hidden and denied the reality of my existence.[5]

For additional information about late discovery in adoption, visit Child Welfare Information Gateway at https://www.childwelfare.gov/adoption/adopt_people/discovery.cfm.

Parents who withhold or distort key information about a child's past may be, in effect, protecting themselves from a task they find difficult: talking about the birth family, adoption, and the circumstances that led up to the adoption.

For healthy psychological adjustment, an adoptive child needs "the creation of an open, honest, non-defensive and emotionally attuned family dialogue, not only about adoption issues, but any issue that impacts the child."[6]

The adoptive family's task is to integrate diversity and use it to form a permanent bridge to and from the wider world. In forming that permanent bridge, the adoptive family, through their child, becomes connected to the social problems that resulted in the adoption plan: alcoholism, drug addiction, teenage pregnancy, child abuse and neglect, mental illness, and so on.[7]

Because of that connection to a difficult past, adoptive parents have a lifelong responsibility—communicating the circumstances of their child's past in a manner that will lead to understanding, resolution, and healing. As parents assume the lifelong commitment of adoption, they should examine the debate surrounding adoption disclosure.

THE DEBATE OF ADOPTION SECRECY: MYTHS AND REALITIES

Adoptive or foster parents may be reluctant to share the knowledge that their child is adopted or that very difficult circumstances surround his separation from his birth family. Sometimes, well-meaning relatives or friends may even advise foster and adoptive parents that what a child doesn't know can't hurt him. The debate can rage on within the minds of adoptive parents setting up personal struggles. The debate can also impact relationships within the immediate family as family members debate amongst themselves. It is a subject that must be addressed openly, and myths serving to fuel a lack of honesty should be dispelled.

Fear of Losing the Love and Loyalty of the Child

Myth: The child will not be tortured by divided loyalties to both birth and adoptive parents if he simply does not know he is adopted. Or, it is acceptable to distort the truth with stories of birth parents who "died in a car crash" as a way of trying to remove the birth parents from the child's thoughts and loyalties.

Reality: One of the paradoxes of parenthood is that, when parents try to hold on to their children too tightly, they will only ensure the loss of those children. Those who try to keep their children too close to home when the children are old enough to emancipate, for example, may find that their young adult children decide to move hundreds of miles away. Or step-parents who try to compete for the love and attachment of their children may find that those children turn away from them. Adoptive parents must remember that the child's love of the birth family does not detract from love of the adoptive family. When adopted children are encouraged by secure adoptive parents to acknowledge feelings for their birth families, the children are free to attach to the adoptive family. They are not caught in a competitive, divisive tug of war. As Dr. Gordon Neufeld, author *Hold Onto Your Kids*, says, it doesn't set up competing attachment.[8] By giving them honesty and understanding, adoptive parents give their children permission to love and attach to both the birth family and the adoptive family.

Mindy, a nine-year-old child, was adopted at age three. She has only vague memories about her birth mother. Mindy was adopted due to neglect resulting from her birth mother's chronic depression. Mother's Day used to be a troubling day for Mindy as she struggled to honor her adoptive mother without being disloyal to her birth mother. Mindy's adoptive mother recognized her daughter's dilemma and suggested that Mindy write her birth mother a card every Mother's Day, telling her about her accomplishments and feelings, and including drawings and collages about her life. Mindy works very hard on the letters she makes for her birth mother every year, and they are kept in a special album for Mindy to review when she wants to feel close to her birth mother or proud of herself. The understanding and acceptance of the adoptive mother have given Mindy "permission" to love both mothers. Mindy no longer holds herself behind a wall of fear in her relationship with her adoptive mother; she is now free to love her mother because she understands that, to do so, she does not have to stop loving her birth mother.

Fear That the Child Will Have a Poor Self-Image

Myth: Children should not be told that their parents were addicted to drugs or alcohol, incarcerated, abusive, mentally ill, developmentally delayed, and so on. Children will have negative self-esteem if they know their family had serious problems. For this reason, it is acceptable to hide or distort information, or to omit significant facts.

Reality: When children do not have parental support in learning about their history, they are forced to develop an image of themselves and their family based solely on misinformation and imagination. What they imagine and are unable to discuss with supportive adults may be far worse than the real situation. Further, it may be the parents' judgments about the circumstances leading to adoption or foster care that could create poor self-esteem. Adoptive and foster parents can learn to present even very difficult information in nonjudgmental ways, giving the children support and love while they are learning about their life circumstances.

Willy, age 12, was adopted at the age of 3 following years of neglect by his developmentally delayed mother. His adoptive parents were reluctant to tell him that his parent was cognitively impaired. Willy assumed that his mother neglected him because she did not care about him. Willy's parents shared his history with him when he expressed tremendous rage about his birth mother's lack of concern. Willy understood that his mother had cognitive problems that made it impossible for her to care for her son. With the help of the child welfare agency, the adoptive family was able to obtain information about the extended birth family. Willy finally could feel proud of his ethnic heritage, his birth grandfather's and aunt's artistic talents, and, most important, his birth mother's loving attempts to care for him in spite of her handicap.

Fear of Telling Children Information at the Wrong Time, before They Are Able to Understand the Circumstances

Myth: Children are, and will always be, "too young" to understand prostitution, rape, mental illness, criminal behavior, and so on.

Reality: It is true that small children are not ready to hear the entire story, as they are unable to understand the complex social situations that led to separation from the birth family. Instead, children are able to understand the life story in layers. What they are told at age three may be a simplified version of reality, with more information supplied when they are better able to understand. Children receive another layer of understanding as they mature, and so on until they have all the information the parent has. This will be addressed more in-depth in Chapter 5.

Amanda, age 15, understands today that she was adopted because both of her birth parents were alcoholic and unable to care for her. When Amanda was a preschooler, her adoptive parents explained to her that her birth parents could not take care of her because they were not healthy and were unable to meet the responsibilities of parenthood. As Amanda reached the school-age years, she understood that she was removed from her parents' care by child protective social workers because her parents did not care for her properly. As a middle school child, Amanda learned about the disease of alcoholism and the history of her parents' ongoing struggle with sobriety. As an adolescent, Amanda is learning that her grandparents were also alcoholic. She is being taught about the genetic predisposition to this disease, and her parents are helping her learn strategies to avoid a future of alcohol abuse for herself.

Fear of a Self-Fulfilling Prophecy—Children May Try to Model Themselves after the Birth Parent

Myth: If children know that their birth mother was promiscuous, they might behave in sexually provocative ways during their own adolescence.

Reality: It is normal for all adolescents to try on multiple identities and to experiment with independence by being very different from their parents. It is likely that adopted youth, then, will try on identities that are different from those of their adoptive parents. They may choose to be like the birth parents (or what they imagine the birth parents to be like) during this process of identity formation, particularly if they find this identity to be troubling to their parents! This behavior is normal and to be expected. Problems can become more serious when adoptive parents, fearful of behavior that appears similar to the dysfunctional behavior of the birth family, overreact to their children's age-appropriate experimentation.

Beau was adopted as an infant. His birth mother had been a promiscuous adolescent who surrendered him for adoption when she became a parent at the age of 16. Beau began dating seriously just before his 16th birthday, and his adoptive parents were concerned that he might try to recreate the scenario of his own birth. Adoption had not been an open topic within the household for many years; the parents had assumed that Beau knew everything they knew, and there was nothing else to talk about. With help from a skilled post-adoption social worker, the parents learned that Beau needed to continue to talk about his history and his birth parents, as his development allowed him to understand and integrate the complexities of his background. Just knowing the facts isn't always enough. Following an increase in open communication in the family, the adoptive parents were surprised by Beau's confused attitudes and feelings toward his birth mother. When Beau had his adoptive parents' help and support in sorting out these feelings, he no longer felt that he had to transfer a need to be close to his birth mother to his adolescent girlfriend.

Fear That the Information Cannot Be Shared in a Positive Light—The Adoptive Parent Does Not Know How to Tell

Myth: My children will be scarred for life if I don't find the right words to tell them about their past.

Reality: Adoptive and foster parents can learn to discuss histories in an age-appropriate, nonjudgmental way. The help of skilled post adoption specialists can also be used when parents feel overwhelmed by very difficult information. While secrets can almost always be lethal, open communication rarely is.

Ben is 10 years old now, and his adopted parents believe he has a right to know about his two older birth brothers. They worried about telling him that he was born to an older birth mother, a divorced woman with two older children. They worried that he would feel rejected because the birth mother made an adoptive plan for Ben but kept the older children. The parents decided to take Ben back to the agency that handled the adoption to talk to a social worker about his history. His parents remained with him throughout the interview, during which Ben was able to ask questions about his past and his mother's reasons for seeking an adoptive family for him. Ben initially expressed anger and feelings of rejection. He became interested in his birth brothers, however, and asked his adoptive parents if he might write to or visit them sometime in the future. The parents were supportive of his feelings and, with the help of the social worker, obtained a picture of the brothers from the birth mother for Ben's room. He displays it proudly on his dresser. As he matures and understands more about the complexities of adult responsibilities, it is likely he will be more empathetic about the reason his birth mother felt overwhelmed by a third child. Because of these fears and myths, parents can be tempted to withhold or change information. The consequences of changing the truth, however, can be devastating to the child and the adoptive family.

THE CONSEQUENCES OF NOT TELLING THE CHILD AT ALL

Few parents today attempt to withhold the fact of adoption from the child. However, some families have been counseled to adhere to the "ignorance is bliss" policy: what he doesn't know can't hurt him. This is comparable to a doctor withholding communication about a terminal disease with the belief that, if the patient doesn't know he is dying, he won't.

Many individuals can relate stories about their cousin or neighbor who was adopted and never told. Everyone else in the family or community seems to know about the adoption, except those at the center of the story, the children themselves. Rarely can this secret be successfully maintained. Sometimes, a secret is only revealed when an adopted adult, following the death of her parents, discovers a final decree of adoption. Imagine the sense of betrayal when this secret is uncovered after an opportunity for communication with the parents is lost forever! When children or adults discover they are adopted, they may feel disconnected from the adoptive family (and, often, from the rest of humanity), an overwhelming rage at the parents' lack of honesty, and a tremendous sense of shame that this information was regarded as so negative that it had to be hidden.

Guy, an adult adoptee, shared "When I was 12 years old, my father took me to the basement and showed me a picture of a woman I did not know. He said to me, 'You have the right to know this is your birth mother. But whatever you do, don't tell your mother that I told you about your adoption—it would kill her!' My father never spoke to me again about my adoption."

The implicit message in this situation is that the youth's status as an adopted child is somehow shameful, secreted from society and the child himself. This young man was adrift throughout the remainder of his life, unable to ask questions about his heritage, his ethnicity, or his personal and family histories.

Often, adoptive parents ask about the ideal age at which to tell a child he or she is adopted. Many well-adjusted adopted adults tell us that they have always known that they were adopted and cannot remember a "telling moment." These adults grew up knowing that they were adopted in the same way they grew up knowing that they were male or female, Catholic or Jewish, tall or short. When parents search for the appropriate telling moment, they find that it never comes. The child has just been sick, is about to begin school, just lost a beloved pet, and so on. The longer parents wait, the more difficult it becomes to tell the child; the parents are embarrassed that they have not found a moment of honesty before. And so the waiting for a perfect telling moment continues, sometimes until the parents lose the opportunity to tell because another person, almost always less concerned about the child's feelings, shares the information with the adoptee. This will be explored in more depth in Chapter 5.

THE CONSEQUENCES OF TELLING THE "HOLE TRUTH" INSTEAD OF THE "WHOLE TRUTH"

Many parents fall into the trap of withholding complete information, either permanently or "until my child is older and can understand." Key pieces of information are withheld, making it difficult for the child to fully integrate the circumstances surrounding his birth.

In this type of communication, the adoptive parent might relate partial information regarding the child's ethnicity, medical history, or placement history in foster care. However, the parent decides not to tell the child that he or she was born to a drug-addicted mother who was engaging in prostitution to support her habit.

Omission or simplification of some facts may be necessary while the child is very young but harmful when the omission continues beyond the child's ability to understand. In determining when the child is old enough to know full information, parents can make the most accurate judgments. However, parents should remember that they usually underestimate their child's sophistication. Betty Jean Lifton, an adult adopted person and author of numerous books about adoption, asserts that all children should have complete information about their birth family history by the time they reach adolescence. It is important that parents share this information prior to, not during, the child's difficult journey through identity formation and individuation (separation from the family), key developmental tasks of adolescence.

A post-adoption counselor explained to 12-year-old Cory that he was surrendered for adoption because he was conceived when his mother was raped by an unknown assailant. Cory, surprisingly, expressed relief that his mother "was not a slut." The child understood that his mother signed the surrender, not to reject him, but to reject the circumstances surrounding his conception.

In subsequent chapters, readers will learn techniques of talking with children about difficult topics in an honest, nonjudgmental, and age-appropriate way.

THE CONSEQUENCES OF AVOIDING CONVERSATION THAT MIGHT BE UPSETTING TO THE CHILD

Talking about the circumstances that surround adoption often leads children to ask challenging questions, cry, express concern about siblings or birth parents, or display behaviors that indicate they are sad, angry, or confused. It is tempting for adoptive parents to cope with these challenges through silence about adoption or birth histories. They decide, "If he doesn't talk about his history, he won't think about it, and he will be able to forget about it."

Adoptive parents need to understand that children think about their adoptions and their birth families often, sometimes continuously. Studies have repeatedly demonstrated the surprisingly large incidence of attentional problems within the population of adopted children. Some studies indicate that one-third of all adopted children have attention deficit disorder with or without hyperactivity.[9] It is unlikely that all of these children have neurological problems resulting from genetics or exposure to drugs, alcohol, or other stresses in utero. It is more likely that many of these children are so preoccupied with trying to make sense of the losses that have occurred in their lives (and with preventing future losses from occurring) that they have difficulty concentrating. By discouraging communication about the topic most on the child's mind, the parent surrenders an important opportunity to influence the child's self-esteem, to promote attachment to the adoptive family, and to promote healthy forms of communication the child will be able to carry into his adult life.

Adoptive parents might assume that their children never think about adoption because they never bring up the topic. When these children are encouraged to talk about adoption through support group meetings with other children or through counseling with skilled post-adoption therapists, they often reveal that they have been consumed by a topic that is never addressed directly in the family.

A significant concept for adoptive and foster parents to understand is "psychological presence." Dr. Deborah Fravel defines psychological presence as "the symbolic existence of an individual in the perception of other family members in a way that influences thoughts, emotions, behavior, identity or unity of remaining family members." Psychological presence was first identified by Pauline Boss, family therapist and professor of family science, toward the end of the U.S. war in Vietnam. Boss was working with families of missing-in-action soldiers. She observed the missing, physically absent soldier/father was psychologically present in the family in a way that kept his presence a reality in the ongoing life of the family. Decisions made by remaining family members, for example, may reflect the understood wishes of the physically absent, but psychologically present, father. Dr. Deborah Fravel from Indiana University, in completing her doctoral dissertation on adoptive family life, noted that this issue of psychological presence is true in adoptive families as well. The physically absent, but psychologically present, birth family is very much on the mind of adopted or foster children, and on the minds of their adoptive or foster parents as well. In other words, silence does not mean a lack of thought or feeling![10]

Jermaine, an 11-year-old boy, asked if he thinks about his birth mother, responded, "I am thinking about her right now. I think about her every minute of the day." His parents were very surprised to learn of Jermaine's concern, as he had never asked a question about her.

Parents of 18-year-old Greg, hospitalized following a suicide attempt, were shocked to hear his girlfriend say, "Greg cries about his birth family all the time." The young man had been adopted shortly after birth and repeatedly assured his adoptive parents that he never thought about his adoption.

Some adoptive parents believe that they should respond honestly to questions asked by the child, but that they should not raise the issue of adoption themselves. Such a policy ensures that adoption will be little discussed in the family. Many children rarely raise the subject of adoption themselves. They believe that they are being disloyal to the adoptive parents if they continue to have feelings about the birth parents. When some children ask questions about adoption, they pick up cues that the topic is uncomfortable for the adoptive parent and should be avoided in the future.

VALUES/BELIEFS OF ADOPTION DISCLOSURE

Certainly, then, we should affirm the following values and beliefs in talking with children and adults about adoption:

- All persons have a right to know their personal histories.
- All healthy relationships involve hard work, open, two-way communication, and mutual respect.
- Adoption is a way of creating a family; it is not better or worse than other ways. Adoption should be celebrated, not hidden.
- Knowing about adoption includes an awareness that children will have questions and feelings about their birth parents. These questions and feelings should be acknowledged and addressed with honesty and respect.

- Birth parents and adoptive parents both care about the same child. They are not in competition for the affections and loyalty of the child. Parents can love more than one child, and children can care about more than one set of parents. Withholding information about adoption because of a desire to have all of the child's loyalty and affection has a paradoxical outcome: the erosion of the child's trust, loyalty, and attachment to the adoptive family.

SUMMARY

Adoptive parents may be tempted to withhold some or even all information from their children in an attempt to "protect" them from experiencing feelings of rejection or poor self-esteem. Such "protection" so often backfires when the child discovers parents have not been honest. In today's world of readily available information, such secret-keeping is almost impossible. While parents are justified in having concerns about sharing difficult information with their children, they will learn principles and strategies in this book that will enable them to be honest in a sensitive and constructive way.

QUESTIONS

1. What "fear" or worries have you experienced in relation to telling your child the truth about his birth family?
2. Of those fears discussed in this chapter, which is most intense for you?
3. What is the "worst case scenario" if you share information you have been withholding from your child?
4. If you had a terminal illness, would you want to have that information withheld from you by the doctor?
5. What might be some consequences of withholding information from your child?

CHAPTER 3

Just the Facts, Ma'am: Why Do Children Need Them?

Isn't fiction better than fact if the truth is painful and disruptive? Isn't it better to protect our children from difficult truths that might overburden them, destroying self-image and confidence? Can't we wait until our children are adults to share their story with them?

Sally, age 16, had been adopted at two months into a loving family with two other adopted children. She lived in a rural community with a sizable Hispanic population. Sally's Anglo peers at school occasionally hurled racial slurs at the Mexican American teens. Sally, a dark-haired, olive-skinned girl, began to wonder if she might be of Mexican American heritage. She announced to her shocked adoptive parents that she no longer wished to be part of their family and that she was going to find and live with her birth mother. Counseled to obtain more information about her past, the parents took Sally back to the placing agency to begin an informational search for her roots. When the social worker mentioned that Sally's birth parents were both of German ancestry, Sally immediately stopped her and insistently asked, "Are you sure?" When she had the information she needed to understand where she came from, Sally quickly abandoned her need to meet or live with her birth family—she only needed information about them to learn more about who she was becoming.

While it can be very tempting for adoptive parents to "protect" children from painful realities, we must question our motives. Are we protecting the feelings of the children, or protecting ourselves from those realities? By refusing to talk about painful history, we can pretend these circumstances don't really matter. When we try to ignore realities, they can become even larger, threatening to overwhelm the child with fantasies, guesses, and assumptions (many of which are more hurtful than the truth).

Adult adopted persons have taught us the importance of communicating information about a child's adoption as he moves from one side of childhood to the other. Why are facts so important to an adopted individual as he grows up and sorts out his identity? There are a number of reasons.

- Uninformed adopted persons develop unrealistic fantasies about their histories. These unrealistic fantasies can range, often for the same youth, between ridiculously positive and painfully negative. Sometimes adopted youth, in an effort to connect emotionally with the lost birth family, will model their own behavior and identity after the fantasy birth family.
- Many adopted persons with little or no information about their histories become confused about their identities and experience long periods of experimentation, at times self-destructive experimentation.
- All children are magical thinkers. Adopted or foster children might believe themselves to be the "cause" of their separation from the birth family, negatively impacting self-esteem.
- Children separated from their families of origin may not feel "free" to attach to new families; they may believe that they are being loyal to their birth families if they refuse to attach to another family. Or, separated children may refuse to have positive feelings toward the birth family, feeling disloyal in that case to the adoptive family. Without positive regard for the family of origin, the child's self-esteem suffers.
- Children who have experienced separation from earlier families may fear a reenactment of this separation, thus impacting their ability to trust and feel safe in their new families. Attachment is built upon the foundation of trust.
- Separated children may lack trust in adults who should have protected and cared for them. They may feel that others are lying to them or withholding information. This lack of trust can lead to serious difficulties with control battles as the children enter adolescence.
- Children with little or no information about their histories may develop anxiety about their histories, dating relatives, developing

serious health or mental health problems, being "genetically" unable to be good parents or even good people.

These potential outcomes of limited background information create compelling reasons to share histories with children who have been separated from their birth families. Let's examine each in more depth.

UNREALISTIC FANTASIES

Without knowing the truth about his adoption status and the circumstances surrounding the plan, a child can develop unrealistic fantasies involving birth parents, former foster parents, and his new adoptive family. Sometimes a child begins to develop fantasies about the "ideal" birth parents who look like movie stars, never nag about picking up wet towels, and never insist that all of the green beans are eaten. Another child may develop negative fantasies about birth parents who were drug addicts, abusive, violent, mentally ill "street people," and so on. It is not uncommon to see adopted children who vacillate between positive and negative fantasies, changing their beliefs about themselves and their histories almost weekly.

Cathy was only five years old when she joined her foster family. Her birth father had disappeared before she entered foster care, and her birth mother was in and out of jail. When Cathy was six, her mother was convicted of murder in connection with a drug-related robbery. Her mother would be in jail for many, many years. Cathy's foster parents adopted her. Because Cathy was so young when the birth family blew apart, her adoptive parents never shared the complete truth with her. They simply told her that her mother could not care for her. One afternoon when Cathy was 10, she was coloring a beautiful picture of a house surrounded by flowers and trees. When her mother asked her about it, Cathy replied, "This is my birth mother's house. I will visit her there when I get bigger. I know this is where she lives." Susan, Cathy's adoptive mom, knew that she had neglected some very important facts regarding Cathy's history. The youngster was searching for information about her past but was forced to resort to fantasy.

When children are unable to discuss their life situations as they develop more understanding about adoption, they may begin to hope or worry that their birth parents will re-enter their lives and "kidnap" them from the adoptive family. Fantasies often revolve around the fear of, or the hope for, reunification with the birth family. Children who consistently refuse to sleep with their windows shut may be hoping for such a reunification. Those who refuse to sleep with their windows open may fear such a kidnapping.

IDENTITY CONFUSION

Identity formation for all teens refers to the need to explore and answer these questions:[1]

- Who am I? Who do I want to be like? Who are my role models?
- How am I like my parents? How do I want to be like them? Different from them?
- What are my values, my beliefs?
- Who are the people I want as friends?
- How do I want to spend my time? What are my unique talents and interests?
- What might I want to be when I grow up?

For adopted youth, the questions become more complicated:

- How am I like my adoptive parents? How do I want to be like them? Do they respect my birth culture, my ethnicity?
- How am I like my birth parents? Based on what I know about them, and what I have learned about my heritage (possibly my ethnicity, my birth country, my culture), how much of that is a part of me? How much more do I want to add to what I am now?
- Do I want to be more involved with people who might be more like my birth parents? (Or closer to those who share my ethnicity, culture?) How do I do that?
- Who are my role models? Do I have role models who share my adoptive experience? (Do they share my ethnicity? My birth culture?)

Yet, establishing one's identity is not something that happens only during a certain period in one's life. Adoption therapist Joyce Maguire Pavao notes that "identity issues are an ongoing process, they just don't start in adolescence. However, the teen years are certainly the major developmental zone for identity formation. Every young person is trying to figure out who he is not—and who he is. He is trying to play different roles, experiment with different looks and figure out who he is along the way."

Maguire Pavao observes that "for adoptees, especially when there is little to no information about where they came from, there is an awareness that they don't really have the genetic information to do that kind of sorting out of their identity. They are basing it on their family of intimacy—the adoptive family, but that's not necessarily where their abilities, interests and traits have come from." Settling one's identity is more difficult for an adopted teen. "For most children," according to Maguire Pavao, "the people around them are mirrors on which they measure themselves, until the adolescent years. At that point they look in the mirror and see themselves. They become more and more aware of how different they are. I think it is a complicated process for adoptees during the teen years. It is at this point that they begin to realize that they do not know another person in the world genetically related to them."[2]

For some, the struggle for identity brings about major behavioral changes. The children may struggle to be like their birth parents or, in the absence of concrete information, what they imagine their birth parents to be.

Michelle, adopted at birth, began to change her looks and behavior when she was 16 years old. She dyed her hair such a jet-black color that she looked like a caricature of Morticia from *The Addams Family*. She wore black leather clothes, "goth" make-up, and she had shoes that looked like combat boots. Her friends presented a similarly "tough" image and were heavy drinkers. While growing up, the only information she had about her birth parents was that they were both 23 years old when she was born. She also knew that she was born in a hospital affiliated with the university, on the "poor" side of town. She envisioned her birth parents to be hard-drinking, poor, uneducated, and dysfunctional. This youth was very surprised to learn, with the help of post-adoption counseling, that her birth parents had been graduate students who had experienced an untimely pregnancy. She was amazed to find that they were even more middle class and conventional than her adoptive parents!

Some older adopted youth may not even have sufficient information about their own ethnicity on which to build an identity.

MAGICAL THINKING

All young children believe themselves to be the center of the universe and therefore responsible for everything that happens in their world. Young children believe that, if one event happens after another, then the first event caused the second. Inappropriate assumptions about cause and effect, while holding oneself as the cause of virtually everything, are called magical thinking by developmental psychologists. Children who have entered the worlds of foster care and adoption often struggle with shame and guilt as they interpret their life circumstances to be their "fault." Even children who have never lived with their birth parents may believe that they were not attractive enough, or not the "right" gender, or that they cried too much to be loved and wanted by their birth parents.

Doretha was placed in a kinship adoption with her maternal aunt shortly after birth when her birth parents went through a bitter divorce. As Doretha grew into adulthood, she remained positive that her birth father would have remained in the family, negating the necessity of the adoptive placement, if only she had been a boy. Doretha had never been told that either of her birth parents had desired a boy. However, as a young child, she needed an explanation for her father's desertion and could find only her own gender to be the reason for the family's breakdown. Even as she grew older, she clung to the notion that she, not her birth mother or father, was responsible for her family's collapse and her subsequent adoption. She struggled with depression and poor self-esteem throughout most of her life.

DIVIDED LOYALTIES

If communication about adoption is not part of the adoptive family life, a child can develop confusion and conflict when emotions about birth parents remain strong. When new feelings for the adoptive family emerge, the child may feel that he is not "allowed" to love and care about more than one family at the same time. The system of closed or confidential adoption, existing in our culture for the past 30 to 40 years, reinforces the concept that a child will be able to love only one mother and father. Therefore, birth parents must be erased from the child's life in an attempt to erase them from his thinking. Adult adopted persons have taught us that this system of adoption practice does not have the desired result. If anything, disconnected adopted persons spend more time and energy struggling with allegiances and trying to decide who they belong to and who they should be attached to. One youngster whose family did not discuss any adoption-related issues blurted out one day to his adoptive parents, "What do I do about you? I still love my birth mom and dad. What do I do about my feelings for you?" This family needed to share the facts regarding his adoption and also assure the child that it is possible to love more than one set of parents. A child who does not receive this critical reassurance may not feel free to attach to his adoptive family. Permission to know about, and care about, his birth family actually frees a child to know and care about his adoptive family. Children, and adoptive parents, must understand that humans do not have to stop loving one person to start loving another. Parents are allowed, and expected, to love more than one child. Children must be allowed, by themselves and others, to love more than one parent.

John, adopted domestically after chronic neglect by his depressed mother, could not bring himself to attach to his adoptive mother, even after eight years in the home. As a very young child, John had been responsible for nurturing his depressed parent. John firmly believed that he had deserted his birth mother and that any positive feeling for his adoptive mother was a sign of further disloyalty. While John could connect with his adoptive father, he continued to hold himself emotionally distant from his mother, believing that this was the honorable thing for him to do. Mother's Day was a particularly difficult time for John, as he could not bring himself to give his adoptive mother gifts or cards. John had frequent behavior problems during the spring months preceding Mother's Day; his behavior was an indicator of his conflict and confusion. With intensive post adoption counseling, John was able to understand that he did not have to stop loving his birth mother in order to feel love and attachment for his adoptive mother. As he entered young adulthood, John was finally able to become a full member of the adoptive family.

FEARS OF FUTURE ABANDONMENT

Adopted children have all experienced a separation from at least one family, their birth family. They may also have been moved numerous times from one foster home to another. Or their placement may have occurred suddenly, as often happens when children are removed due to turmoil—abuse or severe neglect—or due to international adoption. The children have been traumatized by abrupt moves and the disappearance from their lives of trusted caregivers. They learn to fear another such move and are reluctant to allow themselves the vulnerability of believing that this new family is indeed a "forever family." Children who are fearful of future abandonment may be unable to attend school without severe school phobia, to attend summer camps for several days away from home, or even to spend the night with grandparents or school friends. They may become terrified if Mom or Dad is a few minutes late picking them up from soccer practice. Discussions about a family move may become unmanageable to a child who believes that he will not accompany the rest of the family when they move.

Kim was a 14-year-old Korean child who had been adopted at age 2 and a half. She had made a wonderful adjustment in the adoptive home, but was continually concerned about remaining close to her adoptive mother. As Kim was preparing to enter high school, her family decided to purchase a new home in a neighborhood with better schools for Kim. The young teen became extremely agitated, insisted that she would NOT move, and remained tearfully locked in her bedroom for several days. The situation reached crisis proportions when Kim attempted to commit suicide to avoid the move, signaling the family she was experiencing extreme panic. In the counseling that followed this crisis, it became clear that Kim had been devastated as a toddler by her separations from her birth mother, foster mother, and culture. She continued to have intense anxiety throughout her childhood that a similar abandonment would occur in her new home. When the adoptive parents began to talk about a move, Kim was convinced that she would be left behind; the abandonment she feared throughout her childhood was finally becoming, in her mind, a reality.

A parallel concern appears evident in children who may believe they were inappropriately kidnapped by the adoptive or foster family, by the social workers, or by police. They may see their birth parents as searching frantically to be reunited with the lost child. These fantasies can be reinforced by children's fables such as "Hansel and Gretel" and even by Fievel the Mouse in the movie *An American Tale* (singing "Somewhere, Out There" as he yearns for the birth family to find him). In both scenarios, fear of abandonment or anger over "kidnapping" the result is the same. Children who believe that they are not going to remain in the adoptive family will not attach. They worry about the pain of becoming close to a family who will be lost—forever.

FEELING DISCONNECTED

Having little or no information about one's past does create, for many, a deep and pervasive feeling of disconnectedness, of having a piece of themselves missing, of being incomplete. Many adoptees feel an extreme sense of sadness, pain, and confusion. There is a sense of unreality, of not being born properly-not being real or not being a part of society.[3] Another term for this sense of disconnectedness is genealogical bewilderment. This term was first coined in 1964 by psychologist H. J. Sants, referring to the plight of children who have uncertain, little, or no knowledge of one or both of their natural parents. Sants argued that genealogical bewilderment constituted a large part of the additional stress that adoptees experienced that is not experienced by children being raised by their natural parents.[4] Providing an adopted child with information about his birth family, the circumstances of the adoption, and any other pertinent information can do much to alleviate this sense of disconnectedness.

"I feel just like a doughnut—someone with a gigantic hole in the center." Many adopted youth can identify with this young man's analogy of his feeling of being incomplete because he has been disconnected from his own history. Another young adopted adult comments, "I have always felt like a victim of amnesia. I can't remember who I am." Mary, an adopted person exclaimed that she felt as though her parents were ignoring "an elephant standing in the living room." She knew she was adopted, but the family never discussed the adoption or her birth family. And some young people express a feeling of never having been born, but being alien . . . arriving on this planet from another world, completely mysterious to them.[5]

LACK OF TRUST IN AUTHORITY FIGURES AND CONTROL ISSUES

Children and teens must feel that issues of importance to them are shared honestly in order to develop a sense of trust within their family. A study conducted in 1983 of adults who were adopted as older children revealed that much of their discontent came as a result of never being consulted about what was happening in their lives, being moved with little or no preparation, and, finally, never being asked about their feelings. This need for control is evidenced in the mantra of youth in foster care: "Nothing about us without us!" (Foster Club, website https://www.fosterclub.com). All of those in the study felt an incredible lack of control, the consequences of which have followed them into adulthood.[6]

Children also must know that talking about their feelings and histories openly and freely is permitted in their adoptive home. This awareness, along with the opportunity to be a part of the major decisions made for them, will add to their much-needed sense of control. If children and youth believe they have little or no control over their own life histories, they often try to seize control in the family through negative means: power struggles, lying, chronic behavioral problems, or sending the adoptive family into crisis by running away from home.

Laura, age 17, was adopted at age 3. Her teenage birth mother had struggled with the decision to make an adoption plan for her child, and Laura remained in foster care until her birth mother felt ready to sign a permanent surrender. Laura knew very little about her birth mother or her struggle with this decision. She was a very angry teen who often lied to others, as she felt deceived herself. Laura felt most in control when she ran away. She knew that her adoptive parents would experience a crisis when she did so, and that gave Laura an incredible sense of power. Laura always ran to areas of town where she imagined her birth mother would be. In essence, Laura was controlling her adoptive family and "searching" for her birth mother at the same time.

CURIOSITY

Understandably, children are curious about their birth families and origins, regardless of the amount of information they possess about them.[7]

Children who are intelligent and sensitive are likely to have a natural curiosity. And if this curiosity is not satisfied, it will intensify. When adoptive parents are not able to support their children's natural curiosity in a sensitive manner, they create a barrier to closeness with that child, creating a greater possibility for future adjustment problems.[8]

Adopted children are curious and have repeatedly asked post adoption counselors about two particular issues:

1. What do my birth parents look like? Do I look like them?

If parents or social workers can take pictures of the birth parents, these will be very important to the children as they makes sense of their history. Pictures should be protected (digitized, if possible), so they cannot be destroyed or lost. These pictures should be available to the children, perhaps framed in their bedroom, in their lifebook, included in the adoptive family album, or all of the above.

2. Why couldn't my birth parents take care of me?

Children need the unvarnished truth about how they came to be separated from their birth parents, so they can relinquish guilt (magical thinking). The child must also be assured the adoptive family will not make a similar decision.

FEARS AND UNANSWERED QUESTIONS ABOUT GENETICS AND MEDICAL HISTORY

Having little or no knowledge about one's genetic background and/or medical history can add to the sense of disconnectedness. One adoptee summed up the feeling like this:

> Where did I get my red hair? What nationality am I? What kind of body am I growing into? What talents or special skills are in my family line? What hidden illness may show up in my life? All these questions follow me as I move into adulthood, and no one has an answer. I feel like I am walking around with gaps and holes in my life which I cannot fill without answers.

Some young people worry that they might date or even marry a sibling or a cousin.

George, age 16, knew that both of his birth parents had severe mental illness, requiring frequent hospitalizations. As he approached adulthood, George felt like a ticking bomb; he was convinced that he was genetically doomed to develop unmanageable mental health problems. While George had information about his medical history, he also needed help in interpreting, or making sense of, the information about his birth parents. He needed to meet with a person knowledgeable about the link between genetics and the mental health conditions of his birth parents so that he could more accurately assess his level of risk. And he needed the "whole picture;" that is, who in his birth family was not mentally ill? Often, the focus may be on birth parents, ignoring the fact that many healthy, productive, talented people are present in the extended family or gene pool.

ANNE'S STORY

Let's look at the history of one young woman, Anne Ginther of Columbus, Ohio. Anne's story demonstrates the multiple impacts of a "mystery history" on a child as she matures. In 1972, Anne's adoptive parents, Norma and Jeff Ginther, were a young, white married couple with one birth son, almost age three. They were living in Colorado and had applied to adopt an infant girl of mixed racial heritage. One Monday, the agency called to tell the Ginthers a seven-month-old child was available for adoption. The social worker said that the birth mother was Caucasian, but she was unsure if the birth father was African American, Hispanic, or Native American. The Ginthers were told that they could see the baby on Thursday of that week and that placement could occur (with no pre-placement visitation) on the same day if they "approved of the baby." If the Ginthers could not see the baby on Thursday, they would have to wait one month for placement while the social worker went on vacation.

Today, Norma remembers the adoption as a "drive-by placement." At the time, the young couple believed that birth history was unimportant; the child's future would be molded by the adoptive parents, and the impact of her genetic background would be negligible. Over the next 20 years, they learned that they had gravely underestimated the importance of Anne's history. When they tried to get the information years later, they were unable to locate the birth family and received almost no assistance from the placing agency.

Jeff and Norma were told, when they arrived at the agency on that exciting Thursday in 1972, that the baby's mother had been 19 years old, had graduated from high school, and was originally from Kentucky or Tennessee. She had liked music and art and had been an average student. She came to Denver a short time before becoming pregnant. There were three possible birth fathers: one African American, one Hispanic, and one Native American. The mother tried to parent the baby for six weeks. When she could not manage, she called her family. They would not accept a "mixed" baby. The birth mother returned to her parents' home in another state but left the baby with a neighbor. The neighbor cared for the baby for approximately two to three weeks but became concerned when she realized she had no authority to get medical care for the baby.

When Anne became sick, the neighbor called the child protective services agency for assistance. The baby was placed in an emergency foster home and then, later, in a regular foster home. The mother never returned to Colorado, and a permanent surrender was arranged through interstate authorities. Foster parents, in the 1960s and 1970s, were not allowed to adopt.

After meeting Anne on Thursday morning, the Ginthers returned to the agency in the afternoon to pick her up. One of the social workers accidentally used Anne's whole name at the time of placement. Norma remembered the name and shared it with Anne years later. The adoptive parents were told the adoption story verbally, but they never received written information from the agency.

The adoptive family had so little information to share with Anne that they told her everything they knew about her history while she was still in preschool. By the time Anne was ten years old, her anger was building to unmanageable levels. She often became violent, destroyed things in her room, and suffered uncontrollable crying bouts. Due to Anne's explosive behavior, the adoptive parents took her to a professional counselor when she was 10 years old. He advised Anne needed more information about her history and the reasons surrounding her adoption. Anne told the therapist that she particularly wanted to know "who I look like." The Ginthers, now living in Ohio, wrote to the Colorado agency that arranged the adoption. The agency social workers wrote Anne a nice letter, reinforcing the limited information that had been shared at the time of placement. That letter was very helpful to Anne. She was struggling because she had no pictures of herself prior to her adoption, but the agency was unfortunately unable to help her find pictures of herself as a very young infant. The agency sent a separate letter to the adoptive parents, questioning their motives for wanting additional information, expressing concern (and judgment) that they wanted to "give her back." Nothing could have been farther from the truth.

At about this same time, Anne received a school assignment to draw a family tree. This assignment proved challenging for Anne. She commented that she would "lie" and use the adoptive family for her family tree. Clearly, she needed help in understanding that all family trees hold multiple families. Her most realistic or honest family tree would hold both birth and adoptive families, perhaps depicting the birth family in the roots, and the branches of the adoptive family in the "branches" of the tree (see Chapter 9, Tools for Telling for more information).

Also at that time, the movie *Annie* appeared in local theaters. The movie depicted the plight of an orphan who longed for a family. In the movie, Annie could not consent to her adoption by the benevolent Daddy Warbucks until she was positive that there was no hope of reunification with her birth family. The real Anne became obsessed with this movie, whose central character ironically had a name so similar to hers, and owned four or five videotaped copies. She watched the film so often that she wore out the videotapes.

By the time Anne was 11 or 12 years old, she began tirades that included, "You are not my real mom!" Her adoptive mother found her sobbing one day, "How could someone who didn't even know me give me away?"

Anne, now more than 40 years old and the mother of three children, remembers her longing to know more about her history. She always knew that she was adopted, and she feels that her adoptive parents were always very supportive of her need to have more information. However, Anne remembers believing firmly, when she was 10 to 13 years old, that her parents had information that they were concealing from her (lack of trust in authority figures). She was extremely angry about her inability to access this information, and she projected that anger in outbursts directed at her parents.

Anne had many fantasies about her birth parents. She was convinced for some time that they had been rich and famous. When she was particularly angry at her adoptive parents, she would fantasize that her birth parents would send a limousine to pick her up for a joyous reunion (unrealistic fantasies). Another fantasy held for some time was that her adoptive mother had an affair with a man of color, conceived her, and kept the baby. According to this latter fantasy, the adoption itself was a lie because Anne believed she was with her birth mother (magical thinking)!

Control battles and power struggles were common during Anne's adolescence. Even though her parents were very sensitive to Anne's need for information, the constant control battles were wearing for everyone in the family (need for control).

One of Anne's most difficult challenges has been identity formation. She is not certain about her ethnicity, and her appearance really does not confirm any ancestry. She knows that she is a multiracial person, but does not know exactly what constitutes "multi." She could be African American, but also appears to have Native American or Hispanic ancestors. During her adolescence, she identified with several different ethnicities and, as an adult, still has questions about her roots (identity confusion).

Anne shares, however, that her greatest struggles revolve around fears of future abandonment. She commented that she worried incessantly about losing significant people. She tried to push people away from her to avoid the pain of being rejected. In other words, she tried to "quit before she got fired." The adult Anne comments that she worries about losing those who are close to her, and she still overreacts to losses and separations. For example, when in the military, Anne found it too painful and panic inducing to be far away from her parents. She was married and had a child at the time but missed her parents so much that she received an honorable discharge due to intense anxiety around separation from her parents.

CONCLUSION

When caring parents consider the discomfort of talking about adoption and the very real dangers of not talking about adoption issues, they must conclude that:

1. Parents need to talk openly and honestly with the child in an age-appropriate way about the adoption, the birth family, and the circumstances of the adoption.
2. Parents need the tools and knowledge to talk about adoption effectively.

See Appendix A for information needed to fully prepare a case for adoption.

QUESTIONS

1. How would chidren's "unrealistic fantasies" impact their relationship with their adoptive parents?
2. What are signs that an adolescent may be struggling with identity confusion as it relates to adoption?
3. What are signs that an adolescent may be struggling with loyalty issues as it relates to adoption?
4. What behaviors and feelings might a parent see if a child is struggling with fear of future abandonment?
5. What behaviors and feelings might a parent see if a child is struggling with control issues?

CHAPTER 4

Learning about Your Child: A Fact-Finding Mission

Information on a child's heredity and life experiences helps parents to understand their child, have realistic expectations, and address their child's specific needs both in their parenting and through outside resources. Knowledge of the particular losses and traumas that their child experienced is essential for helping their child make sense of these past events and heal.

Susan Livingston Smith[1]

Carlton had just stopped at home for lunch when the phone rang. It was the adoption agency. A birth mother had just made an adoption decision and had chosen them to be the family for her unborn child. Were they interested in discussing the prospective adoptive placement in further detail? Could they come to the agency this evening?

Carlton and LaVonne had waited over five years for this call. For them, life without a child and the intense emotional rollercoaster ride of infertility was almost over. "Yes, of course, we will be there," Carlton responded.

Sandy Ridden hung up the phone. She could hardly dial her husband's office number to tell him the news. The adoption social worker at their public agency had just called, asking Sandy and David to come in the next day to discuss the possible adoptive placement of two children: a four-year-old boy and a one-year old girl. Neither one of them could rest well that evening. The following day they would face a decision that would affect them and two very special youngsters for the rest of their lives.

Each and every day in this country, prospective adoptive parents receive such phone calls. Those calls create a myriad of intense emotions: fear, excitement, curiosity, doubt. Questions and concerns engulf their hearts and minds as they begin to process this monumental endeavor. "What will the children look like? What is their history? Why are they available for adoption? Do they have any significant medical concerns? What is their history of trauma, abuse, neglect? Loss? What is in their background that we should know? And, most important, is it appropriate to ask? Do we have a right to know?" Information these families will hear and the openness they will experience regarding their children's social and medical history have been influenced by decades of controversy on the duty to disclose. For over 70 years, contention over the issue of complete honesty and openness challenged those in the social work profession. In the last two decades, many agencies have attempted to return full circle to complete and honest disclosure, but the road back has not been easy.

A HISTORICAL PERSPECTIVE: HOW WORKERS VIEWED ADOPTION BACKGROUND DISCLOSURE AND THE IMPACT ON FAMILIES TODAY

As the practice of adoption entered the twentieth century, significant issues confronted adoption social workers. One of the most important questions, however, centered on adoption background disclosure. Workers faced an ethically and emotionally inflamed question: How much information should the adoptive family be given about the birth family, the child's history, and potential physical, emotional, or psychological concerns?

The 1920s and 1930s

For workers in the 1920s and 1930s, the question of full and accurate background disclosure was not an issue at all. Against the backdrop of extensive openness between birth family and adoptive family, disclosure was an obvious conclusion. Honesty, openness, and accuracy guided communication.

A worker's perspective on disclosure in adoption in the early part of the twentieth century would go something like this:

> When children, whether infants or older children, came into care, it was the duty of the agency to do a thorough case study. Families needed this information to make a decision as to whether to receive the child or not. The study required a thorough analysis of the child's family—the physical condition of the parents, their personal habits in regard to intemperance, gambling, begging or other objectionable practices. The agency studied the child itself. They studied the child's heredity to discover, if possible, whether it is likely to be a victim of feeblemindedness, insanity, epilepsy, or syphilis, or tuberculosis. They studied the child's mentality and in some cases additional study was required if the children were found erratic, emotionally upset, or nervously disordered.[2]

Agencies always believed that the adoptive family should have all the information in their possession in order to fully know the child. They felt that the prospective parents should be as fully informed as possible regarding the child's history. Not only is this history of usually great assistance . . . in the intelligent bringing up of the child, but, in later life, when the child realizes that he is adopted, he should be allowed to know that facts concerning his forebears.[3]

In 1932, the Child Welfare League of America (CWLA) issued the following statement on adoption disclosure:

> No child that is . . . diseased and no child of feeble-minded parents should be placed in any home for adoption until the adoptive parents know the full facts of the case. Children with special handicaps of a physical nature or related to personality or behavior, and those whose heredity suggests that difficult problems may arise, should be placed for adoption only when the adoptive parents thoroughly understand the child's needs and concerns.[4]

The Fifties Bring Change

By the early 1950s, the number of adoptions rose dramatically, fueled by the postwar era—the baby boom. Early in the decade of the 1950s, confidentiality and, eventually, secrecy filtered into adoption practice. It was assumed that if anonymity of all individuals involved was protected, then the birth mother could more easily resolve her feelings about the placement, the child would be more easily integrated into the family, and the adoptive parents could present their children as being biologically their own.

Along with the evolution of secrecy in adoption practice came the practice of withholding information about a child's social and medical history from adoptive parents. Two issues, according to adoption researchers Freundlich and Peterson, were at the core of these policies. The first concern centered on the need to protect adopted children from the stigma associated with illegitimacy. The second force that drove the movement to withhold information grew out of a need to accommodate what social workers construed as a general reluctance on the part of adoptive families to discuss adoption with their children.[5]

In 1954, one social worker wrote in defense of this policy, "Because of the possibility of neurotic character traits in the adoptive parents, they and the child must be protected by keeping from them any knowledge about the child's background." There was a fear that adoptive parents who were "hostilely envious of those who can bear children would use this negative information as a weapon when angered by this child's misbehavior."[6] Other workers felt that if the parents and child knew anything about the birth parents it would be devastating to the child's self-esteem.[7]

Still more workers labeled prospective adoptive parents who demanded knowledge of the child's past as "very anxious, narcissistic, and unconsciously sadistic." Many adoption workers were convinced that not disclosing information "would ease adoptive parents' discomfort in discussing the issue, would relieve them of the burden of possessing information they were not 'mature' enough to absorb," and would "avoid stigmatizing the adopted child."[8]

For some agencies, nondisclosure of background information became a matter of agency practice. All social information about the birth family was cleared through a few selected adoption agency supervisors. Caseworkers insulated from that information, along with these supervisors, would certify the child's adoptability. The worker would only have to say, "I know this to be a fine baby because my investigating chief and consultants have so agreed, and that is fine enough for me."[9]

Some workers adamantly disagreed about adoption disclosure. It was not so much a question of total disclosure or total withholding, but of how much and what type of family information should be disclosed. By the mid-1950s, most agencies gave families only selected information and left out sordid or "irrelevant" details.

In January of 1955, during a CWLA National Conference on Adoption, a general consensus grew that "agencies should select pertinent facts helpful to the adoptive parents and child and withhold facts that were prejudicial and stigmatizing." A new adoption standard practice was later issued which read: "Member Agencies of CWLA are instructed not to give adoptive parents information, which is not relevant to the child's development and would only arouse anxiety."[10]

The 1970s and 1980s

Policies on adoption disclosure began to shift again in the seventies and eighties toward a greater degree of information sharing. This change came about for a number of reasons. First, the majority of the population of children needing adoption shifted from infant to special needs. Second, adoption professionals realized that parents were willing to adopt children with special needs and that background information did not discourage them. Finally, advocacy movements led to greater demands by all members of the triad.[11]

By 1988, the Child Welfare League further elaborated on their standards concerning disclosure of background information. Those standards, which remain in effect today, require a developmental history and family history, a medical examination, and psychological testing as needed.[12]

What about Today?

In spite of the legal developments that require full and open disclosure to adoptive parents, it still today has not become a uniform mode of practice for all adoption professionals. The process is better, but challenges remain. Some agencies fail to disclose fully to a family because of the fear that the child would be "unadoptable" if all were known. Agencies have failed to disclose because they have not been able to locate information (due to understaffing). Perhaps the staff has not been adequately trained on how to gather critical information about the child's history and birth family.[13] Maybe they don't recognize the critical need to make the effort to obtain all pertinent information. In the case of international adoption, often the country of origin has not obtained a child's social history, accurately diagnosed a child's medical problems, or fully understood the lifelong value such information would provide for an adoptive family.

When families do not have adequate information, it can lead to grave consequences, according to Susan Livingston Smith:

> Parents' cognitive appraisal of their child helps to shape their efforts to cope with challenges and their overall commitment to parenting. When parents lack understanding about the causes of a child's adjustment difficulties, it can lead to negative or blaming perceptions of both their child and themselves as parents as well as failure to access the best information or other resources to effectively support them and their child.[14]

Without a full understanding of what happened to their child, parents can form unrealistic expectations. An important means of achieving realistic expectations in parents and in older children placed for adoption is thorough preparation. For parents, this includes accurate and up-to-date background information on the child. Yet many families report not having received enough information. For example, in a study of 259 families adopting from foster care, 58 percent reported getting insufficient information on the child, and 37 percent reported the child's problems were more serious than the placement agency originally described.[15]

What Do Parents Need to Know?

Seth was five years old when he joined his adoptive family. Prior to his arrival in his adoptive family, Seth had experienced abuse and neglect. Due to the expertise of his trauma-informed caseworker and therapist, the family was given a significant amount of information.

"We were given a real gift," said Johanna, his adoptive mom. "When our caseworker, Kelly, sat down with us and described his trauma and loss history with us extensively, we felt so much better prepared. She shared so much with us, gave us opportunities to ask a lot of questions and provided resources for our further understanding. When we first learned about Seth and saw his picture on the state photo listing, we began to dream what life would be like with this precious five-year-old. Our expectations are far more realistic now, and we know that just love isn't enough. We know we need 'well-informed love.' It is our greatest hope."

So what did Seth's caseworker share with the family? She conveyed to them their important role in the information-gathering stage of adoption decisions. She explained five essential tasks in learning about their prospective new son. She discussed the importance of understanding the impact of trauma and loss on a child. She talked to them about Seth's sensory and developmental issues, birth family history, and much more. She not only talked to them about these potential challenges but gave them tools to understand the information on a very practical level.

LEARNING ABOUT YOUR CHILD: FIVE ESSENTIAL TASKS TO FIND OUT WHAT YOU NEED TO KNOW

A Parent's First Essential Task: For Adoptive Parents to Recognize Their Right to All Social and Medical History Regarding Their Child and the Benefit of Obtaining and Maintaining It

Adoptive parents, often intimidated by the adoption process because of lack of experience, may be hesitant to ask questions about the child they are considering for adoption. They may feel that their questions are intrusive, unkind, or insensitive to the child. Some feel that the information is not that important because the child will be in a new family with a new start. Some say, "It is best I don't know anything; then I don't have to lie to my child about the truth." However, gathering and maintaining that information is important not only for them, but essential for the child in the future.

What Are the Benefits of Having a Complete and Accurate Background History?

- It provides an opportunity for early diagnosis, treatment, and intervention for developmental problems and conditions.
- It eliminates the need for repetitive testing for the children.
- It provides an opportunity for the adoptees, as children, and eventually as adults, to develop an accurate sense of history about themselves and a more fully integrated identity.

There Are Limits on the Extent to Which Health and Other Background Information May Be Obtained

Adoptive parents must realize that generally the sole source of information for most domestic infant adoptions is the birth family. In many cases, this information may come only from the birth mother. Information may be incomplete or inaccurate (intentionally or unintentionally). Many U.S. states, however, have Safe Haven laws enacted as "an incentive for mothers in crisis to safely relinquish their babies to designated locations where the babies are protected and provided with medical care until a permanent home is found. Safe Haven laws generally allow the parent, or an agent of the parent, to remain anonymous and to be shielded from prosecution for abandonment or neglect in exchange for surrendering the baby to a safe haven."[16] Safe Haven providers vary according to state laws but are typically fire or police stations, hospitals, or possibly churches. These laws attempt to prevent unnecessary deaths caused by panicky young parents, but they do leave children with no information about their roots.

In international adoptions, generally the only source of information is the agency in the country of origin. Their capacity to get full and complete background information from the birth family is very limited due to the circumstances of the relinquishment. Many times, children are left at orphanage doorsteps with no way to trace the birth family. Other times, children are brought to an orphanage for "temporary" care, and the family disappears. Agency staff is then left with the task of putting together information in a vacuum, even guessing about the child's age.

When children move into adoption from the domestic foster care system, health and other background information may or may not be more readily available. Again, the primary source for that information is the birth family, and complete and accurate information may not be available. A second hurdle in gathering information about a foster child is that collection, maintenance, and communication are often handled by various units of a public service agency before the information reaches the adoption worker. Improving the flow of information is a task that many agencies are tackling with determination.

A Parent's Second Essential Task: To Gain Understanding Regarding the Impact of Trauma on Child Development

When early life trauma and neglect is the child's story, that child is set on a trajectory path that leads them to behavioral issues and possible mental health issues well into adulthood—unless that trajectory is interrupted with trauma-informed care by trauma-competent healing parents and social workers. An essential task of competent, compassionate adoptive and foster parents is to have a growing understanding of the impact of complex developmental trauma on a child. Complex developmental trauma is defined in the following way:

> Complex traumatic exposure refers to children's experiences of multiple traumatic events that occur within the caregiving system—the social environment that is supposed to be the source of safety and stability in a child's life. Typically, complex trauma exposure refers to the simultaneous or sequential occurrences of child maltreatment—including emotional abuse and neglect, sexual abuse, physical abuse, and witnessing domestic violence—that are chronic and begin in early childhood. Moreover, the initial traumatic experiences (e.g., parental neglect and emotional abuse) and the resulting emotional dysregulation (poorly modulated emotional responses), loss of a safe base, loss of direction, and inability to detect or respond to danger cues, often lead to subsequent trauma exposure (e.g., physical and sexual abuse, or community violence).[17]

There are four elements that comprise complex developmental trauma:

1. **Early** – Trauma can occur even before birth. According to Dr. Karyn Purvis, Director of the Institute of Child Development at Texas Christian University, there are three risk factors that can happen early to a

child that could result in emotional and behavioral difficulties. These risk factors are:
   a. A difficult pregnancy
   b. A difficult birth
   c. Separation/hospitalization immediately after birth
2. **Chronic** – A young child is exposed to danger over time that is unpredictable or uncontrollable. The child never experiences what it feels like to feel safe.
3. **Maltreatment** – This danger is **always a form of maltreatment**—physical, emotional, psychological, sexual abuse or neglect.
4. **Failure/absence of a caregiver** who reliably and responsively protects and nurtures the child.[18]

Tools to Understand the Impact of Complex Developmental Trauma

- Trauma loss history tool
- Sensory processing assessment
- Developmental checklist

Trauma Loss / History Tool

One of the most helpful tools to understand complex developmental trauma is the trauma/loss history tool developed by the Chadwick Center for Children and Families.[19] Although this tool was originally designed to help child welfare workers make more trauma-informed decisions about the need for referral to trauma-specific and general mental health services, many agencies are now using it when presenting children to families for adoption. This tool helps parents get a clearer picture of the timeline of their child's trauma experiences. Trauma derails development, and the timeline offers parents insight into what developmental pieces may be compromised or missing. For more information about the trauma and loss tool, visit the National Child Traumatic Stress Network at www.nctsn.org.

Sensory Processing Assessment

Recent neurological research indicates a number of damaging things happen to a child's brain as a result of trauma. One of the life-impacting results of trauma is in the area of sensory processing. "Trauma disrupts the sensory processing system," according to Dr. Karyn Purvis. How important is it that parents have an understanding of sensory issues before their prospective child arrives? According to Lindsey Biel, occupational therapist, author, and sensory expert, it is critically important: "Children first learn about the world through their senses. What they see, hear, touch, smell, and taste and how they experience movement all work together to give children a reliable picture of the world and their place in it."

Adopted children are at an increased risk for sensory challenges—especially those adopted from overseas orphanages—due to low or absent prenatal care and an environment in which there is often poor sensory stimulation, little contact with affectionate people, and minimal opportunities to explore the world and all of its rich sensory information. This can lead to hypersensitivity or even fear of certain types of noises, lights, textures, smells, foods, and movement challenges. Another child may become undersensitive or somewhat numb to sensory input, needing greater input to become alert and interested.

Once adopted and brought home, children with sensory processing challenges may become quickly overwhelmed by all the new sensory input they face. A child used to being in the same limited spaces may be quickly overwhelmed by how big and exciting the world is, with so many faces, places, and things to discover. New, unfamiliar clothing will feel different on the skin, and colorful new toys and room decorations may be disorienting. A child used to being bottled propped in a crib for hours or fed the same bland foods day after day may have feeding issues when presented with what parents consider a typical child's diet.

"The great news is that most children adapt fairly quickly, especially when adoptive parents tune in to their child's sensory needs and introduce new sensory experiences in a thoughtful, careful way."[20] To view a Sensory Checklist, visit www.sensorysmarts.com/signs_of_spd.html.

Developmental Checklist

As with sensory processing issues, trauma also impacts a child's development. "Two basic processes, neurodevelopment and psychosocial development, are affected by early abuse and neglect. Scientists have begun to understand the mechanisms through which these adverse experiences alter child development and produce damaging mental, medical, and social outcomes."[21] A helpful checklist that compares normal child development with possible indicators of trauma can assist parents in developing realistic expectations. To view a developmental checklist, http://www.dhs.vic.gov.au/for-service-providers/children,-youth-and-families/child-protection/specialist-practice-resources-for-child-protection-workers/child-development-and-trauma-specialist-practice-resource.[22]

Understanding the impact of trauma and strategies to gather information about that portion of the child's history is essential. Another essential task is equally important.

A Parent's Third Essential Task: To Develop a List of Questions for the Information-Sharing Meetings with Their Child's Caseworker and Others Involved in the Child's Life

During the decision-making time prior to an adoption, families will have the opportunity to talk with their child's caseworker. In cases of older child adoption, parents should also ask for the opportunity to talk with other professionals who have been involved with the child, including former foster parents, therapists, child care providers, and schoolteachers. The following are "starter" lists (older child and/or infant adoption) parents can use when asking questions about their prospective adoptive child:

Questions When Considering the Adoption of an Older Child

1. How complete is the social/medical history on the birth family, including the extended family? What is missing? Is it possible to obtain more information?
2. Is there a history of drug or alcohol abuse?
3. Is there any history of mental illness?
4. Is there any history of other genetically related illnesses such as diabetes, heart disease, and so on?
5. What is known about this child's prenatal care and birth history?
6. What is known about this child's developmental history—physically, emotionally, and cognitively, including language development?
7. What is the child's current health? Allergies? ADHD-related problems?
8. Why was the child removed from his or her biological family? Physical abuse? If so, what kind, how often, and from whom? Sexual abuse? If so, what kind, how often, and from whom?
9. What does the child understand about the reasons for removal?
10. When was the last contact the child had with the biological family?
11. Are there any brothers and sisters? If so, what contact has this child had with these siblings? Is it expected that these contacts will continue, and to what degree? Who is responsible for seeing that it happens?
12. In what ways is the child manifesting behaviors related to his abuse, separation, or other trauma? Are other children "victimized" by the behavior? In what way?

13. How has this child functioned in foster care? How many moves has this child experienced in foster care, and why was the child moved?
14. What methods of discipline does this child respond to most often?
15. How does this child relate to his peers in the neighborhood and school?
16. What level of openness, if any, is possible with birth family members?
17. What special skills/abilities/talents/interests did birth family members have?

Questions When Considering the Adoption of an Infant

1. How complete is the social/medical history on the birth family, including the extended family? What is missing? Is it possible to obtain more information?
2. What is known about the birth parents' developmental history—physically, emotionally, and cognitively, including language development?
3. Is there a history of drug or alcohol abuse?
4. Is there any history of mental illness? Is there any history of other genetically related illnesses such as diabetes, heart disease, and so on?
5. What is known about this child's prenatal care and birth history?
6. Are there any brothers and sisters? If so, what contact, if any, is planned with these siblings? How often and to what degree will these contacts be expected to continue? Who is responsible for seeing that it happens?
7. What special skills/abilities/talents/interests did birth family members have?

A Parent's Fourth Essential Task: How to Read a Waiting Child's Description and Social Summary

In pursuing an adoptive placement, many families spend time either looking through sources such as Adopt US Kids,[23] Adoption.com,[24] or Holt International Children Services[25] to find available adoptable children. Each state and many public and private agencies also have their own photo-listings of waiting children.

Before even visiting the photo listings, it is most helpful for parents to understand the purpose of the photo listing. Its main purpose is to provide an "acquaintance"-level introduction to a waiting child. When we meet a new person, that person is still just an acquaintance. We don't share everything with that new person. That is similar to the purpose of the photo listing. It is just an introduction. There is much more to learn. One easy, emotional mistake parents make when looking at the listing is to "fall in love" with a picture, therefore ignoring the crucial steps in learning if they can truly meet the child's needs.

In *Adopting and Advocating for the Special Needs Child*, Anne Babb and Rita Laws note that adoptive parents need to understand how to interpret information given on a photo listing or social summary. Because brevity rules each listing, certain phrases or comments are used as shortcuts. The following is a type of matching quiz for prospective adoptive parents who read the photo listing:

In reading a child's description the following information will generally be available to prospective parents:

- Child's first name, date of birth, state and possibly county of residence, an ID number, and the date the listing was added
- A brief social/medical history
- Where the child is currently living (i.e., foster or group home, residential treatment center)
- What type of adoptive family is needed (i.e., single parent, married couple, other children in the home, older or younger children, etc.)
- The agency contact person's name and phone number[26]

As parents read these shortcuts, it then becomes imperative to explore the meaning behind the words with caseworkers and professionals.

Recognizing an adoptive parent's right to information, learning about the impact of trauma and the tools that will help that understanding, developing a list of questions for the information-sharing meeting, and understanding how to read the child's description on the photo-listing are four tasks for prospective parents in the information gathering phase of adoption. There is one more.

A Parent's Fifth Essential Task: For Adoptive Parents to Realize That They Also Have a Responsibility with Regard to Background Disclosure

One of the responsibilities that adoptive parents must assume is the awareness and understanding that there are risks involved in adoption, just as in parenting a child born to them. Prospective adoptive parents should understand that by pursuing adoption, they will be assuming responsibilities for which there are no guarantees of specific results or outcomes. It is not possible, according to Freundlich and Peterson, to be given an assurance "that all existing information has been discovered, nor is it possible to predict the future health status of a child."[27]

Adoptive parents should pursue diagnosis and prognosis of a mental or medical health concern from professionals skilled and experienced in the area in question. In an effort to fully disclose information to adoptive parents, adoption professionals may say that they have a suspicion about a particular problem, or they may attempt to interpret information given on the social/medical history form. To avoid misinformation and errors, prospective adoptive parents should consult with professionals in the appropriate field (medical, mental health, education, etc.) for help in understanding the facts and reports shared by the adoption worker.

WHAT IF YOU DON'T KNOW THE FACTS?

Many adoptive parents find that they have only skeletal information about their child's history. Because the agency may have terminated a formal relationship with the adoptive family at the time of finalization, the parents believe that what they see is what they get—and all they will ever get. However, attitudes and laws about the importance of full disclosure to adoptive families have changed dramatically over the last 10 to 15 years in the world of adoption practice. Adoptive parents should not hesitate to re-contact the agent of the adoption to request a meeting regarding the child's history. The child, depending on the age and circumstance, might be included in this meeting or invited to a future meeting with agency staff. The agency should share all non-identifying information about the child's history. Although practice regarding full disclosure to adoptive parents including identifying information (in cases of foster parent adoption) is changing, there are still some states whose policies do not allow the following to be shared:

- Name of the birth family
- Address of the birth family
- Social Security numbers of birth family members
- Birth dates of family members
- Identifying school information about birth family members
- Places of employment of birth family members

All other information (medical, social, ethnic, religious, psychological information/ history) must be shared with the adoptive family. Many families who return to their placing agencies after eight to ten years find that workers disclose much more information than was the practice at the time of the adoption.

However, in some situations it is difficult or impossible for parents to obtain additional information from the placing agent. Sometimes agencies do not have the desired information. Families can ask the placing agency to re-contact persons in the birth family who might be willing to share information to help the child better understand why the separation from the birth family occurred. If the birth parents are not accessible or cooperative, perhaps grandparents or other relatives can be contacted.

The agency can serve as an intermediary in gathering information if the adoptive family is uncomfortable with opening the adoption, or if a relationship between the child and birth family relatives is not in the best interests of the child. At times, extended birth family relatives are willing to share mementos or pictures with the child as well as significant information that they were not willing to impart at the time of the adoption.

Occasionally, agencies place children who were abandoned as in Safe Haven situations or in out-of-country adoptions, and there is no access to information about the birth family. These situations are especially problematic for the adoptive family and for the child. A child who has been abandoned may believe, at least during adolescence that the adoptive family has a complete history of the birth family and is withholding that information. If the child was in fact abandoned, the adoptive family should go with the child to the agency to hear that information from the social workers or attorneys who facilitated the adoption. Ways to share information about abandonment will be explored in a later chapter.

At times, families who have adopted internationally have very little information about the birth family, or they may be told that the child was abandoned. Those families adopting Korean children should be aware that "abandonment" is the way children are freed for adoption in that country. Birth mothers who wish to make an adoption plan for their child may leave the child at a police box and hide until they are sure that an appropriate authority has taken charge of the child's welfare. It is critical that international adoptive parents research and understand the social situation in the country at the time of the adoptive placement.

Some families have adopted privately through a physician or an attorney who may have retired or moved out of the area. Adoptive families can petition the probate or family courts that finalized their adoptions to determine whether the files can be opened for purposes of sharing more complete information.

SUMMARY

Gathering background information is an important task for foster and adoptive parents. It is crucial that they understand the importance of having the information. It is their right and that of their child to full and complete disclosure.

QUESTIONS

1. What barriers have you encountered in obtaining social, medical information from your child's agency?
2. What type of information do you feel is most valuable to you in making a decision to adopt a specific child?
3. What information is missing from your child's history? Why is it missing?
4. If you have missing information about your child, what are your options in obtaining that information?
5. What do you see as your responsibility regarding responding to background information?

CHAPTER 5

Adoption Through a Child's Eyes: Developmental Stage

Johnny, who is 13, just refuses to talk about his adoption with me, said one adoptive mother. He displays a lot of anger about it, but shuts down. Is it his age? What could be going on with him?

As adopted children grow up, their understanding of adoption dynamics also matures. An incredible sense of loss and rejection may begin to shadow some adopted children during late childhood. This sense of loss and rejection can steal the excitement and joys of the teen years. This chapter explores the developmental stages children and teens experience and their perceptions of the adoption experience. When adoptive parents understand the sensitive nature of adoption through their child's eyes, they'll be better prepared to communicate effectively during each stage.

INFANCY—BIRTH TO AGE 3

Child's Developmental Characteristics and Tasks Impacted by Adoption

According to Eric Erikson, the most significant developmental task of infants and toddlers is to develop trust. Attachment is built over time but begins optimally during infancy, when consistent caregivers predictably meet children's needs. After thousands of repetitions, children learn that their needs will be met and that they are safe; they become attached to those caregivers reliably meeting their needs.

Acquisition of language also occurs during infancy and toddlerhood. Children's understood language is far greater than the language they are able to articulate. How does this impact adopted children?

Children under three years of age need to hear appropriate language related to adoption issues so that they may begin, as they mature, to understand the concepts underlying the words. Children need to begin using phrases like "birth mother," for example, instead of "real mother" because the connotations of words chosen are so important to the understanding of children as they mature.

Children's Perception of Adoption

Adoption is a very abstract concept. The idea involves a basic understanding of human sexuality, and such understanding is not found among infants and toddlers. Further, the notion of "letting go" of a beloved person or thing is much too sophisticated for very young children. While children at this age are too young to understand the concepts of adoption, parents can begin foundational work to assist children in developing positive attitudes about adoption, their birth parents, and themselves during these early years.

Some parents may have adopted infants or toddlers who have experienced traumatic, abrupt losses, or children who have experienced institutionalization or serious abuse or neglect. Instead of learning that the world is a safe, predictable place, these children have learned that they cannot rely on their caregivers to meet their needs.

While the children cannot verbalize their panic and distress, they communicate these feelings through behaviors. Clinging, night terrors, and other problematic behaviors signal that their comprehension of the parent/child relationship has been impaired. Infants and toddlers who have experienced institutionalization, maltreatment, or abrupt separations must essentially be "re-parented" until they can unlearn that the world is unreliable and dangerous. Such lessons are not easily or quickly taught, and adoptive parents may find that extreme patience and many years are required to assure these children that they will be safe, protected, and secure in their new homes.

Behaviors Related to Adoption During This Stage

A child who has experienced maltreatment or abrupt separations may cling to parents, cry inconsolably during brief separations, experience night terrors, or turn to self-nurturing or self-protection through obsession with food, rocking by oneself, or emotional withdrawal and isolation.

Strategies for Adoptive Parents

Talk about adoption comfortably from the time the child enters your home. If parents adopt a child who is preverbal (an infant or a child who does not yet speak English), they have a wonderful opportunity to practice talking about adoption and the birth family, building their skills and comfort level before the child is able to understand.

"Parents who project an attitude of acceptance and comfort with adoption are better able to help their children explore their own feelings and fears. With young children, how you say something is more important than what you say. Stay relaxed and matter of fact. Your tone of voice is important. Parents who grimace or tense up when the topic of adoption is raised may send the message that something is wrong with being adopted. Similarly, keeping information "secret" implies that adoption is negative, bad, or scary."[1]

Children who are adopted during infancy should grow up knowing that they are adopted in the same way they grow up knowing that they are male or female. Parents who wait for the "right" moment often find reasons why they should postpone telling their child about adoption. Parents who talk comfortably about adoption from the time the child arrives ("Here are pictures of the day we brought you home from the agency [hospital; airport]. We were so excited when we adopted you!"). Adopted children at this developmental stage first understand in a limited way that they gained a family through adoption.

When talking about adoption with very young children, model correct adoption language. Parents should not tell children they were "given up" or "given away," as young children will almost certainly develop anxiety that this type of abandonment will recur. Birth parents should certainly not be called "real parents" or "natural parents;" after all, adoptive parents are not unreal or unnatural! More information about correct terminology to use when talking about adoption or the birth family will follow in Chapter 7.

Gather as much information as possible about the child's history while the trail is still fresh. Adoptive parents should use these early years to gather as much information as possible about the child's history. Remember that the child may have important questions during early adolescence, but birth parents may, by that time, have different names, may have moved out of state, or may be involved in new relationships that do not allow for ongoing contact with the adoptive family or agency. The placing social worker may have retired or moved on to other employment. When the child has questions or asks for mementos or pictures from the birth family years after the adoptive placement, it can be difficult to meet those needs. Parents should anticipate the child's needs for information and concrete mementos from his history and use early years of the child's life to gather the information as completely as possible.

PRESCHOOL—AGE 3 TO AGE 7

Child's Developmental Characteristics and Tasks Impacted by Adoption

Preschool-age children are only capable of concrete thinking. Preschool children love to hear their "adoption story" and often ask to have it repeated as a favorite bedtime story. By the age of three or four, many adopted children can repeat the story verbatim as it was told to them. When sharing the story, remember that "preschoolers are limited in how much they can understand about adoption, so simple explanations will work best. Be concrete and use props such as dolls, simple drawings, and storybooks. Don't feel you have to cover everything at once; you and your child will have many chances to talk about adoption."[2]

Children between the ages of three and seven are developing independence from primary caregivers. They are moving out into the world, interacting with others as they participate in play dates with other children and go to preschool and on to elementary school. Most children spend several hours a day away from their families as they reach the end of this developmental period.

Preschoolers believe in magical things like fairies and monsters. As magical and self-absorbed thinkers, preschoolers are likely to assume that they cause everything that happens to them. For example, if a young boy pulls the dog's tail and the dog becomes sick the following day, he may assume that he caused the dog to become sick by pulling his tail. The phenomenon of imagining one's behavior to cause unrelated events is known as magical thinking. An adopted preschool-aged girl may assume her birth parents are not caring for her because of something she has done. Or another little girl who has experienced multiple moves may have extreme fears of monsters who will come and take her away.

Children's Perception of Adoption

While children between the ages of three and seven have acquired language to talk about adoption, they are repeating words they really do not understand. For example, the concepts of growing "inside the birth mother's tummy" and living with another family are very abstract and essentially unintelligible to young children. Children under the age of seven rarely have the cognitive ability to understand the concepts behind the words in their adoption story. While they can parrot the words, the light bulb of understanding has not yet clicked on.

Adopted children at this stage may have fears of separation from the adoptive family. Separation from parents can be extremely threatening to children who have already lost parents. The first day of school is a challenge for most children, but such "emancipation" from the family can inspire full-blown panic in a child who has already experienced permanent parental loss.

Children under the age of seven, as magical thinkers, often believe that they caused their birth parents to "abandon" them. Young children may believe they cried too much, were the "wrong" gender, were too ugly, or in some other way so offended their birth parents that these people left their lives permanently. In other words, children assume responsibility for the adult decisions and behaviors that led to adoption.

Some parents who have more open relationships with birth parents worry their adopted preschoolers will be confused by multiple sets of parents. However, even very young children are absolutely clear about who is meeting their needs and filling parental roles! Birth parents should be addressed by their first names, and correct adoption terminology ("birth parent") should be used from the beginning.

Behaviors Related to Adoption During This Stage

Adopted children ask a lot of questions about "being in Mommy's tummy" and about birth parents as they develop language and a limited understanding about their histories. They love to hear their adoption story and may repeat it to anyone who will listen. Children at this stage are quite ingenuous about sharing their histories, and they may tell playmates in the neighborhood or at school about their adoption. Children at this stage often play out their story with dolls or stuffed animals and may develop some highly creative ideas about how babies are made and how families are formed!

Children struggling with independence from the family may develop school phobias. They may become anxious when parents become sick or are away from home on business. As they become older, children may worry more and more about how the first family was lost, and wonder if this kind of loss will recur. If, as magical thinkers, they have assumed guilt for the original adoption because of an imagined flaw in themselves, they will wonder when the adoptive parents will discover this flaw and abandon them in the same way the birth parents did. Some young children fearing such a calamity may struggle to be "perfect" in an attempt to keep the adoptive parents from discovering their faults. The adopted child at this developmental stage begins to understand in a limited way that he not only gained a family through adoption, but lost one in the process. Questions can begin in earnest toward the end of this stage.

Children in transracial adoptions will notice differences during this stage and may question why they look different from other family members. They may express a desire to be like the adoptive parents in skin color, eye shape, hair texture, and so on.

Strategies for Adoptive Parents

Encourage questions and answer concretely and simply. Children under the age of seven will not have sufficient cognitive ability, knowledge of human sexuality, or understanding of adult problems such as drug addiction, poverty, or war to understand their entire story. Parents, better than anyone else, know the child's limited ability to understand the concepts being presented. Parents should answer the child's questions in an honest but simplistic way.

Listen for cues about misperceptions when the child is playing or talking with peers. Parents or older siblings may hear a young child playing out his adoption story, expressing beliefs that are quite inaccurate. When these situations occur, "replay" the scenario in an accurate way.

Ron, a six-year-old boy adopted from Korea, was playing at home with his best friend. His 12-year-old brother heard Ron explain his history this way to his friend: "I was born to my parents and went to live with another woman in Korea for a year. Now I am back with my real parents." It was important to Ron to be with real parents, to be where he "should" be. He understood that another woman was involved in his history, but he misunderstood her role. Ron's older brother made a brief correction for Ron in front of his friend and shared the incident with the parents so that the story could be re-explained to Ron in private. It was important to Ron to hear about real parents, to understand that both his birth parents and his adoptive parents are real, and they have played different roles in his life. It was especially important for him to understand that he is, in fact, where he should be.

Don't assume that telling the adoption story every once in a while is adequate. The adoption story is often a favorite bedtime story, but parents should not assume that they can stop talking about adoption when the child seems to know the story. Remember that the child's perceptions about the circumstances of the adoption, the birth parents, and even himself will change as he matures and becomes more sophisticated in his thinking.

Tell the adoption story positively but realistically. Birth parents should not be painted in a totally positive or totally negative light. Both positive and negative aspects of the birth parents' situation are important in helping the child understand why a separation from the birth parents was necessary. In telling the adoption story, parents must be careful about using glowingly positive scenarios. If the explanation is "Your birth parents loved you so much, they placed you for adoption," the child may wonder if the adoptive parents will do the same! Further, many adult adopted persons have expressed their discomfort with the "chosen child" story: "We picked you to be our child—other parents had to settle for whatever they got." Adult adoptees have told us that they felt enormous pressure to be worthy of being chosen. They also worried that they might be "unchosen" if they did not measure up.

Reassure the children that they will not lose the adoptive family. A terrifying fear of young children, underlying most school phobias and night terrors, is separation from parents and family. This fear is graphically portrayed in many children's movies (*Bambi, An American Tale, Annie)* and stories ("Hansel and Gretel"). For adopted children, this common childhood fear has become a reality—they have been separated from at least one family. They must be reassured that their position in the adoptive family is permanent.

Children who have traumatic histories often feel more secure in a predictable home with structure and routine. When children have lived with chaos, they crave certainty and security. Many preschoolers have difficulty with transitions, so plan for plenty of time to get ready for day care, bed, and so on. Young children who are trauma survivors are more likely to feel secure in an "unhurried" home.

SCHOOL AGE—AGE 8 TO AGE 12

Child's Developmental Characteristics and Tasks Impacted by Adoption

By the time children reach the age of eight, their ability to think in abstract terms increases dramatically. At this point, children comprehend the meaning behind the words in their adoption story.

Children in the "middle childhood" years are striving to be successful and industrious in school, in sports, and with same-sex peers. It is important to preadolescents to be capable and to be similar to their friends.

Children's Perception of Adoption

Because children comprehend the concept of adoption for the first time around the age of seven or eight, they realize at that time that a significant loss has occurred in their lives. If they were adopted as infants, the children are now mature enough to understand the significance of this loss. Children have lost connections and a relationship with the birth family, knowledge of their own history and roots, and perhaps cultural understanding and continuity. Even if adoptions are open, children have still lost the lives they would have lived with their birth families. Because they become aware at this age of the significance of these losses, a grieving process begins, even though several years may have already lapsed since the separation.

Children at this age are very concerned about fairness. The game playing of school-age children quickly displays their preoccupation with rules and fairness. Many children of this age worry about the fairness of adoption. They wonder if they are with the "right" family and fantasize about lives that might be spent with the birth family or with another adoptive family. Children at this stage may also worry that they are not being fair to the adoptive family if they have feelings or questions about the birth family. For this reason, they may be reluctant to ask questions about the adoption or about the birth family, particularly if they sense discomfort on the part of their parents.

Behaviors Related to Adoption During This Stage

One reaction to the grieving process, according to Elisabeth Kubler-Ross, is denial. Adopted children may stop asking questions about their birth parents or the adoption as part of this initial stage of grieving. A common behavior among eight- and nine-year-old adopted children is an insistence they were not adopted, even when the adoption may be a transracial placement.

Adopted children in preadolescence will probably stop asking about the adoption story. They may refuse to talk about adoption as a form of denial, or they may be concerned about showing disloyalty to the adoptive family, thereby violating the "rules" of adoptive family life. Even though children in this stage may not be talking about adoption, they are most likely thinking about it. The 8- to 12-year-old begins to consider that he not only gained a family through adoption and lost one in the process, but was actually given away. He may wonder, but never discuss a potentially damaging thought. "People don't give away valuables; I must not be worth much."

Megan, a nine-year-old child adopted as a toddler, never asked her parents about her birth family or how she came to be part of her adoptive family. If her parents raised the subject, Megan stated she did not want to talk about adoption and asked her parents to stop asking her about it. Near the time of her ninth birthday, Megan began to display some troubling behaviors (destroying pictures in her lifebook, stealing from a birth child in the adoptive family). Her family consulted a post adoption therapist who asked Megan, "Do you ever wonder about your birth mother?" Megan's response, "I think about her every minute of the day. I'm thinking about her right now." This is an excellent example of the concept of psychological presence. Megan shared that she did not want to talk about her feelings with her adoptive family, as she felt it was disloyal and "ungrateful" for her to have such strong feelings about her birth family.

Strategies for Adoptive Parents

When children are not talking about adoption, don't assume they aren't thinking about it. Adoptive parents sometimes interpret children's reluctance to discuss adoption as an indication that they know their story and no longer need to talk about it. There may even be some relief for the adoptive parents in the child's silence on this sensitive topic.

While children should not be forced to discuss adoption-related issues, they should be aware that parents are open and comfortable with the subject when he is ready. Parents can periodically remark about the children's skills, looks, or interests, indicating that some of these positive attributes might have come from his birth family ("You have such beautiful eyelashes/great musical ability. I wonder if anyone in your birth family has eyelashes/talent in music like yours. Do you ever wonder about that?").

Learn to be alert for anniversary reactions. As with other grief reactions, children may begin to experience anniversary reactions at the time of their birthday or their adoption. Instead of allowing the children to suffer in silence with these feelings, parents should anticipate the children's feeling and help them express it ("I always think about your birth mother when it's time for your birthday. Do you think about her too? Do you have any questions about her that I could answer now that you are a year older and able to understand more fully?"). Because children will rarely bring up the subject of adoption, parents should look for opportunities to let children know they are not threatened or angry about questions regarding birth family and history.

Let children know they can love two sets of parents. Because children at this stage are concerned about fairness and loyalty, they are likely to believe that they are disloyal to the adoptive family if they have feelings, or even questions, about the birth family. Children need to know it is expected that they can love both sets of parents. They do not have to choose. Explaining to the child that adults are allowed to love more than one child in a family can alleviate some of that struggle. When additional children join a family, parents do not have to stop loving the children who were already there in order to start loving the children who have just arrived. In the same way, children are able to love more than one set of parents. They do not have to stop having feelings about the birth family when they become part of the adoptive family.

Remember that attachment occurs when parents repeatedly meet the needs of children. The same holds true for older children and teens. Meeting children's needs is the best way to build attachment. However, one of the dynamics challenging one's efforts to meet the needs of their school-age children is that they may not be able to express their needs verbally. If their needs were not met during their early years due to neglect or institutionalization, children may have learned to stop asking. They may express their needs not through language, but through negative behavior. Dr. Karyn Purvis of Texas Christian University states, "Behavior is the language of children who have lost their voice." *If you believe children's misbehavior is an expression of need, teach them to "use their words"* so that they can learn how to express their needs through words. This strategy will help your children develop skills they should have learned years before, and it will enable you to meet their needs, building essential attachment to you.

Find *age-appropriate ways to provide physical contact*: combing hair, hugs, and celebratory pats on the back for successes.

Use "time in" rather than "time out" with children who have attachment issues.[3] Instead of isolating children in their room when they misbehave, spend time interacting with them by completing chores together, talking about other options for handling conflict, and offering them opportunities to "re-do" problematic situations in a more appropriate manner.

Parents may have appropriately withheld some of the more troubling details of children's history while they were too young to comprehend the information. However, as the children approach adolescence, adoptive parents must provide the details to help them make sense of their own histories. Because adolescents often do not believe what they are told by adults (especially by their parents), adoptive parents should try to share whatever information they have *before the children enter adolescence.* If more information is needed, parents should contact the placing agent and take the children to that agency to learn all of the non-identifying information in the case record. Parents should take the children with them to hear the information firsthand so that they are not later accused of distorting or withholding information. While some adoptive parents are tempted to omit information until the child reaches adulthood, they find, often too late, that the children *must* learn about their history in order to successfully navigate through the identity formation struggles of adolescence. These tasks cannot be accomplished in a vacuum. Strategies for disclosing especially troubling information will be shared in Chapter 7.

EARLY ADOLESCENCE—AGE 12 TO AGE 15

Child's Developmental Characteristics and Tasks Impacted by Adoption

The early adolescent is working on two important developmental tasks: identity formation and separation/individuation. Both tasks are challenging for all young people, and both are impacted by adoption.

Identity formation begins as youth examine their own roots, question their beginnings, and begin to experiment with identities different than those of their parents. We are often perplexed or amused, depending on our perspective, by young people who look very different from the larger culture—those with long hair, no hair, purple spiked hair, and so on. The adopted youth may seek to try on identities different from those of their parents by emulating the identities of their birth parents. If information about their birth parents is limited, they may try on identities they *imagine* to be like those of their birth parents. They may seem to reject the values, customs, religion, and appearance of the adoptive family and adopt those codes of conduct or values they believe are held by their birth family.

> Adopted teens may feel that parts of their identity are missing. Unknown or missing information may prevent them from knowing where certain characteristics, abilities, or talents come from. They may worry that they will take on undesirable characteristics or repeat behaviors, tendencies, or mistakes of a birth parent. Teens whose race or ethnic background is unknown (completely or to some degree) or whose race or ethnicity is different from their adoptive parents may feel that they do not fully belong in their family or community. They may have a strong interest in meeting or spending time with birth family members or others of a similar race or ethnic background.[4]

All young people, some more forcefully than others, demand independence. But remember that adopted youth have already lost at least one family. They may be particularly threatened by the need to assert their independence, or individuation. Paradoxically, adopted youth who are nervous about separation from their adoptive family may actually go overboard during early adolescence, angrily asserting their independence and ranting about wishing they had never been adopted: "You can't tell *me* what to do! You're *not* my *real* mother!" "As soon as I am 18, I'm moving far away (or back to my birth family) and you will *never* see me again!"

Adopted youth continue to work on resolution of their grief, begun with the realization of their loss during an earlier developmental stage. Another emotional reaction to grieving is anger. Adopted youth may experience this grief reaction at the same time they are rejecting the family's identity and support. While adolescence can be an angry period for most young people, it is even more exaggerated for adopted persons. Many parents find that the anger begins to build when children are 12 years old (even earlier for some girls) and peaks when they reaches 13 or 14.

Children's Perception of Adoption

Early adolescents, capable now of sophisticated, abstract thought, are confused about the reasons their birth parents have "abandoned" them. Teens' understanding of adoption progresses at this age. Adopted teens have moved from gaining a family to losing a family, to being given away, to arriving at the conclusion that "I was rejected."

Teens may be angry about a lack of control in their adoption, and they may look for someone to blame for earlier separations and the lack of information about their history. Often, the adoptive parents are selected to be the scapegoats for children's rage and confusion. If the history has not been discussed since the children were preschoolers, as happens in too many adoptive families, the children may have used fantasy to create a web of new information, implicating the adoptive parents as kidnappers responsible for the separation. Adopted youth may firmly believe that the adoptive parents know full information about the children's history but, in collaboration with social workers, have chosen to withhold the information or even actively lie about it.

Behaviors Related to Adoption During This Stage

Early adolescents can be angry, confused young people who often resist authority and seem to constantly seek control. They may seek control through lying, even telling lies that seem to give them no advantage. They may seek control over the family by creating chaos, a family crisis precipitated by their own angry outbursts. Adopted youth struggling to separate and individuate will engage in "distancing behavior," behavior that pushes others away from them. Assertions that he hates the adoptive family and that they are not really his parents are excellent examples of distancing behavior.

Adopted youth may try on multiple identities, seeming to be a different person every few weeks. Their identity may fluctuate with their current fantasy of the birth family. Some adopted youth may seek to be like the birth family in some way, getting tattoos, dying their hair, or adopting a tough exterior.

Anne, whose story is described in Chapter 3, knew that her birth father was one of three men: one African American, one Native American, and one Latino. During her high school years, Anne would cycle through all of these identities from week to week. Her parents never knew if Anne would display her Latina persona or her Native American identity! And she could shift to hip hop music and language at the drop of a hat.

Strategies for Adoptive Parents

This angry stage can be a real challenge for adoptive parents. Several strategies will enable parents to emerge successfully from a difficult three-year period.

Allow children to exercise control whenever possible. Providing opportunities to make some decisions creates a sense of control for young people. It may be necessary for parents to lose a few battles during this stage in order to win the war. For example, parents should examine, when engaged in a power struggle with their teens, if the issue at hand is really dangerous to the teens or to others. Hair or clothing styles, for example, do not pose a threat to anyone. Children should be allowed freedom to make decisions that do not pose any threats to themselves or others.

Try to keep from responding to children's anger with more anger. If parents can understand that much of their children's anger is generated by their "rejection" by the birth parents and not aimed at the adoptive parents, they might not overreact to angry outbursts. When angry teens assert that they wants to leave the family, try to hear this as a question instead of a statement. They are not saying, "I am leaving!" They are asking, "Will you keep me, no matter what? Will you abandon me too?"

Be firm in setting limits. Sometimes adoptive parents do not feel really entitled to be the parents of their children, and they treat their children as though they belong to the neighbor. Remember that you are the only parents they have, and you must take responsibility for being very firm about limits that protect their safety. A good rule of thumb is to have only a few rules, but enforce those completely. Decide what is most important, and stick to it.

Establish consequences for broken rules prior to misbehavior. Parents should not try to respond to misbehavior by developing a consequence after the problem, when they are angry. Reasonable, logical consequences can only be developed by parents in reasonable, logical frames of mind. Once logical consequences have been established, parents should not make excuses for children or "bend" on consequences when children test their authority. Teens learn from mistakes by experiencing consequences, positive and negative, for their behavior.

Do not agree or join in if children criticize their birth parents. Teens can be judgmental and lack empathy regarding some of the adult situations that may have led to their separation from the birth family. While teens have a right to their angry feelings, the wise adoptive parent will refrain from criticism of the birth family.

Keep a sense of humor. Remember that adolescence is chronic, but not terminal. Adoptive parents should network with other parents of teens, particularly *adoptive* parents of teens, so that they can share successes and learn from each other's experiences.

LATE ADOLESCENCE—AGE 16 TO AGE 19

Children's Developmental Characteristics and Tasks Impacted by Adoption

Late adolescents are preparing to leave the family. They will soon emancipate or live independently. Emancipation, like many life transitions, involves loss: loss of dependency and childhood, loss of life with the family, loss of the familiar and safe. Again, while emancipation presents a stressful challenge to most young adults, the losses associated with independence are even more threatening to the adopted young person.

> Adopted teens, especially those adopted as older children, may fear leaving the security of the home and family. Some may adapt by acting more mature, more independent, or "tougher" than they feel to cope with fears and intimacy issues. Again, this is not unlike typical adolescent behavior but may be more evident in adopted teens. Adopted children who experienced previous neglect or abuse often need extra time and practice to learn life skills. Newly adopted adolescents face the task of establishing themselves into the family at a time when normal development would have them pushing away from family.[5]

Many adolescents begin to have their first experiences with romantic intimacy between the ages of 16 and 19. While younger adolescents may have a "steady," relationships during early adolescence tend to be superficial and fleeting. Older adolescents are ready for a relationships with more depth and commitment. Older teens, threatened by the loss of intimacy they experience when emancipating from their family, often turn to a romantic involvement as a replacement for that lost intimacy. Romantic relationships during late adolescence, especially for youth needing assurance that they are lovable, can become extremely intense.

Many young people between the ages of 16 and 19 have their first experiences with sexuality. Adolescents are often faced with value conflicts related to religious, family, and cultural beliefs about morality as they approach their first sexual encounters. Adopted youth who perceive their birth parents as sexually irresponsible or promiscuous will have even greater challenges as they become involved in romantic relationships. If young people experienced sexual abuse in the past, they may view sex as a way to gain attention and love. Counseling for abuse survivors may be important as they consider intimate relationships.

Children's Perception of Adoption

Again, adopted youth may be anxious about growing up and leaving home. Losing the adoptive family may be a reenactment of their earlier "abandonment" by the birth family. While connections to family remain after emancipation, adopted youth probably experienced a permanent termination of their relationship to the birth family when the adoption occurred. In other words, the last time they lost a family, it was forever.

As adopted youth approach legal adulthood, they may have conflicts about beginning a search. They may fear a "second" rejection by the birth family, and they may worry that the adoptive family will see their interest in their birth family as disloyal or hurtful. Some adopted youth may feel pressure from peers, the media, or family to search (or not to search). Some adoptive parents, in an attempt to be helpful, may even initiate a search for the birth family. A search for birth family members needs to be in the control of those who have been adopted. If a reunion is thrust upon them before they are ready for this relationship, irrevocable damage can be done. It is critical that adoptive parents understand that adopted persons have already experienced tremendous loss of control in the original termination of parental rights. They need to maintain control over a re-establishment of a connection to the birth family. Only they can know if, and when, they are ready for such a relationship. Of course, emotional support for the searcher is always welcome!

Adopted youth may be fearful of intimacy or may feel unlovable. This fear of close personal relationships may be expressed either through avoidance or through over-involvement in romantic relationships and sexuality before individuals are really mature enough to handle the consequences of that decision. If the youth are very enmeshed in a romantic entanglement that ends abruptly, as many adolescent relationships do, this may feel very much like another abandonment, leaving the teens devastated, and confirming their belief that they are unworthy of love.

As the youth continue the work of resolving their grief related to loss of their family, they may experience yet another grief reaction: depression. Adoptive parents may experience tremendous relief, as their children are no longer so angry. However, parents should be alert for signs of serious depression, particularly around times of loss (graduation from high school, moving to college or the armed forces, breakups of significant relationships, loss of grandparents). The depressed youth will withdraw into their own world, and knowledgeable parents should be available for support and guidance as the older teens progress toward resolution of his grief.

Behaviors Related to Adoption During This Stage

Older teens afraid of independence from the family may fail in school to delay emancipation. While this type of academic "backsliding" is not uncommon for high school seniors (humorously dubbed "senioritis"), it can be more serious for young people who unconsciously try to sabotage their own successful independence.

Separating from the adoptive family may be so threatening to adopted youth that they "replace" parents with intense romantic entanglements. When these relationships fail, the adopted teens are shattered. Older teens may overreact to such losses and strive irrationally to remain in relationships that are unhealthy or unproductive.

Chantel, age 17, was anxious about her upcoming high school graduation and move to a college on the other side of the state. She was very worried about losing the "secure base" of the only family she could count on to care for her. Chantel became involved in a relationship with an older boyfriend and relied on this relationship as a "replacement" for the family she felt she was leaving (or in Chantel's emotional experience, the family that was leaving her). When the boyfriend broke up with her, Chantel had a dramatic and emotional reaction. She swallowed an overdose of aspirin in an effort to bring her "caregivers" and protectors (both the adoptive family and the boyfriend) closer to her. Chantel needed assurance from her adoptive family they would continue to be her support and secure base after her 18th birthday and high school graduation. The parents and Chantel together reconsidered her college plans and decided to enroll her in a college less than an hour's drive from the adoptive home.

Older teens may be troubled and withdrawn as they consider their transition to adulthood. "Should I search for my birth family? Will they want to see me? How will my adoptive parents feel? Will they understand? Why can't my friends understand my need to know?"

Strategies for Adoptive Parents

Make it clear that children may remain at home for a time following graduation. They may live at home and work, go to a commuter college, or board at a college near enough to allow for frequent visitation and parental support. Adopted youth must feel in control of the timing of their departure from the nest.

Be alert for overreactions when relationships with peers fail. Without hovering, parents of older adolescents should be observant of those older children's struggle for independence, and they should be available for support and reassurance when needed.

Prepare emotionally for a search for, and possible reunion with, members of the birth family. This can be an emotional roller coaster for adoptive parents; even those who cognitively support the search may find they have some anxiety about the child's continued allegiance to the adoptive family following a reunion with the birth family.

OTHER TRIGGER TIMES FOR ADOPTION ISSUES

There are other predictable times, not related to child development, when adoption issues can become more difficult for children. Adoptive parents should be aware of their child's development and be alert as well to these potential triggers of emotional pain, grief, divided loyalties, or anxiety. *See Appendix B to learn more about adoption issues triggered by situations.*

The Children's Birthday

The children's birthday may be the time of separation from the birth family if the birth parent's parental rights were terminated shortly after birth. Even those children who experienced separation at much older ages, however, will wonder if their birth parents even remember the children's birthday. Sadness and anger, both part of a grief reaction, can begin building a month or so before the birthday and continue for a week or two following the birthday. Adoptive parents should be alert to see if this common pattern of triggered grief occurs annually. If so, direct communication about feelings of loss, powerlessness, and fear of being forgotten can ameliorate the children's grief.

Mother's Day

Mother's Day can be a time of divided loyalties for many adopted or foster children. Because Mother's Day occurs during the school year, many younger children make lacy, flowery cards for their mothers at school. Adopted or foster children may feel disloyal because the birth mother is not acknowledged. It is not uncommon for adopted and foster children to have a stronger tie to the birth mother and little or no connection to, or memory of, the birth father. For these reasons, early May can be an extremely difficult time for adoptive and foster families. Recognition of the children's divided loyalties and acceptance of the children's feelings for the birth mother can be tremendously helpful. Some adoptive parents have encouraged children to make Mother's Day cards for their birth mothers to be kept in a special scrapbook. The cards may be shared with the birth mother in open adoption relationships or saved in confidential adoptions and later given to the birth mother if a reunion occurs at some point in the child's future. Merely making such cards for the birth mother seems to help many adopted children express feelings and cope more effectively with this difficult time.

Placement or Separation Anniversaries

Obviously, we all experience grief reactions at the time of anniversaries of losses. We feel sadness, for example, on the anniversary of a miscarriage or the death of a parent. Adopted children experience many of these same anniversary reactions. It can be extremely helpful for adoptive parents to chart a Life Map (see Chapter 9) for their children. They may be surprised to note that many children experienced sadness or anger at the same time of the year—in the fall, or at holiday time. During these seasons, parents will need to be especially alert and supportive to assist children in coping with grief.

Holidays

When anyone has experienced the loss of a significant person, holidays can become sad, difficult times when the loved one is particularly missed.

Those children who remember holidays with birth or foster families may find it especially difficult to cope with the intense family atmosphere of the holidays. Adoptive parents should keep the intensity of holiday visits with extended family to a manageable level (easier said than done!) and try to keep their own expectations for close holiday memories manageable as well.

Any Experience of Loss (School Transitions; Loss of a Pet, Grandparent, Best Friend, etc.)

Any loss can trigger the grief experience. People who have suffered the loss of one significant person understand that they re-grieve that loss when a second or third loss occurs. Many adopted children overreact to seemingly small losses. They are re-experiencing the pain of the initial separation (abandonment) from the birth family.

Perceived Loss of the Adoptive Parents Through Illness, Death, Divorce

Obviously, children who have lost parents will have anxiety about a recurrence of that traumatic experience. Because children so often believe that they caused the original loss of the birth family to occur, they believe that they are vulnerable to another such loss, loss of the adoptive family, simply because of their own unworthiness to have a family. If adoptive parents become ill, particularly if hospitalization is necessary, adopted or foster children might experience unmanageable panic. If loss of an adoptive parent actually occurs, through death or divorce, adopted children will likely have an even more severe reaction, with more self-blame, more anxiety, and more anger than their non-adopted counterparts. Even when the "loss" of the parent is temporary and seems inconsequential to the adoptive parents (e.g., parent out of town on business, child's first day of school, child goes to sleep-over camp, parents leave for a getaway weekend without the children), adopted children and teens may respond with behavior that represents an extreme fear of abandonment. The intensity of this fear results from earlier separation experiences.

Moving

Moving the family is another form of loss, one that is particularly significant to a child who has lost family or families forever through moves. Many young children believe that they will be left behind when the family moves, and even teenagers can have an irrational fear of being abandoned at the time of a move. Allowing children to have as much control as possible during a move (selecting new bedroom colors, for example) can reduce the sense of powerlessness and fear they experience during moves.

Roxie, age 14, was adopted as a toddler from Korea. Her move from that country was of course abrupt, with no opportunity for pre-placement visitation. She met her adoptive family when her plane landed in this country. Of course, this was a terrifying transition for a child who was barely two years old. Roxie settled in with her family and was adjusting well until the parents announced they planned a move to another community, so Roxie could attend better schools. The prospect of moving triggered a panic reaction in Roxie. Her association with moving was losing everything and everyone she loved. Significant counseling was needed to assure Roxie she would be safe with her family, her pets, and her belongings after the move.

Problematic or Insensitive School Assignments

Children often experience confusion or anger over school assignments related to family or adoption issues (see Chapter 15). Many adoptive parents have "war" stories to tell about problematic assignments involving family trees, genetics studies, and so on that have created thorny problems for their children. Adoptive parents should be alert to assignments or experiences that can trigger pain for their children. Adoptive parents can give their children support or assistance to help them cope with both the assignment and the resulting feelings.

Greg, age 15, was studying genetics in his high school biology class. The teacher assigned students to create Mendel's boxes in their own families to show whether each family member had ear lobes or no ear lobes. Greg was adopted into a family that had one other adopted child, not biologically related to Greg, and one birth child. Greg was dismayed to find that he was the only person in his family that had ear lobes. This reality underscored his "differentness, his otherness." The triggering assignment became even worse, however, when the teacher held up Greg's diagram of his family's boxes and said to the entire class, "Clearly, Greg did not understand the assignment, because this is genetically impossible."

Films or Television Programs That Depict Adoption Insensitively

Sometimes children or teens watch a film or television show that triggers feelings of discomfort with adoption or issues related to the birth family (or birth country). When these programs engender emotional upheaval in children, adoptive parents may find an excellent opportunity to directly address the child's perceptions and engage the child in a dialogue about feelings. When programs or films are extremely negative (case in point, the 1990 film *Problem Child,* whose theme song was "Bad to the Bone"), parents can talk with children about the mistaken ideas that some uninformed people have about adoption. The child may be helped to write a letter to the television station or theater to set the record straight.

Emancipation from the Adoptive Family

Most teenagers find emancipation from the family to be a challenging task. Adopted teens have already lost at least one family, perhaps forever. The prospect of separating from the adoptive family can be particularly challenging. Support and sensitivity from the adoptive parents, as well as "gentle" emancipation (not sending the child to the other side of the continent for college), can be helpful.

Trauma Triggers

Children who have experienced trauma may associate sensory information like sounds, smells, sights, or tastes with the traumatic event. It may appear that children, seemingly unprovoked, completely lose self-regulation, or control of their emotional state. Thorough knowledge of the circumstances surrounding children's traumatic past will help adoptive parents to be alert for situations that can derail children.

Evelyn joined her adoptive family when she was five years old. Her depressed mother had neglected her, not providing adequate supervision or medical care for her preschool age daughter. Her first weeks with her new family seemed uneventful. One evening, her father decided to save time by giving Evelyn shower instead of a bath. Evelyn had a complete meltdown: sobbing, screaming, totally out of control. Her confused father thought she was simply afraid of the shower. Once out of the bathroom, however, Evelyn was able to recover sufficiently to disclose to her horrified adoptive mother that she had been sexually abused. Her mother's boyfriend had fondled her in the shower.

SUMMARY

While adoption does not really alter the stages of typical human growth, developmental tasks are impacted by the fact of adoption. Adoptive parents will recognize the difficulty of differentiating which behaviors are related to typical child development and which are caused by adoption-related issues. Certainly, most toddlers are demanding and strive for control, and many adolescents experiment with different identities. However, when children have also experienced adoption and/or maltreatment, their journey through some of these developmental tasks becomes even more challenging. While their history does not *change* typical tasks, the behaviors associated with those tasks may become more extreme in nature; in other words, the intensity of the children's struggle with the task will likely increase due to their history of trauma or earlier separations. Many adoptive parents ask, "How do I know what is 'adoption' and what is 'normal development'?" The most accurate response is, "If your hair is turning gray, it's typical child development. If your hair is falling out in clumps, it's probably adoption."

QUESTIONS

1. What is a child's perception of adoption at ages three to seven?
2. What is a child's perception of adoption at ages 8 to 12?
3. What is a child's perception of adoption at ages 13 to 15?
4. What is a child's perception of adoption at ages 16 to 19?
5. What is your child's chronological age? What is the child's developmental age?
6. What parenting strategies can you use in developing your child's understanding of adoption?

CHAPTER 6

Through a Parent's Eyes: The Challenges in Creating an Environment of Ongoing Adoption Communication

Adopted children will only ask the questions they feel they have the permission to ask.

Jane Hoyt-Oliver, MSW, PhD—Adoption Mom

Comments from adoptive parents...

Mark is seventeen now. He used to ask a lot of questions about his birth family. I just told him that we are his family now, and that is all that matters. He just doesn't bring it up anymore. I am glad he doesn't.

Kelly came into my room the other night and asked me why her birth mother got rid of her. We have always talked to her about adoption and the fact that she is our chosen child and that we really love her. I just always thought that would be enough for a 10-year-old.

Robert, who is 14 now, has always had a lot of questions about his birth mother. We were given detailed information about her and have always answered his questions completely. I generally asked him about what he was feeling when he asked questions. He knows that talking about adoption in this house is always welcomed.

Helping to give meaning to a child's life narrative is one of the key essential tasks for adoptive parents.[1] However, as important as it is to talk with children and teens about their adoption histories, and answer their questions, it is still one of the greatest challenges for adoptive parents. Stepping into a child's story of abuse, neglect, and loss is difficult for some parents. All adoptive parents face choices about how and when to talk to their children about the past, and it is a task that must be managed with care, sensitivity, and honesty.

THINGS WE KNOW

- Every family communicates differently.
- Parents perceive adoption communication differently than children.
- When there are two parents within a household, they each have a different level of communication.
- Parents' degree of difficulty in communication differs from one child to another and from one history to another.
- Adoption communication can be a critical factor in a child's successful adoption adjustment.

Every family communicates differently.

Every adoptive family is different. "The way an individual adoptive family deals with communication about a child's background may be affected by family factors:

- Individual parenting style
- Type of adoption (open or closed, domestic, or international)
- Age of child at adoption
- Whether the adopted child is an only child or there are other biological or adopted children in the family
- Background circumstances leading to adoption
- Child's apparent curiosity and self-confidence"[2]

Parents perceive adoption communication differently than children.

In a study conducted with adoptive parents and their children, the researchers posed a question: Do adoptive parents and children share views about the ease of adoption communication in the household? The study found that there was a difference of viewpoints between parents and children. The parents reported much lower levels of difficulty in talking about adoption than their children reported themselves.[3]

> "I have always thought that we did a good job of communicating with Rachel about adoption issues," said Katherine, an adoptive mom of 14-year-old Rachel. "I was a bit shocked to learn that she didn't feel that way." The day she asked me, "Mom, the only time we talk about stuff around adoption is when I bring it up, and that is sometimes hard to do. Why don't you ever bring it up?"

Parents each have a different level of communication.

Both parents in the household are important in the process of adoption communication. However, it is the adoptive mother who holds the key to adoption-related conversation at home. The adoptive mother is central to adoptive family communication. How she deals with such issues as the psychological presence of the birth mother (discussed in Chapter 2) is the consistent factor in how adoption is handled.

Dr. Gretchen Wrobel observed "that adoptive mothers consistently maintained active communication with their children about adoption-related issues. However, adoptive fathers communicated more actively when the adoption was more open. In other words, adoptive father/child communication increased when the adoption was structured in a way (by the adoptive mother) that made the birth mother a more regular presence (both psychologically and physically), a part of their family's life.[4]

Parents' degree of difficulty of communication differs from one child to another and from one history to another.

One of the interesting discoveries in recent adoption communication research is that parents reported varying degrees of difficulty in talking about adoption among their adopted children.[5] One adoptive mom commented:

> We do struggle with how we communicate about John's past versus how we deal with Micah's story. Micah's story is heartbreaking, and I think we avoid it to avoid the pain ourselves. John's story has no drama—it has loss, of course, but that is much easier for us to talk about.

Adoption communication can be a critical factor in a child's successful adoption adjustment.

How important is healthy adoption communication for adopted children and youth? Extremely! It is key to a sense of belonging in the family and to a child or teen's self-esteem.

Two interesting insights come out of research regarding "differentness" and self-esteem. First, children who could not talk openly about adoption with their parents were more likely to feel different from their adoptive families compared to those who could talk easily about questions and feelings.[6] Second, children who found it harder to talk about adoption within the family experienced lower self-esteem.[7]

Dr. James Gritter, a prolific writer in the field of adoption, explains adoption communication is not just about the content—the dissemination of information—but it is about "the sharing and supporting of adoption-related emotions both within the adoptive family and between the adoptive and birth families, in the case of open adoption." It has much more to do with how all the parties touched by the adoption experience manage intrapersonal emotions, and interpersonal relationships, rather than a specific type of family or systemic structure. Its emphasis is on the adoption communication process, both informational and emotional with the individual, between adoptive family members, and for those involved in a structurally open arrangement, between members of the two family systems.[8]

Research, according to Dr. David Brodzinsky, indicates that family process factors, such as parental warmth, emotional sensitivity, nurturance, and communicative openness play a much more important role in the child's development than the specific type of family structure. What is foundational for an adoptive child for healthy psychological adjustment, before any suggestion of openness arrangements with the birth family can be considered, is "the creation of an open, honest, non-defensive and emotionally attuned family dialogue not only about adoption issues, but any issue that impacts the child."[9]

WHAT GETS IN THE WAY: CORE ISSUES FOR PARENTS

Much work and research have been done on the core issues of adoption as they relate to adopted persons. However, adoptees are not the only members of the adoption triad that confront concerns related to their adoption experiences. Adoptive parents experience adoption-related challenges as well. How parents process these questions in their lives will have much to do with how they handle adoption as a family system and how they communicate about adoption to their child. Three important issues for adoptive parents are loss, shame, and rejection.

Loss

We became parents at thirty-eight years of age. Christopher came home when he was three days old. We were ecstatic! However, we

> suddenly began to realize we didn't have a peer group as parents. The children of all our friends were teenagers. Who wanted to run around with a couple with a fussy infant? (Mark and Sheila, adoptive parents)

Adoption is the only relationship in life that creates loss for each person in the relationship. "Without loss, there would be no adoption. Loss is the hub of the wheel."[10] Jean Pierre Bourguignon, a pioneer in post adoption services, once stated, "Loss is the stage on which the drama of adoption is played."[11] For many adoptive parents, the initial issue of loss is created by infertility. Most young people think and dream of the day when they will become parents, never giving a thought to the possibility it may not occur. Parents entering adoption through this loss forfeit the dream of a biological child and the family as planned. Other losses occur as well, such as:

- The loss of status as a biological parent
- The loss of providing grandparents with a biological grandchild
- The loss of a biological connection to the future
- The loss of a parent peer group due to the age of the child

When parents adopt older children, loss is also a subtle part of the relationship for them as well. When parents adopt an older child, they lose the early years of development. They can't answer questions like: "How much hair did I have when I was born?" or "When did I walk?" or "What was my first word?" They have also lost the ability to protect their child from the early pain of abuse and neglect. Understanding the dynamics loss can play in the parent-child relationship in adoption is an important task throughout the years. Consequences can occur when loss is not processed well. Robert Anderson, in *Second Choices*, comments about loss:

> Life consists of a series of losses, which by themselves do not cause psychopathology. One does better to confront a loss directly; ignoring it or wrapping it with platitudes may obviate the need for grief over a short term, but invites a problem with self-esteem over the long term.[12]

If adoptive parents fail to resolve loss in a healthy manner, it could have a domino effect on how they deal with adoption issues and their child. Failure to resolve loss could have the following effects:

- It could impair parents' ability to recognize pain associated with adoption issues and offer support through that pain.

- It could force parents into self-protection that will inhibit them from forming strong emotional attachments with the child.
- It could cause adoptive parents to project past fears and beliefs into present moments and relationships.

Unresolved loss can extend to every aspect of our lives: physical, emotional, relational, and spiritual. Another issue impacting adoptive parents is shame.

Shame

> For years I struggled with the issue of infertility. My friends were having their second and third children, and I was left with empty arms. I began to believe that something was terribly wrong with me. I couldn't decide if it was because I just didn't deserve a child or it was something that I did to create this painful problem in our lives. (Terry and Teresa, adoptive parents)

"It is a very heavy feeling, this pervasive sense of shame. It is the ongoing premise that one is fundamentally bad, inadequate, defective, unworthy or not fully valid as a human being," according to author Merle Fossum.[13] The feeling of shame is not about what we did or did not do. It is about our very selves. It is about who we are. Shame tells us we are unworthy, horribly unworthy. "Shame is without parallel—a sickness of the soul."[14]

For some parents who embark on the journey into adoption because of infertility, the sense of shame is a dark shadow over their lives. Shame steals joy from their lives and their marriage. They ask, "What is so bad about us that we have been robbed of parenthood?" says Fossum. Loss and shame can impact adoptive parents as they communicate about adoption with their youngster.

At times, the issues of loss and shame can snowball into disappointment when the "dream child" does not match the real child adopted into the family. It should be acknowledged that all parents, those who add children by birth or adoption, experience some gap between their imagination and expectations of parenting and the reality of day-to-day care (married couples also experience moments of ambivalence about their partners!). However, when a child joins the family through adoption, the sense of disappointment and loss may be greater as an adoptive parent wonders how the child's experience of parenting would have been different with a birth child.

Rejection

Rejection is a third issue that can impact healthy adoptive family communication. Rejection is most often considered when discussing emotional difficulties faced by adopted children and adults, not as an issue faced by adoptive parents. Nevertheless, rejection, often in a subtle form, can significantly impact the lives of adoptive parents. It has to do with validation of the parent-child relationship. When family and friends fail to validate the child as a "true" member of the family, it feels like rejection to parents. A personal encounter by H. David Kirk, the father of three adopted children, and his family many years ago paints a clear picture of such a rejecting experience:

> On my return from a Chicago conference, I found that our landlady wanted our little cottage for her own use. It was time to search for a house of our own. We settled on the plan for a tract house that was to be built by late summer, but by the end of August, only the foundation was visible. Within a week we would have no roof over our heads, an emergency that called for fast action. Both my family and my wife's family lived in California, but only my in-laws had room to spare. So a year after arriving in Montreal, my family took off without me. I stayed behind to get on with my university studies and to try to speed up the builder. . . . Weeks later everyone was anxious to end the enforced separation. Our house would soon be livable, and we made plans for Ruth and the children to return to Montreal. Just before they left, Ruth asked her mother about the crib, the old family heirloom, in which Debbie had slept while at the maternal grandparents' house. "Could we have the crib for Debbie at our new house?" After a moment's hesitation her mother said: "I'm afraid not." [It had been promised to their first grandchild, soon to be born to Ruth's younger sister.][15]

Tim and Traci Miller, adoptive parents of Justin, experienced a similar experience of rejection and lack of validation. Justin was adopted as a five-month-old from Guatemala. Three birth children later joined him.

Traci shares the experience:

> I was shopping at a grocery story near our home. Justin, who was three and one-half at the time, was standing up in the cart along with two-year-old Jeb and one-year-old Allison. The three children are quite a contrast as Justin is dark-complected, the other two extremely fair. A woman came up to me and asked about the children.

> "Are these your children?" she asked.
>
> "Yes," I replied.
>
> "I can tell that these two are your own, but where did you get him?" she said, pointing at Justin.
>
> I was dumbfounded by such a comment, and quickly said, "South America," and continued to move down the aisle. I desperately hoped that Justin had not overheard the conversation.

This type of subtle rejection and invalidation cuts to the heart of adoptive parents and children as well. Dee Paddock says of this experience, "People often ask adoptive parents, in front of their children, 'do you have any children of your own?' Over and over, our children breathe into their souls this toxic cultural dismissal of who they are in relation to US!"[16] (*Note:* See Chapter 14 on Adoption Communication Outside the Family for more information.)

Another type of rejection felt by some adoptive parents is the anxiety that children will, either now or in the future, prefer the birth family to the adoptive family. This fear of rejection by the children themselves is the root of queasiness some adoptive families feel about open adoption or about search and reunion for adult adopted persons.

Issues of loss, rejection, and shame do influence how parents develop coping styles to deal with adoption issues. What are those styles of coping?

WHAT DO WE DO WITH THE ISSUES OF ADOPTION?

Is adoptive parenting just like raising a child born into the family? Yes, almost. Of course, the day-to-day needs of any child—whether born into a family or entering the family through adoption—are the same. Each child needs the same care and nurturing to ensure healthy physical and emotional growth. It is almost the same. The differences that make adoptive parenting unique stem from the family's need to recognize the adoption-related issues and struggles. Families develop unhealthy or healthy coping styles to deal with those differences created by traditional or closed adoption.

Rejection of Differences

With an impending move out of state, 14-year-old Judy was given the task of cleaning out and packing the contents of the family attic. On that cold, rainy February afternoon, Judy set about the task with less than minimal enthusiasm. She came across an unfamiliar box filled with all sorts of documents and memorabilia. What she found there set her adrift on a course of uncharted emotions and events:

> Before I taped the box, I decided to just go through it for fun. I found a large envelope that read "Court papers." My first thought was that one of my parents had been in trouble and never told us. When I opened the envelope a certificate of adoption fell out. It was a court paper finalizing the adoption of Judith Marie Walker. Adoption! I couldn't believe what I read. I didn't even know what to think or what to do. I put that paper back in the box and finished my job. I was very teary for the next week. My mother kept saying, "Judy, I know you are sad about our moving, but you will be fine." I finally couldn't hold it in any longer and started shouting at her. "You don't understand. I am not sad about leaving."
>
> I began to tell her what I had found in the attic. The only thing she could say was, "At least now you know the truth. We never wanted you to know." "Why didn't you tell me?" I pleaded.
>
> Mother quietly told me, "We thought of ourselves as your family, your only family. I planned never to let you know."
>
> Later that afternoon, she told me more of the family secrets—my older sister Katherine was adopted, one of my cousins was also, and they didn't know either. Everything in my world changed for me that day.

At the time of Judy's adoption and in the ensuing years, her parents faced a critical decision encountered by all adoptive families. They must ask and answer key questions: "As we raise this adopted child, will we be truthful and open regarding the adoption, or will we pretend it never happened and that this child is ours by birth? Will we deal with this adoption by rejecting the differences adoption creates in our family?"

Sociologist and adoption expert H. David Kirk says that "some couples in reacting to their role handicap of adoptive parenthood (due to infertility) try to take the 'sting' out of adoption by simulating non-adoptive families as closely as possible."[17] In relating to their child, parents send the message loud and clear to forget about being adopted and everything that goes with it. Kirk calls this style of managing adoption communication *rejection of differences.*

Such a view only breeds negative consequences in the future for the adopted child and family. Kirk suggests that this rejection of differences pattern potentially blocks "the development of an accepting and trusting family atmosphere—an atmosphere conducive to open, honest exploration of adoption related issues."[18]

As an adult, Becca recalls with incredible pain how her family dealt with the issue of adoption as she was growing up. A lack of communication left an aching emptiness in her life.

> My parents lost their only birth child in a car accident when she was only five years old. Two years after her death, they adopted me as a newborn. I can remember only one conversation about adoption when I started school. If I ever brought it up as I was growing up, my mother would get terribly upset. She would say to me, "We just don't talk about those things, you are our little girl, now."
>
> As I reached my teen years, I had many, many unanswered questions. But for everyone in my world, the adoption never happened.

David Brodzinsky, in exploring the pattern of denial or rejection of differences, comments:

> It [is] simply not dealing [with] the issues that the child deals with.
>
> - The child says, "I feel bad because my parents didn't want me."
> - The parents say, "Don't think about that now, we love you."
>
> It becomes a series of behaviors that create an atmosphere in which discussions about adoption just don't happen. Parents ignore the issues. When there is an opportunity to talk about it, they choose not to. They sidestep the issues and discourage the child from ever bringing it up.[19]

Why do parents adopt this approach? Brodzinsky feels that there are several underlying reasons:

- It is an attempt on the parents' part to minimize their sense of pain around loss.
- It is an attempt to protect the child from feeling the pain of loss and rejection.
- It is an attempt on the part of the parents to protect themselves from potential loss—not the physical loss of the child, but the loss of the child's love, trust and commitment to them.[20]

Acceptance of Differences

Acknowledging differences is in direct contrast to rejecting differences within adoption and creating a closed communication system in the family.

Adoptive parents realize the importance of talking openly and freely about adoption. Children learn early that "in this house, it is okay to ask questions." Children learn that it is okay to explore their issues and feelings, not going through life as if those concerns didn't exist. For one teen, Anna, growing up in a family that acknowledged the differences created by adoption meant developing a healthy identity and self-esteem:

> I always knew I was adopted. My parents shared my adoption story with me from a very young age. One special thing that my adoptive parents asked for from the adoption agency was to get a picture of my birth mother and a letter from her. I will never forget the day that my mom took me to lunch and gave them to me. I was probably about eight. What she did for me on that day over nine years ago opened doors for me in terms of finding out what I needed to know about my birth family, my background and myself. As I continue to occasionally deal with adoption stuff, I walk through those doors she opened for me that afternoon.

What does the acknowledging style within a family do for the parent/child relationship?

- It creates an atmosphere of empathy and sensitivity in which feelings, thoughts, and struggles can not only be expressed, but recognized as valid.
- It builds a firm foundation of trust between parents and child.
- It fills in information gaps from the child's past.
- It corrects fears and fantasies that a child may have developed.
- It provides a firm footing for the development of identity.

One particular concern of adoptive parents who understand the importance of open communication about adoption is that they may be talking about it too much. Is it possible to approach this need somewhere in the middle between the rejection of difference style and acknowledgment of differences? David Brodzinsky suggests how:

> Parents have to create a balance between talking about adoption and living daily life. One way to do this is to ask oneself, "When was the last time we talked about adoption in this house?" If one doesn't remember, there is probably a need to address it in some way.[21]

Insistence Upon Difference

The *insistence upon difference* style—one that places the adopted child outside the emotional security of the family—is a management technique found in families in crisis. This pattern often leads family members to view adoption as the foundational reason for family chaos and disconnectedness. It also absolves everyone—except the adopted child—of responsibility for the problems.

A number of years ago, an angry adoptive parent contacted the adoption worker in her agency to bring her up to date on the family. Nancy, mother of Cassandra (age 16 and adopted at birth) and Katherine (age 15, the family's birth child) was enraged. "Cassandra told us last week that she is pregnant. I told her that if she wanted to keep the baby, she would have to find another place to live. If she would place the baby for adoption, she could come back home. How could she have done this to us? Katherine, our own daughter, would have never done this to us!" Families can move into an insistence upon differences style without real awareness. It is a subtle slide into family disharmony and blame.

Jonathan joined his adoptive family when he was a year old. He had been in two foster placements prior to coming to his family. In the early years, Jonathan experienced a warm, nurturing family environment. However, by the time he was 11, Jonathan and his parents began to experience difficulties. Jonathan started getting in trouble at school, on the school bus, on the playground. Just about anywhere he went, Jonathan encountered problems. At home, his parents argued a lot and occasionally his father didn't come home at night. Jonathan became the target for his family's problems. He no longer lived up to his parents' dream of a child, and they began to talk in terms of "this adopted child" when referring to him to other family members or friends. Jonathan and his adoptive status became the center of family discussion. The "adopted child" caused these family problems. Although the family never legally dissolved the adoption, Jonathan was seen as the problem, and his parents emotionally dissolved ties to him.

Families do not usually begin using the insistence upon differences style until conflict and crisis erupt. According to Brodzinksy, it is generally found in families of teenagers where there has been a long history of parent-child conflict. Parents begin subtly to move from seeing the problems as issues of normal family growth and development to viewing all family problems through the lens of adoption. That is when they step right into the pattern of insistence upon differences. Adoption then becomes the rationalization for explaining problems, and it becomes the only one.[22]

The self-assessment in Table 6.1 is also a helpful guide to examining the adoptive family relationship and can aid adoptive parents in assessing their own style of coping with the differences that adoption creates.[23]

Table 6.1. Since your child's legal adoption, how frequently have you:

1. Wondered whether the birth mother or father thinks about the child?	Never	Infrequently	Sometimes	Often
2. Recalled that at one time the child legally belonged to someone else?				
3. Remembered the child's original name (either first or both)?				
4. Wondered whether your child's birth parent worries about the child he/she relinquished?				
5. Talked with someone about your child's birth parents?				
6. Wondered what your words about adoption mean to the child?				
7. Tried to imagine how your child feels about being adopted?				
8. Thought that your child might someday be curious about his/her background?				
9. Wished that you might understand adoption from the point of view of the child?				
10. Talked about adoption with your child?				
11. Celebrated the adoption day anniversary?				
12. Personally been asked by your child the reasons for his/her adoption?				

(*Continued*)

Table 6.1 (*Continued*)

13. Answered your child's questions about his/her birth parents' history as honestly and completely as possible?
14. Found yourself referring to your child as "your adopted child" to family and friends?
15. Found yourself dreaming about how much easier parenting would be if you had a birth child instead of an adopted child?
16. Found yourself saying that this "adopted" child is the source of all family problems?
17. Asked yourself if there is any way to end the relationship with the child?

What Your Scores Indicate:
Never =1; Infrequently = 2; Sometimes = 3; Often = 4

Questions 1-5 deal with acknowledgment of differences. A low score means a coping style or a tendency to deny differences. A high score means a tendency to acknowledge differences.
Low <5 High >20

Questions 6-10 deal with levels of empathy toward the child. A low score means a tendency to have little empathy toward the child. A high score means high levels of empathy toward the child.
Low <5 High >20

Questions 11-13 deal with levels of communication. A low score means a tendency to communicate little about adoption. A high score indicates a high level of adoption communication.
Low <3 >High 12

Questions 14-17 deal with insistence upon differences. A low score means a tendency not to insist upon differences when the child is in crisis. A high score means a tendency to insist on differences.
Low <4 High >16

SUMMARY

Adoptive parents do have unique challenges before them to understand the subtle issues in adoption that impact their families, their children, and themselves. Parents demonstrate growing understanding of these issues as they adapt coping styles in talking with their children about adoption. It is also critical for parents to be aware of their own feelings and concerns as they relate to the communication needs of their adopted children.

QUESTIONS

1. How has your life been impacted by the three core issues—loss, shame, rejection—discussed in this chapter?
2. What style of coping with adoption issues best describes you—denial, acknowledgment, insistence? Why?
3. What aspect of talking to your child about adoption is the most difficult for you? Why?

CHAPTER 7

Principles of Talking about Adoption

"Do I really have to tell the whole truth?"
"How old should my child be when I do?"

These are questions frequently asked by adoptive parents. This chapter will respond to those questions and share other "principles of telling" that will aid parents in this vital task. While few rules are really written in stone, some principles, applied consistently, will enhance communication about adoption. These principles can also provide some welcome direction to adoptive parents besieged with well-intentioned advice from family and friends who really do not understand the complexities of adoptive parenting.

PRINCIPLES TO GUIDE ADOPTION COMMUNICATION

1. Initiate Conversation about Adoption.

Parents often handle discussions about adoption in the same way they handle conversations about sex. They believe they should wait until the child asks questions and answer only the questions asked by the child. This strategy is not helpful in assuring that children understand their histories.

Children often believe that they are being disloyal to the adoptive family when they have feelings and questions about the birth family. As a result, they may avoid conversation about the adoption and the birth family, even when they have burdensome questions or troubling feelings. Adoptive parents must look for opportunities to raise the issue for adoption and elicit questions from children. In this way, the adoptive parents assure children that their feelings are normal and expected and that they, as parents, do not feel threatened or believe the children are disloyal.

Elise had been adopted as an infant. Her parents had talked with her when she was three and four years old about her history, but they had not mentioned the adoption or her birth family since that time. Now, at age 13, Elise was dating a 26-year-old man who was an alcoholic and, when drunk, physically abusive. She had a "gothic" appearance, wearing black leather, very heavy make-up, and a punk hairstyle. Elise, only 13, was completely out of the control of her parents and was dangerously close to losing control of her own self. When her parents contacted a post-adoption therapist, the counselor asked how they communicated about Elise's adoption issues. The parents responded that they never discussed adoption within their family because Elise never raised the topic. They assumed her silence on the subject meant that she did not have any concerns or questions about her adoption. The therapist soon discovered, in talking with Elise, that she was consumed with fantasies, identity conflicts and confusion, and serious trust issues. Yet she did not feel comfortable in discussing her concerns because she feared her parents would be hurt if they knew she wondered about her birth family. Her struggle was displayed in behaviors and appearances because she felt blocked in addressing her questions directly and honestly.

There are a number of ways that parents can introduce the topic of adoption within the household and nurture the child's self-esteem at the same time:

1. When a program or movie with an adoption theme is on television or at the theater, watch the program or film with the child. Draw parallels and contrasts between the situation in the program and the child's own adoption. Use this conversation as a springboard to elicit additional questions.
2. Parents can also use key times of the year (often birthdays, Mother's Day, holidays, anniversaries of the placement) to discuss adoption issues. Example:

   "I always think about your birth mother on Mother's Day. I'm sure she is thinking about you today, too. Would you like to make a card for her and keep it in a special scrapbook?"

3. Adoptive parents can comment on the child's positive characteristics and wonder aloud from whom the child inherited them. Examples:
   "You have such beautiful long eyelashes. I wonder who in your birth family has eyelashes like yours. Do you ever wonder that?"
   "You are so good at drawing (music, soccer, math)! Do you wonder if anyone in your birth family is as talented as you are?"
4. Finally, adoptive parents can comment on the child's accomplishments, including the birth parents in their own feelings of pride. Example:
   "What a great job! Your birth parents would be as proud of you today as we are!"

2. Use Positive Adoption Language.

When parents talk with their children, friends, and extended family members, they must model positive adoption terminology. Careless use of language may inadvertently connote negative ideas about the birth parents, the child's history, or adoption itself.

Table 7.1 contains some excellent examples of both positive and negative adoption terminology, adapted from work by Holt International Children's Services.[1]

3. Never Lie to a Child about the Past or a Birth Family Member.

Lying about a child's birth parents or history generates serious trust fissures. When the truth is revealed in the future due to a search, a slip by either the adoptive parent or extended family, or an accidental discovery of adoption-related documents, a serious rift in the parent/ child relationship occurs—a rift that is difficult to repair with an apology or explanation. What began as "protection" of the relationship with the adopted child can become a "termination" of trust and intimacy in that relationship.

Rachel was removed from her birth family as a toddler due to child neglect. She was placed with her adoptive family when she was four years old. The adoptive family, Orthodox Jews, were very observant of conservative religious traditions. As Rachel grew up, she asked several times if her birth parents were also Jewish. The adoptive family had been told that Rachel's birth family was not Jewish, but they were concerned that Rachel, a strong-willed adolescent, would reject their family's religious and cultural practices if she knew this history. Therefore, they told her that they did not know her birth family's religious/cultural background and that her family might or might not have been Jewish. Not satisfied at age 17

Table 7.1.

Positive	Negative
Adoption triad	Adoption triangle
Biological parent Birth parent	Natural parent Real parent
Birth child	Own child
Birth father Birth mother	Real or natural father Real or natural mother
Born to unmarried parents	Illegitimate
Child with special needs	Handicapped child
Court termination	Child taken away
Make an adoption plan Choose adoption	Gave away Gave up
Intercountry adoption	Foreign adoption
Interracial	Mixed race
Making contact with	Reunion
My child	Adopted child
Parent	Adoptive parent
Search	Track down parents
To parent	To keep
Waiting child	Adoptable child Available child

with this ambiguity about her birth family's culture, Rachel contacted her placement worker and asked if her birth family had been Jewish. The social worker, not realizing that the adoptive parents had been less than honest with Rachel, shared with her that the birth family had been Protestant. Rachel was much more troubled by her parents' lack of honesty than she was about the information she received.

4. Allow a Child to Express Anger Toward a Birth Family Member Without Joining In.

Many adults remember that as children they became enraged when someone outside the family criticized any family member, even a family member who drove them absolutely crazy! Adoptive and foster parents find themselves in a similar position. They "share" the child with another family without being an "insider" in that family. While the child should be allowed to express both positive and negative feelings about birth family members, foster/adoptive parents cannot echo the negative sentiments.

Many children who are caught up in multiple family systems (stepchildren, foster children, and adopted children) find themselves torn by divided loyalties. If members of any of those family systems berate other involved families, the child's conflict is greatly intensified.

Refusal to join the child's anger can be an easy concept to grasp, but a difficult task to accomplish. After all, many foster and adoptive parents *are* angry at birth family members who harmed their children through substance abuse (during and after the pregnancy), physical and sexual abuse, neglect, abandonment, or emotional maltreatment. When the child expresses anger or outrage, it can be extremely difficult to restrain oneself from sharing that outrage. Maltreatment of a child should never be acceptable, but the adoptive parents cannot allow themselves the indulgence of speaking negatively of the perpetrators.

The following types of comments are acceptable and helpful to the child:

- "I'm glad that we are able to keep you safe now."
- "I can understand why you are so angry."
- "That must have been an awfully hard time for you. Is there anything I can do to help you now?"

Comments like the following are unacceptable and potentially harmful to the child:

- "If your mother had any sense in choosing boyfriends, you never would have been abused."
- "I cannot imagine how anyone could abuse a child. They must have been awful people."
- "They should lock up your parents and throw away the key. What they did to you was unforgivable."

5. Share Information in a Developmentally Appropriate Way.

No one knows better than the parent about a child's ability to cognitively and emotionally make sense of information. Adoptive and foster parents realize that many of their children may have some level of delay due to frequent moves, lack of nurture and enrichment, institutionalization, or trauma. Use language that's easily understood by your child and remember that many children and even teens have limited attention spans, particularly when dealing with painful topics. Several short, simple communications are generally easier for young children to understand than a lengthy "lecture" with multiple messages. Tools and strategies will be presented in Chapters 8 and 9 to help parents communicate about sensitive issues with preschoolers, school-age children, and teens.

6. Omissions Are Okay Until Age 12, but, by Adolescence, All Information Should Be Shared.

The complete history may be too complicated or too "adult" to share with a toddler or even a school-age child. For example, explaining prostitution to a child who does not understand human sexuality is not at all appropriate or advisable. It is sometimes in children's best interests to learn about their history in increments appropriate to their developmental level. Chapter 8 discusses how to impart difficult information in developmental stages to a child.

Parents know their child's developmental level better than anyone. There are no rules about the right age for giving details to a child. This decision depends on the child's developmental level and understanding. Parents must assess each situation individually.

Almost all teenagers, unless developmentally delayed, have the cognitive skills and sophistication to know all of their histories. "In response to the question, 'What do you say to an adopted teenager?', the answer is everything. Adopted people deserve to hear all the facts, all the information that concerns their own lives, their own histories. In other words, an adopted person deserves to know his or her story. So if, for whatever reason, the full story has not yet been told during childhood, it should be told during adolescence."[2]

However, most teens believe very few of the things they hear from adults. It is part of the job description of the adolescent to challenge whatever messages come from adults, particularly from their own parents. Therefore, adoptive parents are advised to share information before their child enters the argumentative, stormy stage of adolescence. Paradoxically, children of eleven or twelve will understand and accept information that an older youth might not.

Holly van Gulden writes,

> The instinct of parents who plan to share difficult information is to wait until the child is older, perhaps in their teens. In my experience,

> this is not the optimum developmental time to share difficult information. Adolescents face two tasks which make processing and externalizing difficult information potentially problematic: individuation and separation. Teens are re-evaluating the question "Who am I?" based in part on their sense of their history to date. Teens are also preparing to leave the family nest . . . this is a critical and complex stage during which to offer new, different and negative information about the young person's heritage. Though they appear more vulnerable, younger children in middle childhood generally process negative information more easily—not without pain, confusion and some self-blame, but with less potential for internalizing self blame/shame for the actions/choices of others. Children ages 8–10 have more time to work and rework material and come to a positive sense of self before they begin to emotionally leave the family nest.[3]

7. Consider Asking Instead of Telling.

When broaching the subject of adoption or birth family history, a good place to start is by asking questions rather than sharing information. Inquiries about what the child remembers, wonders, worries, or fantasizes about will give parents an opportunity to "start where the child is." Some examples of questions that might be conversation-starters are:

- What do you remember about the time you lived with your birth family (foster family, relative)?
- Do you have questions or worries about your birth parents (birth siblings)?
- Do you ever wonder about your adoption and how you came to be part of our family?
- Now that you are getting older, I bet you have questions about your birth family (how you joined our family). Would you like to talk about that?

8. Repeat, Repeat, Repeat!

Adoption and birth family histories are not "one and done" conversations. As children mature or develop additional questions, the topic should be revisited. "In order to gain a full understanding of adoption, repeated discussions should take place across time into early adolescence."[4] Children may have misunderstood information previously shared if parents used language or concepts they were not yet able to comprehend. Or children may have been so focused on one portion of the information, particularly if they have attentional challenges, that they missed other, equally important, parts of the message. They may have developed new worries or fears that need to be addressed. Or they may need facts during one conversation and an opportunity to express feelings during another. While parents want to avoid obsessively insisting on adoption communication until children feel overwhelmed by a barrage of painful discussion, it is important to remember that adoption should be addressed throughout children's maturation. As psychologist and researcher Dr.David Brodzinsky suggests, "If you can't remember the last time you talked about adoption, it's time for another conversation."

9. Be Realistic, and Don't Paint a Picture That Is Overly Positive or Negative.

Some parents, understanding their children's self-esteem will be tied to their attitudes and feelings about their origins or their birth family, will describe the birth parents or the situation in such rosy terms that children may wonder why they were not able to remain a part of the birth family! They may even conclude that the birth family was fine, but there was something wrong with them that caused the family to reject or abandon them.

Other parents, particularly those who have adopted children from the foster care system, may have received a great deal of negative information from their social workers. It is only natural that foster and adoptive parents would have negative feelings about people who abused or neglected their child. Foster and adoptive parents should remember the case records have focused on deficits of birth parents, especially in those situations where court cases are being prepared for an involuntary termination of parental rights.

In reality, all parents have both positive and negative qualities, and mature, empathetic adults should help concrete-thinking children recognize both. Furthermore, those children who were adopted at an older age remember times during which they may have been neglected, but they also remember times when their birth parents tenderly cared for them or played with them. They may be confused when therapists or foster/adoptive parents focus on poor parenting, excluding or ignoring moments of nurture. Duality of positive and negative attributes or memories should be acknowledged, and the child can be helped to understand her birth parents were doing as well as they could, under trying circumstances and with limited resources. However, a child separated from her birth family should also understand all children have a right to a safe, permanent home in which their needs can be more consistently met.

10. If Information Is Negative, Use a Third Party, Such as a Therapist, to Relate the Most Troublesome Details.

Because adoptive parents must be careful to avoid sharing extremely negative information about the birth family, they might choose to seek out a post-adoption specialist, a therapist who is sensitive to adoption issues, or an agency social worker to give the child particularly negative information. There is an old saying about "killing the messenger" that applies here. In some cases, it is wise to avoid becoming the messenger!

Many parents are concerned about knowing when to choose a third party to handle difficult information. If you feel the information is very negative and you are uncomfortable sharing it, it's time to look for a skilled and adoption-competent person to help.

Adoptive parents who decide to use a third party to share especially troubling information with their child must be careful to choose their helper wisely. Not all therapists are skilled in working with adoptive families, and some agency workers may even be insensitive to the needs of the child or the parents. Parents would be wise to interview the counselor prior to the meeting with the child to discuss parameters and engage in some form of "rehearsal" to avoid unpleasant surprises during the interview.

While parents may enlist the support of a professional in talking with their children about their history, they are not off the hook. It is critically important that parents are present for the interview for three reasons. First, they must provide emotional support to their children during a difficult interview. Second, they must be present to remember details that might be forgotten or misunderstood by the children. In fact, parents may want to audiotape the interview, with the permission of the children. The children will hear different information at different stages of maturity and may greatly value the ability to replay the interview as a young adult. Finally, parents must communicate to their children, throughout the interview and after, that they have heard "the worst" about their history and that they still love them unconditionally. Their presence sends a powerful message of love, support, and commitment to the children.

11. Don't Try to "Fix" the Pain of Adoption.

All parents naturally try to protect their children from pain. However, adoptive parents must recognize that their children must experience some pain in the normal resolution of adoption-related grief. The only way "out" is "through." Do not impose unrealistic expectations that parents can, by saying exactly the right thing, erase all of the pain and sadness caused by separation from the birth family.

When talking with anyone about a serious problem, particularly a loss, platitudes (e.g., "You'll have another child." or "She was so old—it's better that she's no longer suffering.") are not helpful. Listening ears, soft shoulders, and understanding attitudes are very helpful. Sometimes in parental eagerness to take pain away from children, we instead take away the validity of their feelings. When in pain, children do not necessarily want explanations or reasoned thoughts about what has happened; they only want someone who understands and empathizes, "I know this hurts."

Beth Hall, founding Co-Director of PACT, an adoption alliance, writes that her daughter experienced a crisis when a storyteller at school talked about the importance of naming. The seven-year-old child told her mother, "I don't think my birth mother really loved me. She didn't give me a name. I wanted her to give me a name." Her mother responded, "I can't imagine how hard it must have been for you to realize that right in the midst of your class." The adoptive mother did her best to listen and support, "not to try to fix, not interpret," the child's grief.[5] The mother did not give reasons why the birth mother might have avoided naming the child ("It might have been more difficult to sign the surrender if she had given you a name."). The adoptive mother also did not try to make her child's pain evaporate by ignoring it or redirecting attention from it ("But you are with our family now, and we did give you a name. So it doesn't matter that your birth mother did not give you a name."). Often, the best remedy for emotional pain is the support that comes from awareness that another person understands and accepts our feelings.

12. If the Child Refuses or Resists Communication, Try Again Another Time.

Young children generally love to hear their adoption stories. They are naturally self-absorbed, and they love to hear stories about themselves. However, as children mature and understand there are painful elements of grief and loss as well as confusion over divided loyalties involved in their stories, they may become resistant to adoption communication. Parents may wonder if they are overdoing adoption discussions if the child insists, "I don't want to talk about it. Can't you just drop it?" The child's wishes about adoption communication should be respected, and it's certainly difficult, if not impossible, to have a meaningful conversation with an unwilling partner. You can occasionally make comments like "I'm so proud of the way you handled that tough situation. I bet your birth parents would be proud of you as well" or "Today is a happy anniversary for our family—it's the anniversary of the day you became one of us." Occasional references to adoption or the birth family communicate to the child or teen that you are always available when he is ready to discuss the issue.

Some parents report more success in adoption communication if you are in a natural situation where you are not making eye contact with the child. Driving a child in the car is a great time to talk about sensitive issues. Other "no eye contact" moments might occur when playing pool, braiding a child's hair, or going for a walk.

Finally, some adopted youth are convinced they cannot talk with their parents about adoption because "they wouldn't understand" or "they would be hurt if they knew how much I think about my birth family." If an older child or teen continually refuses to communicate about his adoption or history, he might benefit from participation in a support group with other adopted youth near his age. If no post-adoption groups exist near your community, seek out foster or adoptive family associations so your teen has an opportunity to talk with other children or youth separated from their birth families.

13. Don't Impose Value Judgments on the Information.

Information about a child's history may seem very negative, even horrific, to adoptive parents or social workers, but may be interpreted quite differently by the child. As stated earlier, information about a child's history should never be changed, or given to an older child with significant omissions. Facts must be presented, however, without the overlay of values, without judgment.

Children's feelings for, or memories of, the birth family may alter their perceptions of events. And their need to have positive feelings for their birth family will definitely color their perceptions. If facts are presented in a negative, judgmental fashion, children interpret this judgment as rejection by the adoptive family of their birth family, their origins, and, ultimately, themselves. We do not have the right to judge birth parents; understanding comes from "witnessing" without judgment or censure. Children must develop the maturity to do the same, and this "understanding without judgment" must be modeled for them by the people most important to them: their parents.

This avoidance of judgment can actually be a relief for many adoptive parents. Sometimes they worry for years about the right time and the right way to present information they perceive to be extremely negative. The child, when presented with the facts, may not see the information as negative at all.

Cameron was conceived as the result of a rape. He was placed as a six-month-old infant with Debbie and John. Cameron had never been told the circumstances surrounding his adoption, and he became obsessed as a preteen with curiosity about his story. His family wanted to protect him from learning, as his own awareness of sexuality was beginning to develop, that his birth father had been a rapist. Not wanting to lie, they simply told Cameron that his birth mother had been unable to raise him. Cameron interpreted this to mean that his birth mother had been a horrible person who had rejected him and found him so repulsive that she could not care for him. When told the actual circumstances surrounding his birth and adoption, Cameron expressed relief to learn that his mother was not a "slut." He understood that his mother had rejected the rape, not him. His imagination had created a far worse scenario than the actual one.

14. Children Should Have Control of Telling Their Story Outside the Immediate Family.

Remember that the history belongs to the children, not to the adoptive parents. If friends or extended family members ask about sensitive information, simply tell them that the information belongs to the children. They can ask them about it when they are old enough to understand their questions. Parents should not decide with whom, when, and how intimate details of children's lives are shared.

Parents may want to assist children in developing a short, simple version of their story that they feel comfortable sharing with neighbors, school friends and teachers, relatives, and other acquaintances. This "cover story" may be very similar to the information given your children when they were very young. Let the children know that one does not withhold information from acquaintances because it is shameful, but because one should not have to explain one's history in all its detail to anyone and everyone. Explain that some people don't have a lot of experience with adoption and might ask insensitive questions or make ridiculous remarks. At some point, a child will be very grateful to have developed and rehearsed a cover story that will short-circuit these questions.

Liz Clanton and her two children, Peter, age seven, and Katie, age five, both adopted from Korea, were sitting in a restaurant enjoying a few quiet moments together. A woman came up to them and commented to Liz about how beautiful her children were. The woman then directed her attention to Peter and asked, "Why did your mother get rid of you?" Thankfully, Liz knew that this day would come when her children would need to be prepared to answer uncomfortable questions—and prepared they were. Peter, with respect, said to the inquiring woman, "We only talk about that at home." Peter was prepared.

There are two key points to remember when helping a child to develop a cover story:

1. Discuss questions people might ask and the situations the child might encounter. Such things might include introducing the child to a new neighborhood of friends, experiencing the first day at a new school or church, or, as in Peter and Katie's case, what questions curious people might ask at a mall or restaurant.
2. Talk about what information should be shared. It is not an easy task for children to sort out what should be told and what should be kept private. Children can be instructed to provide three basic responses to questions: their name, their origin, and the date they joined the family. It is important for children to know that they are not obligated to tell everyone everything—that there are personal boundaries others must respect.

15. Remember That Children Probably Know More Than You Think They Do.

Sometimes adoptive parents tell others in the family about "troublesome" details of their children's history, and they believe they will tell the children—but later. No time ever seems like the right time because school is starting, the dog just ran away, or the children just had a fight with their best friend. So parents never get around to telling the children, and someone else does. When information comes to children from someone other than the parents, the children do not have the support of parents in integrating information into a positive self-identity. And, unfortunately, information is sometimes shared that is not entirely accurate because it has been passed through too many tellings.

Jordan, age 16, was placed as an infant with his loving adoptive family. He had two older sisters, both born into the family. Jordan had been born to a woman with significant mental health problems who reported that the father of the baby was African American. Social workers at the placing agency informed the adoptive parents that the baby might be biracial, but certainly did not appear to be a mixed-race child. The mother was described as "unreliable" as a source of information due to her mental instability. The adoptive parents were uncertain about what they should tell Jordan about his racial background. They talked about this dilemma to Jordan's two older sisters, but never spoke to Jordan about the issue. When Jordan and his parents attended a post-adoption support group for parents and adopted youth, the parents were advised to share exactly what the agency had told them: his birth mother, an unreliable source, reported that the birth father was African American. When they did so, Jordan commented, "Oh, I've known that for years. The girls told me all about it." While the parents had agonized over what information to share, their older children had done it for them—though not nearly as well as the parents would have handled it. Though the adoptive parents believed that Jordan would eventually ask about his race/ethnicity, he never had. Jordan struggled with identity issues without the support and guidance his parents could have given him.

SUMMARY

Keeping lines of communication open is vital to adoptive family health. Observation of these principles of truth telling can aid a family in assuring they are creating a safe environment in which their child can develop a healthy sense of self and an experience of honest, healthy family relationships.

QUESTIONS

1. Discuss ways that adoptive parents can initiate conversation about adoption.
2. Discuss the consequences of "lying with good intentions" to an adopted child about the past or a birth family member.
3. Why is it important to allow a child to express anger toward the birth family without joining in?
4. What does the statement "Don't try to 'fix' the pain of adoption" mean to you personally?
5. Do you find it hard to refrain from value judgments on the information about your child's history? What judgments are particularly hard for you to give up? Why?

CHAPTER 8

Sharing the Hard Stuff: The Adoptive Parent's Challenge

If we don't journey with our children to those dark and difficult places in their memory and history, we leave them to journey alone.

To actually have a child, a child of your heart and kindness, who sleeps warm and secure in the blanket after you kiss him goodnight, and to know that this child's life began in horror . . . and that you must tell him and watch his innocence be shattered, and know yourself to be an agent of that shattering, is a duty that no one would wish upon another.[1]

She approached the adoption speaker tentatively, waiting until the last person asked his question and the room cleared. She wanted no one to hear her question. "Excuse me," she said to the speaker, "I need to ask you something. My son is seven years old, almost eight. He came to us through a public agency at the age of seven months. We were told that he is the product of an incestuous relationship between a brother and sister. He doesn't seem to have any major problems or difficulties. This is something we never have to tell him, right?"

This adoptive mom, like hundreds of adoptive parents, holds a secret to her child's past. She looks at the information from every angle, inside and out, upside down and right side up, hoping to find a way to avoid disclosing it. Yet the moment of disclosure is inevitable, unavoidable.

Imparting such information is difficult. The details seem far too painful. Yet, those distressing pieces—the missing pieces—are often the parts of a puzzle that bring understanding to a child and fill in the blanks in an otherwise jumbled perception of his past.

THE HIDDEN PIECES

We all have a storehouse of memories from our childhood. Some of those memories are neutral, in that we may remember the event, but there is no really strong emotion attached to the event. Some of those events provoke warm and comforting memories. They come to mind, because there is a positive and strong emotion connected to the event. A special Christmas, a fun childhood vacation, the first homerun or ballet program are special and warm memorable events.

Although children who come into families through foster care or an orphanage situation may have some good memories, those are often overshadowed by staggering horrific events that provoke pain and deep sorrow. Many of the children who come from early harm have built walls around those events. They will not allow anyone into those shattering events and painful memories until a solid foundation of trust and safety has been laid. Months, even years, may pass before a child opens a small door to invite anyone inside. Parents must be prepared and ready for those moments of opportunity, armed with compassionate truth.[2]

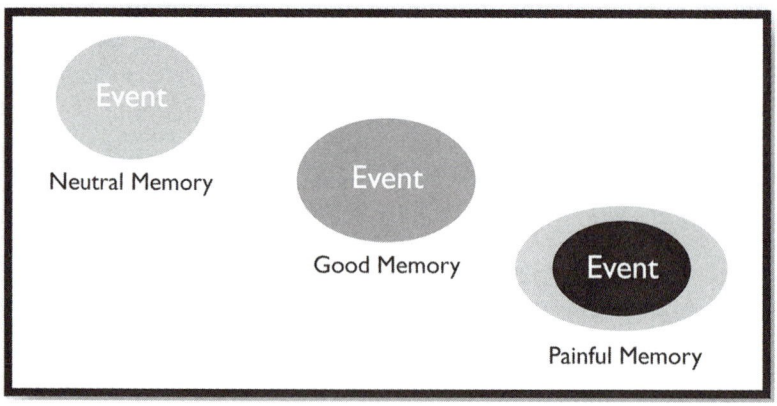

Figure 8.1

For many children, learning the difficult facts comes as a relief. Especially for older children, it affirms the emotional reality for which they have vague, fleeting memories of experiences and feelings.

"Children most often know the truth . . . they lived it," comments Greg Keck, an internationally recognized authority on attachment and bonding. "We need to validate their truth, document their truth, and where possible, show them the truth. Trauma is subjective. Therefore, we must present the facts as they were, and then it becomes the child's job to reframe it, repackage it and put it together in their understandable form."[3]

Keck said, "I think that in our efforts to protect hurt children, we often hurt them more. Somehow we want things to be nice or seem nice. I think that, as a result of this, we want to reframe things so that they are comfortable enough for us to tolerate. In doing this, we often leave [children] incomplete, confused, and more unclear than they were."[4]

"We as parents often want to change our child's past reality. That is not our job," Keck pointed out.

When a child says, "I hate my birth mom," it is better for a parent to affirm this by saying, "I know," or, "I bet you do." Instead, I have heard people say things like, "Oh, Bobby, they had so many problems of their own, they just couldn't take care of you. They drank. They used drugs." This response seems to explain and, even worse, excuse the behavior.

> In working with kids, we want them to stop projecting blame and discontinue externalizing the causes of their problems and misbehavior. If someone thinks that they "hate" someone, the worst response we can give to them is some reason that they should not. When we do not validate their feelings and perceptions as accurate, we further complicate the healing process.[5]

Another response children often receive when facing painful issues of their past is to hear something like "Don't cry, it will be alright." We want to stop the tears because we ourselves are uncomfortable with them. According to Dr. Gordon Neufeld, we shut off the adaptive process when we shut off the tears. In order to move past things we cannot change and do not like, we must first grieve.[6] Within the tears of grief, sorrow and pain are literally toxins that are released in the tears of the broken-hearted or wounded person.[7] Instead of shutting off a child's tears over the pain of the past, a parent can quietly and simply sit and cry with them.

Knowing that sharing the hard stuff is the right thing to do is one thing. Knowing just how to do it is another. Just how does a parent carry out this challenging task?

SHARING ABOUT ABANDONMENT

Josh's Story

Little is known about Josh's story. His adoptive parents have very little information about Josh, his birth family, or any other background. They do not even have his exact birthdate. Josh was found on a warm summer morning on the steps leading to the police station in his small Korean town. He looked to be just a few days old. A note was taped to his blanket. "I am young and alone. I cannot care for him." Someday his parents must attempt to tell Josh his story—without much knowledge or information to help.

For many thousands of children adopted internationally and some domestically, abandonment is the only word that describes their history. No name. No identifying information. Nothing. How does a family relate that information to a growing child?

Sometimes, parents will have to research the situation in the child's community of origin and let the child know, "We are not sure of exact details, but this is the most likely scenario, given the situation in your birth family's community/country at the time of your birth." For example, cultural understanding that male children in China are expected to care for aging parents is very pertinent when those Chinese parents are limited by a "one child only" government policy. To provide for care during their aging years in a country where nursing homes are not part of the cultural scene, Chinese birth parents may make a painful, but necessary, adoption decision for a female child.

Dee Paddock, a nationally respected therapist and adoptive parent, says that adoptive parents need to see sharing their child's story as a process in telling and understanding—not just relating the facts of the event. "Whatever happened in the child's life experience that led to adoptive placement for that child, from the very beginning and in every stage they need to hear the words, 'your birth parent couldn't parent you,'" says Paddock.[8] From that point on, parents can build the story developmentally.

When a child was abandoned at birth or early in life, Paddock suggests telling the story in the following increments:

Preschool years: Your birth mother couldn't take care of you and wanted you to be safe. So she found a safe place for you where safe adults would come and take care of you.

Early Elementary: We feel sad sometimes, and even mad sometimes, that we cannot give you any more information. Do you ever have any sad or mad feelings about not knowing anything? It is important that you understand that you are not responsible for the decision your parents made.

If a single mother: Being a single mother in Korea (or whatever country) may be extremely difficult. A single mother may have difficulty finding a job and being able to provide for her child.

If a large family: Sometimes a family has too many children and is not able to provide for all of them. When the newest baby arrives, as you did, your parents felt they had no other choice but to take you to people who could care for you.

Elementary school years: Although we do not have information directly about your birth parents, we can explore all about your country and learn to understand why birth parents had to make such difficult decisions. When you think about your birth parents, what do you think about? Are you ever sad or angry that you don't know anything about them? What would you like us to do to help you? (Parents can begin to bring into the conversation the societal, economic, and cultural aspects of their child's country that would force birth parents to make such a decision.)

Preteen: Continue using educational resources to fill in a child's cultural and ethnic background. Continue to ask the questions mentioned above in greater depth. Consider locating a peer support group of other adopted preteens and teens that deals with open discussion regarding adoption issues.

Additional points for parents:

- Rough periods for children can create a period of real growth and understanding. Remember the maxim "No pain, no gain."
- One of the most helpful experiences for internationally adopted children has been the homeland tour—a return to their country of origin. "What we are learning from these trips back to the child's country," Paddock suggests, "is that some of these children spent far more time with their birth families than initially reported. As a result, some children do have vague memories of the birth family, and locating some of those families has been possible."
- Be careful not to say that the birth parent could not parent any children. On some trips, adoptive parents discovered that the birth family did have other children they were parenting.
- Many adolescents who have experienced the homeland tour make real strides in understanding the whys of their adoption experience. "They see real people who had to make real life decisions," Paddock comments. "After they return, they realize that they fit more into the culture of the country they grew up in, instead of the one in which they were born."[9]

SHARING ABOUT PROSTITUTION AND DRUGS

Chris and Kimberly's Story

Chaos, confusion, neglect, abuse are words that depict the early years of Chris and Kimberly. The children's birth mother, a single mom, was trapped by a life-threatening problem: drug abuse. A heroin and crack addict, their mother, Sharon, focused only on one thing—getting enough money for the next hit. Care of her toddlers fell to a distant second priority. On many occasions, various men paraded in and out of their small, cramped apartment because the only source of income that could support Sharon's habit was prostitution. Often, the children were left alone when Sharon went out seeking customers. Other times, the children would be locked in the bathroom when their mother was "working." Neighbors, tiring of Sharon's lifestyle, reported the situation to the police and the local child services agency. The children were removed and placed in foster care. Because their mother failed to complete plans for their return, they were eventually adopted. Someday, their adoptive parents will have to tell them their life story.

One of the important things to remember when talking with children who were old enough to have memories of previous families is that they do have memories. Parents often shy away from bringing up this difficult topic, but they must realize that such memories are there, even though the child may not have the words to describe their experiences. A child removed from his mother for child neglect related to involvement with drugs and prostitution might be told the following increments at the following times:

Preschool years: Your first mommy did not take care of you, and it is very important to be sure you are safe. She wasn't ready to be a mommy.

Early elementary years: Your mother had a lot of trouble making sure she could take care of herself. She did not have a "daddy" to help take care of you. She could not protect a small child, so a social worker and a judge made sure you had a safe family who would take care of you forever.

Middle school years: Your mother made some bad choices when she was a very young woman. She began to take drugs that were not good for her. She could not think well when she was taking the drugs. That caused her to make even more bad choices. That's why it was not safe for you to remain with her.

Preteen: Your mother could not support her drug addiction because she was not a reliable employee and could not keep a job. She had dropped

> out of school. Because she was addicted to drugs, she felt really sick when she could not buy and use them. When your mother was feeling this sickness, called withdrawal, she became a victim of human trafficking to raise the money to get the drugs. She worked as a prostitute as this was the only way she could support herself and her habit. While she was looking for customers, she left you alone in her apartment when you were only a baby. Neighbors were worried about you and called the police. They wanted to be sure you were safe.

Notice the way in which details are added as the child's cognitive abilities to understand the information develop. At no time does the parent relate something to the child that has to be contradicted later. More information is added as the child gains maturity.

SHARING ABOUT PHYSICAL ABUSE

Kenneth's Story

Kenneth came to the attention of child protective services workers after he entered Head Start at the age of three. With just one look at him, his teachers could tell he was an angry child. Even at three, he struck out frequently at playmates, slapping, kicking, and biting them. His behavior mystified his teachers. They knew his mother. She was a very quiet woman who rarely said very much when she came to get him each day. He always seemed happy to see her.

On a rainy fall day, Kenneth was soaking wet when he arrived at school. The teacher always had extra clothes in the classroom. As she was helping this youngster change his clothes she was horrified by what she saw. Kenneth's back and legs were covered with varying shades of black, blue, and green, and yellow bruises. She could tell that some of the injuries were older. One seemed as recent as a day or two. She simply asked Kenneth who did this to him, and his reply was, "Daddy and Mommy." That simple question and response changed Kenneth's life forever. The local protection agency became involved with the family. Kenneth was placed in protective custody, and after 18 months of attempts to work with his mother and father, efforts for reunification were discontinued. Kenneth became eligible for adoption. His foster parents adopted him. Someday, Kenneth will have a lot of questions about the how's and why's of his life. His parents must be prepared to answer them.

Parents can aid their child in coming to some understanding about abuse as they move through their developmental stages.

Preschool years: "Your mommy and daddy were not ready to be parents did not take care of you the way that parents are supposed to. Mommies and daddies must keep children safe, and your parents did not do that."

Early elementary years: "You were not hurt because you are a bad child, even if someone told you that. You are not at fault for what your parents did. You were treated badly because your parents were out of control in their lives." Adoptive parents can, at this age, begin to fill in some details about the birth parents, for example, drinking problems, family problems, or financial problems. If the children have memories of the abuse, parents can use joint storytelling and puppets to help them talk about their thoughts and feelings. (This technique is fully explained in Chapter 9.)

Middle school years: "Do you ever get angry at a friend at school or on the playground? Do you ever feel like hitting him? Many children feel that way. Your parents also got very angry. They never learned how to handle anger while they were growing up. So, instead of handling anger in a good way, they took their anger out on you, even when they knew it was wrong. What do you think could make them so angry? Life circumstances were overwhelming to them, and they didn't know how to handle them. What could have been overwhelming for them?" Adoptive parents should fill in all the details they know about the parents' background at this point. (See Chapter 9 for tools to help children deal with their own anger and fears.)

Preteen: Continue to deal with all the child's memories, both positive and negative. Giving information (the rational style—see Chapter 6) and tapping into emotions (the reflective style) are key in helping children move through the stages of their own anger and hurt. Information at this age includes such things as factors that contribute to intergenerational patterns of abuse, social/economic influences, and the psychological makeup of the family of origin. Children age 12 and beyond have developed abstract thinking and can begin to understand their birth family dynamics in these terms.

Defusing the Time Bomb

Not dealing with the issue of abuse can create a "walking time bomb." Randolph Severson, an adoption counselor in Dallas, Texas, sees this in teens or adults who have not talked about their past:

Many come to me saying they feel like a time bomb ready to go off. This happens often in those who were under the age of six and had few verbal skills when the abuse or trauma occurred.

They have not seen their family of origin since that time and, because of their young age, they do not have any context for relating to those persons outside the memory of the abuse.

Life is a continuum of human experience, and the abusive event was so overpowering, it is the only memory from which they can develop a sense of identity from a historical context.

As these adults move through adolescence and attempt to develop self-image from their historical context, two issues present themselves. First, they don't have much memory to serve them and second, what memory they do have is often traumatic and even horrifying.

When I can, I work to get into the historical context of the person's memory. No one person abused a child twenty-four hours a day. I try to help this person recover any memory, however small it may be, that is positive.

I also use what I call "explaining therapy," that is, giving them as much information as possible, as a successful tool. Going back to an agency and getting as much information as is relevant to them is essential. Even if [it] is nothing more than information that can place this child into the social, economic, psychological and family problems that his parents faced it is helpful.[10]

Finding Out More

Agencies may have additional non-identifying information about the child and the birth family's background that was not initially shared with the adoptive family. It is worth the effort to contact the agency to update what information they have available.

SHARING ABOUT SEXUAL ABUSE

Dusty's Story

Dusty was three years old when her stepfather entered her life. Within a year after he came, life changed dramatically for her. John, her stepfather, began "grooming" Dusty for sexual activity. It started when she was four with fondling her genitals. By the time Dusty was in second grade, he would come into her bedroom late at night and force himself upon her. One afternoon when Dusty was in third grade, a teacher overheard her tell a friend at recess about the things her daddy made her do. Within hours, her life dramatically changed again forever. The teacher notified the local child protective services agency. Her birth mother denied all of Dusty's allegations and essentially chose to believe her husband instead of her daughter. Dusty entered foster care and was eventually adopted. Someday, her adoptive parents will have to tell her why.

Children often feel responsible for sexual abuse. Offenders frequently make the child feel responsible for what happened, both as a way of keeping their victims quiet and as a way of rationalizing their own destructive behavior. Perhaps the abuser told the child warm, wonderful things, like "You are a special person to me, and we could share some wonderful things together, but it will be our little secret."

Adoptive parents often have difficulty talking about sexual abuse. It is a subject that most parents would like to avoid. "Parents don't like to hear or say the words that their children use to describe what happened to them," says Greg Keck. "If the child has language, ask her to tell you what happened, without correcting her language or words. Her feelings are attached to her language. However, often parents change the words to much more pleasant ones—one . . . they are more comfortable in using. If parents change how their children say what they say, they will not access their true feelings. They minimize their emotional and psychological reality."[11]

Many children who have been sexually abused ask such questions as "Why did they do it to me? Why did they do it at all?" Parents can make several important points while talking about sexual abuse with a child who has memories of the experience.

- Sexual abuse was never your fault, no matter what anyone said to you.
- (Name) was very selfish when he did that to you. (Name) was only thinking about himself first. He wanted to make himself feel good.
- (Name) touched you in ways that were wrong. (Name) is totally responsible for what he did.
- It took great courage on your part to disclose what (name) did to you. You did the right thing. I'm proud of you. You knew how to keep yourself safe.

WHEN YOUR SEXUALLY ABUSED CHILD WAS TOO YOUNG TO TALK

Cassie's Story

Cassie was four months old when she entered her foster home. It became apparent that her birth mother was unable to care for her. For over

14 months, the agency worked to bring about reunification with her birth mother, but the efforts failed. Up to that point, Cassie's birth father had been out of the picture. Two weeks before the agency was to seek permanent custody of Cassie with plans for adoption, her birth father appeared. Cassie, now 18 months old and having never met her father, began visitation with him. Within two months, the court ordered Cassie be placed into the custody of her father.

The Weldons, Cassie's foster parents, were devastated by the court's decision. However, their devastation was even greater when, less than a year later, the agency called them and asked them if they would take Cassie back into their home. Her father had physically and sexually abused her. When Cassie returned to the Weldons' home at the age of three, she was a different child, now with a traumatized past that carried emotional scars hidden within her memory.

"In healthy adoptive families, the parents are the healers," says Paddock. It is their responsibility to create an environment in which discussion of this difficult subject can occur. What can parents say developmentally to bridge the gap for the nonverbal child who must someday understand his or her earlier life experience?[12]

Preschool years: "Your first parents were not able to take care of you the way a child should be cared for. All children need safe mommies and/or daddies. Your birth parents were not able to keep you safe."

Early elementary years: Continue to reinforce the above story and begin discussion of sexuality. There are appropriate books for children that discuss this subject. (Suggestions are given at the end of this chapter.) Begin discussion about how the offending person made hurtful decisions and was not considering the child's feelings. Parents can begin asking questions like "Do you ever wonder about the time you spent with your birth parents?" The message needed early by the child from his parents, according to Paddock, is that "nothing is too scary or horrible to talk about. Nothing the child can say will cause the parent to send him back. Kids need to learn that no feelings will kill them, nor will any memory kill them either. Sharing it will help heal it."

Middle school years and beyond: As children prepare to enter adolescence, parents might consider counseling or a support group to help with resolution of early sexual abuse. Parents can contact the local child protective services agency to inquire about local resources for children who have been sexually abused. Parents should continue to respond to questions with openness, support, and reflective listening.

SHARING ABOUT MENTAL ILLNESS

Roy's Story

Roy was only three years old when he entered foster care but already had more life experiences than many adults. Although Roy's mother loved him, she suffered with severe depression. She was totally detached from Roy's needs. Filthy and hungry, he often roamed around the apartment complex. Eventually, neighbors reported the severe neglect, and Roy was removed. After 18 months in foster care, it was evident that he could not return home safely. His foster parents ultimately adopted him. Someday his parents will need to share the truth about his past.

Preschool and older children who are placed for adoption because of a parent's mental illness may have memories of strange, even frightening behavior. Perhaps the child remembers his parent being severely depressed and dysfunctional. There were too many days to count, the child might say, when he came home from school only to realize that his parent never got out of bed. Perhaps the child can remember his parent's rapid mood swings, making it hard for him to know what to do. He can recount being locked in a room for doing something, when just the day before the same behavior was okay.

Greta, age 16, Steve, age 11, and Martin, age 9, were removed from their mother, Marinda, as a result of her severe mental health challenges. Marinda was quite paranoid and afraid of getting out of her bed. She kept her three school-age children home from school and insisted they remain in her bed to protect her from unseen threats. Marinda never abused the children, and she clearly loved them. However, as a result of her paranoia, she relied on her children to take care of her instead of providing for their needs.

Although they may have lived in an upside down, chaotic, dysfunctional, and unpredictable home, these children love their birth parents and often ask with words or behavior, "Why couldn't I stay with them?" or, "I need to be there to help take care of her." There are important concerns that parents can address in a developmental sequence.

Preschool years: "Your first daddy is not healthy and needs other people to help take care of him. Your first mommy couldn't manage things alone. Your first daddy has 'good' days when things feel fine and 'bad' days when he especially needs help from others. He and your first mommy could not keep you safe. You need to be with a forever family that can take care of you every day and keep you safe. That's why you are with us."

Early elementary years: "Your birth mother felt sad (or scared) much of the time because your first daddy wasn't healthy. Neither of them could keep you safe. When you have a problem (can't understand your homework), you think about ways to solve it (get help from me, your older brother, your teacher). When your birth parents got so upset and scared, they couldn't figure out what to do. Your first mommy didn't do anything, and the problems just got worse. You know what happens if you never figure out your homework! Your birth dad had trouble thinking clearly about what was happening and how to cope with problems. When thinking problems go on for a long time, we call it mental illness. There is medicine that might help your birth dad feel and think better. But he didn't always take the medicine, and the thinking problems would return. Sometimes, talking to a doctor or social worker helps. We think that your birth mom is safe, but she cannot take care of children. That's why you will always be with us."

Middle school years and beyond: "Your birth father has had mental health problems (depression or other diagnosis, if known) for a long time that were overwhelming for your birth mother. The problems started long before you were born, and you did not cause your birth dad to be depressed or scared. He doesn't choose to be unhappy, but he cannot stop feeling this way. So your birth dad's mental health problems are not your fault, and they are not your mom's fault. Mental health problems happen to some people, and it is not anybody's 'fault.' Your birth parents have trouble with working and taking care of children. Sometimes, your birth father even has to go to a hospital to get help with medicine and to talk with the doctor. What kinds of things worry you about your birth parents? What questions do you have that I can answer for you?"

Additional points that parents can reinforce with their child

- Just because mom or dad couldn't make good decisions doesn't mean that he or she doesn't love you.
- It became very important that you could finish growing up in a stable home where it is safe.
- You did not cause this problem in your parent's life. He had it before you were born.

If your birth parents had mental health problems, this does not necessarily mean that you will develop mental health problems later. We hope that our family can provide a stable environment for you, one where you will not experience the kinds of trauma that may have led to depression or anxiety for your birth parents.

SHARING ABOUT SUBSTANCE ABUSE

Jimmy and Ashley's Story

"Traumatic" and "harsh" are two words that vividly describe the early life of Jimmy and Ashley, a brother and sister. Both children almost daily experienced unpredictable and often abusive treatment from their birth mother, a crack addict. The two children frequently slept all night in the family car, a trashed shell, alone and cold, while their mother attended to her drug addiction. A policeman walking by the car at 2:00 A.M. one morning heard the children's cries. The authorities removed the children from their birth mother. Over time, it was obvious that she would not be able to parent the children, and an out-of-state family adopted them. Someday, their parents will need to share the truth about their past.

Marty's Story

Marty, age six, was removed from her alcoholic mother after five years of neglect. Her mother would provide marginally acceptable care when sober, but would go on binges when she would drink cheap wine until she passed out on the couch. Her blackouts lasted for several hours, leaving Marty terrified and alone. When she could not rouse her mother, she feared her mother had died. No amount of crying or shaking could waken her mother. After the termination of parental rights and the subsequent adoptive placement, Marty, an absolutely delightful child, was adjusting beautifully. Her adoptive family thought that her earlier difficulties were resolved until, one night, they served wine with dinner. Marty took one look at the wine bottle and became hysterical. She was absolutely inconsolable, associating wine with abandonment and lack of nurturing. Someday, her parents will need to help Marty understand the ravages of alcoholism.

Even very young children who were placed for adoption may have vague memories of what life was like with someone who abused alcohol or drugs. Children need the opportunity during their developing years to voice their feelings about those memories of not having food to eat, not having a clean bed to sleep in, or not having clean clothes to wear. These children often have lingering fear of what it was like to live with someone who was chronically absent, leaving them alone or who was abusive or spaced out most of the time. (The suggestions that follow can be adapted to explain alcoholism.)

Preschool years: "Your first mommy took some drugs that weren't good for her. She did not get this medicine from the doctor, and it wasn't good for her. She took the medicine because she thought it would help her feel good, but she was wrong. When she took the medicine, she didn't feel good, and she couldn't take care of you. You need a forever family that can keep you safe. That's why you are with us."

Early elementary years: "Your first mommy made some bad choices before you were even born (when you were very little). She listened to a bad person who said she would be happier if she took drugs. This bad person, a dealer, wanted to make money by selling drugs to people. Once people get started taking drugs, it is very hard for them to stop. They feel really bad whenever they try to stop. When your birth mom tried the drugs, she did feel better for a little while and thought the bad person, the dealer, was right! But the dealer did not tell her how bad she would feel when she stopped taking the drugs. And the dealer did not tell her she would not be able to take care of you, or any children, when she was using drugs because she would be too sleepy. Pretty soon, she was taking drugs every day because she felt sick when she didn't. She wanted the drugs so badly so she could stop feeling sick; sometimes she would even use money for groceries or rent to buy them. You need to be with a family that can always make sure you have a safe place to sleep and good food to eat. That's why you will always be with us."

Middle school years and beyond: "Your birth mom got hooked on drugs or alcohol because she listened to the wrong people and made some bad choices. What do you remember about that time? How do you feel about it now? What questions do you still have?"

Additional points that parents can reinforce with their child:

- You did not cause your parent's drinking or drug problem.
- Your parent treated you as she did because drugs or alcohol controlled her.
- Just because your parent did not always treat you as a child should be treated, doesn't mean that she doesn't love you.
- Your parent did not have control over her life and couldn't give you a safe, happy, and secure place to be.
- You need to grow up in a home where you can be safe from harm.

SHARING ABOUT LAWBREAKING

Kristy's Story

Kristy's life was never quiet. Home life was chaotic, loud, and unpredictable. There were always a lot of people—mean ones—who came at all hours of the day and night. Her parents had a home business that provided money for the family. It wasn't a legal business, but a dangerous one. Her parents would steal cars, repaint them to sell on the black market, or tear them down and sell the parts. Late on a warm fall evening, Kristy's life changed forever. An undercover police officer came to their home to "buy" a car. After the transaction was completed, he arrested both of her parents. At age four and a half, Kristy entered foster care and was eventually placed with an adoptive family. Someday, her parents will need to explain to her the circumstances of her past.

Opening the door of communication regarding law breaking can begin early. For example, here is what parents might say to their children as they grow.

Preschool years: "Do you know how we have rules in our family? Some rules are so important that they are called laws. Everyone has to obey laws, even grownups. Can you think of any laws? When big people don't follow these especially important rules, called laws, they have to go away to a special time-out place to learn how to behave better. Your first parents are at a time-out place now because they did not follow the important rules. You need to have a forever family to keep you safe. That's why you will be here with us until you grow up."

Early elementary years: "Your birth parents broke the law and had to see a judge. The law your birth parents broke was ___ (stealing cars from other people, selling drugs to other people, etc.). We are not sure why your birth parents decided to break the law, but we think it was because they were taking drugs and needed money to buy more when they felt sick, or they were drinking and could not make a good decision about how to act, or they tried to solve their problems with fighting instead of talking, and so on. The judge decided that your birth parents had to think about the bad choices they made, so the judge sent them to jail to think about it. They will be there for ___ years. You cannot wait that long for a family. You need a family to love you and keep you safe right now! That's why you will be with us until you are grown up."

Middle school years and beyond: "Your birth parents probably wish now that they had made a different decision when they were as younger

> so that they didn't have to be separated from you. They love you very much and are probably worried that you will be angry at them or, even worse, will forget them. How do you feel about your mom? What questions do you have about your birth family?"

SHARING ABOUT DIFFICULT CIRCUMSTANCES OF BIRTH: RAPE AND INCEST

Disclosing the circumstances of a child's birth if those circumstances involved rape or incest is not an easy task. Severson catches the intensity of the task for adoptive parents whose child was conceived as the result of incest or rape. This is a quote worth repeating here:

> To actually have a child, a child of your heart and kindness, who sleeps warm and secure in the blanket after you kiss him goodnight, and to know that this child's life began in horror (fear, trauma or confusion as in the case of incest) and that you must tell him and watch his innocence be shattered, and know yourself to be an agent of that shattering, is a duty that no one would wish upon another.[13]

When to tell a child the story of his beginnings under these circumstances continues to be a question faced by adoption professionals whose task it is to guide adoptive parents. Vera Fahlberg, whose experience in the field is widely respected, feels that the door of communication can be opened incrementally. "Waiting until the child is 18 or older and ready to leave home is not a good time for sharing this type of information," she asserts. "Many adopted individuals have a resurgence of feelings of abandonment as they approach moving away from home and family. It is important that the information about their origins . . . not be associated with the experience of parent separation and loss (even though this time the separation is developmentally appropriate)."

Fahlberg also suggests that the first step for parents when disclosing "hard stuff" is to discuss the information between themselves or with another trusted adult enough that they both develop acceptance of the facts and are able to talk about them without becoming emotionally overwhelmed. She continues:

> Whenever people need to discuss difficult things it is probably best to "practice" before the actual event. Practicing with a tape recorder and then listening to oneself can help parents hear what the child will hear. Frequently, that helps adults modify how they will phrase the

facts. Parents need to realize that although they are the custodians of the child's history during his/her early years, ultimately the history belongs to their adopted son or daughter.[14]

Specifically about Rape

The Early Years

The early avenue in, according to Fahlberg, is to mention the birth father in the lifebook. (See Chapter 9 for a full discussion on how to develop a lifebook.) The lifebook can simply reflect in those early years, in the case of rape, that no information was available about the birth father. Most children don't feel a sense of connection to a father they do not know until they are about 8 to 10 years old, Fahlberg points out. At that point, they develop a curiosity about genetic connectedness and usually want to know more about their birth father.

Susan Pelleg, an adoption therapist in Ohio, says that parents can progressively add an explanation, such as "Your mother didn't know your father well (or at all). The relationship was not a happy one. Your mother found herself in a situation that was not safe, but something good came of it: you were born."[15]

Middle School and Beyond

Severson advises that "as soon as your child asks or becomes aware and only your love and instinct will hint at its emergence—that it 'takes two' to make a baby, he should be told that his birthmother and birthfather were not in love and perhaps did not know each other well, and that they did not 'make love,' but rather 'had sex' even though the birthmother didn't want to."[16]

Parents frequently ask the following questions about how to disclose sensitive information:

1. Should I tell my child everything I know about the details of his conception? Severson says, "No, no more than you would explain to any child every detail of his or her conception."
2. When should I use the word "rape"? Severson suggests that parents not "use the word itself until they feel the time is right when they are certain that [the child] understands the meaning, which usually occurs developmentally around late latency age." Severson cautions, however, that, in an effort to defer a child's pain until the right time, the "right time never comes," and the child stumbles onto the truth

from another source. What happens then is that the child is deprived of parental strength and support in coping with the harsh reality. The parents "have also added a new truth to his map of reality. Mom and dad cannot be wholly trusted."[17]

Specifically about Incest

The Early Years

The early avenue to this painful subject, according to Fahlberg, is again the mention of the birth father in the lifebook. The lifebook can simply reflect in those early years, in the case of incest, that the birth father was a member of the birth mother's family. Another possibility, suggests Fahlberg, is for people to include a physical and ethnic history of the father in a way that leads to the logical assumption that the birth father and birth mother shared the same family. The important thing to remember about lifebooks during the early years is that they need to include information that is truthful yet simple so that the information can be expanded as the child gets older. Information can be written in ways that make it easy for further questions to develop as the child gets older.

The Middle School Years and Beyond

Severson's suggestions about the concept of the right time for explaining rape are appropriate here as well. Parents can begin to share with their child that their birth parents grew up in a family that did not know how to show love appropriately. "People didn't know how and to whom to express love. Because of that lack of understanding, you were born."

Vera Fahlberg offers these key points for parents of older children and teens to remember:

- Late latency and early teen years can be used for educating the child about the causes of rape or incest within a family. This can be done by visiting support groups or victim advocate groups, scheduling time with therapists skilled in the subject, or researching the topic in the library or on the Internet. It is important that children and teens learn that rape is about anger and control of others, and that incest is about extreme family dysfunction. Either could be related to other forms of physical abuse, anger and control, lack of boundaries, or an adult incapable of developing intimacy with other adults.
- Children and teens can be challenged to discover what they need to learn about life and about themselves that will enable them to

function well in a family and society, and not make the same type of decisions their birth parents made.

Whenever a child comes into this world as a result of rape or incest, that child is cherished and treasured by his creator. What ultimately does a parent tell a child about himself? Parents tell him the truth. That he was created in the image of God. That God knit him together in his mother's womb. That he, like every child, was fearfully and wonderfully made and that all the days of his life are ordained by God.[18]

SUMMARY

Sharing difficult realities with a child is a challenging task for adoptive parents. It takes courage and insight to impart potentially devastating facts sensitively but truthfully. The information in this chapter, as well as advice from other adoptive parents and professionals will help equip parents for the task ahead.

QUESTIONS

1. For the small group activity and discussion for this chapter, spend the time asking each participant to practice writing their own child's story.
2. If some participants do not have a personal example, they can use the following example with which to practice.

Katie is now eight years old and has been in her adoptive home for six and a half years. A lifebook was never prepared for her, and her adoptive parents have returned to the agency for more information about Katie's past. They knew that her mother was dead, and her father is in jail because of the murder, but they did not have a lot of details. What they learned that day, they felt was important to pass on to her.

Katie came into foster care at 14 months. She had witnessed the brutal stabbing of her birth mother by her birth father. After the stabbing, her father grabbed her and hid from police for two days. When she was eventually found at a friend's home, she was still wearing the bloodstained pajamas she had on the night of the horrific event. Her foster family eventually adopted her at two years of age. How would you write her story?

CHAPTER 9

Twelve Tools of Parent/Child Communication

Without a life story, a child is adrift, disconnected and vulnerable.
Dr. Bruce Perry[1]

Using communication tools within the adoptive family can help both parents and children process the many issues that arise during the growing-up years. This chapter describes 12 interactive tools parents and children can use to explore important issues. Children who joined their adoptive families after living for a period of time with birth family members have memories. Adoptive parents have a special role, for they truly are the storehouses for those memories—the difficult ones as well as the pleasant ones. There are several tools and techniques that adoptive parents can use to store those fading memories and to aid their child in communicating his feelings about his life experiences. The first six tools aid interactive communication from parent to child:

- The Lifebook/Life Story Box
- The Life Map
- The Eco Map
- The Family Tree

- The Family Collage
- Bibliotherapy/films

TOOL 1: THE LIFEBOOK/LIFE STORY BOX

What Is a Lifebook?

Author Beth O'Malley offers this definition: "A Lifebook is a collection of words, photos, graphics, artwork and memorabilia that creates a life record for the child who is adopted."

Why Children Need a Lifebook

Vera Fahlberg, a retired pediatrician and psychotherapist stresses the importance of a Lifebook, saying, "It is difficult to grow up to be a psychologically healthy adult without having had one's own history. It is never too late or too early to make a Lifebook. Each time the Lifebook is read, the child is likely to understand the message in a slightly different way, reflecting her current intellectual abilities and psychological needs."[2]

The Lifebook is useful for all adopted children, whether placed as infants or older children, and is helpful at all stages of child development. A Lifebook records a child's family and placement history, according to Denise Goodman, a nationally recognized expert on adoption. It is a tool that gathers information about a child's growth and development, feelings, ideas, and hopes and dreams for the future. It is a vital resource in helping a child to understand the past and prepare for the future. Goodman provides seven reasons children need a Lifebook.[3]

It Recreates a Child's Life History

This is important, as many of our children have had very confusing lives. They have been in and out of care and shuffled between family members. Each child's reaction to separation from the birth family presents its own set of unique individual responses. These painful feelings weave a common thread throughout the lives of older adopted children. For children whose memories of former relationships smolder vaguely in their minds, themes frequently recur during the healing process. They need to have an accurate record of their past because it will help them look forward to the future without fear.

It Gives Children Information about Their Birth Family

Many foster and adopted children do not have a lot of information about their birth families, and they may not have any positive information at all.

What did their parents look like? What talents did they have? Everyone has a "genetic road map," provided by their parents. This "road map" helps in identity development. Individuals decide what traits they like and keep them. The traits they do not like, they reject. Youngsters who have no information make it up, and usually fantasies are negative. Some children only have negative information about their parents from which to construct their own identity; their information is gleaned from agency records focusing on skill deficits to prepare cases for termination of parental rights in court. Children need both positive and negative details about their birth families.

It Gives Reasons for Placement

Frequently, children have the wrong idea about why they have been removed from their homes. Many times, they believe that it was their fault. This leads to feelings of guilt, and sometimes children will try to punish themselves. Therefore, children must have accurate and honest information about why they are in care.

It Provides Photos and a Pictorial History

Even when information is given in written form, kids generally want to know what their families look like. In addition, photographs also record family events such as holidays, birthdays, and special times. Children need pictures of themselves to trace the changes that have taken place.

It Records Children's Feelings about Their Lives

Too often, children are not given a chance to voice their feelings about their life and being in out-of-home care. The Lifebook, in some ways, is a diary or log children can use to keep a record of their personal thoughts or feelings.

It Gives Children Information about Their Development

How many people have baby books? If you are not the firstborn, you probably don't have one. How would you like a recording of all your important milestones—your first tooth, your first step, your first word along with a record of all the other special things you've done? This is another important role that the Lifebook plays.

It Is a Useful Tool When Working with Children

As a way to organize information, the Lifebook is a helpful tool for foster parents, adoptive parents, caseworkers, and therapists who must assist children struggling to cope with being away from their parents, siblings, and homes.

Developing an Age-Appropriate Lifebook

Examples and Resources Related to Lifebook Development

The U.S. Department of Health and Human Services has collected several excellent resources for Lifebook development. These are available on this website:

https://www.childwelfare.gov/outofhome/casework/children/lifebooks.cfm.

Lifebooks for Infants and Toddlers

Gathering information for the Lifebook for an infant or toddler is far more important than one might assume. Children at these ages have no memory of their birth parents, foster parents, or other significant people who cared for them. They often have no pictures of themselves or any significant person to help fill in the gaps. Completing an infant's Lifebook while in foster care, whether the child's outcome is reunification with the birth family or adoption, is a crucial activity. Table 9.1 lists the information that should be included.

Table 9.1.

What to Include	Where to Find It
Birth Information: Birth certificate, height, weight, time and date of birth, hospital (picture, if possible, from brochure or taken by family), names of doctors, special medical information or circumstances of birth, genogram, pictures of birth family, and cultural history	Bureau of Vital Statistics, case record and social! Medical hospital, WIC clinic, hospital records, birth parents, extended family
Placement Information: Reasons for removal or placement. Include journal entry, chronological list for each move, good-bye letters from caregivers, names of other children child was close to, pictures of their caretakers, their birth and foster homes, bedroom, pets, etc.	Court records, intake worker, birth family, caseworker, previous caretakers

What to Include	Where to Find It
Medical Information: List of medical providers, immunization record, list of childhood diseases, injuries, allergies	Case record, health department, caretakers, pediatrician, WIC clinic
Developmental Information: Significant milestones of development	Case record, health department, caretakers, pediatrician, WIC clinic Previous caretakers, case record, medical history
Adoption Information: Date of finalization, adoption party pictures, any special mementos	Adoptive family and adoption caseworker

Lifebooks for School-Age Children

Children removed from their homes during the early school-age years may have memories of important people in their lives, but those memories are usually vague and fleeting. Those memories may also be attached to the trauma of abuse, neglect, and the experience of removal. The Lifebook should be a tool that fills in the memory gaps for these children and also replaces the fantasies that have developed. In addition to the birth, developmental, and medical information recommended for infants and toddlers (see Table 9.1), the school-age child's Lifebook should also include the information in Table 9.2.

Table 9.2.

What to Include	Where to Find It
Placement Information: Reasons for removal or placement. Include journal entry, chronological list for each move, good-bye letters from caregivers, names of other children the child was close to, pictures of caretakers, their birth and foster homes, bedroom, pets, church activities, neighborhood friends, ball teams, scout troops, letters from birth family or other friends, names and addresses of separated siblings, mementos of special events	Court records, intake worker, birth family, caseworker, previous caretakers, school teachers, counselors, adult leaders, ministers

(*Coninued*)

Table 9.2. (*continued*)

What to Include	Where to Find It
Educational Information: List all daycare and schools attended with dates, names and addresses, and photos if possible, pictures of classmates, teachers, and other important adults, copies of report cards, samples of homework, special projects, pictures and mementos of special events, awards, achievements and certificates	School personnel, teachers, yearbooks, school and community newspapers, coaches, school records
Adoption Information: Tools used to prepare child for adoption (coloring books), date of finalization, adoption day pictures, etc.	Adoptive family, foster care and adoption caseworker

Lifebooks for Teens

Teens who have spent any amount of time in foster care and enter adoption or independent living have probably lost track of the important details of their lives. They probably do not have many mementos of their past, and may have little or no birth information, and few pictures, if any. They may not have a record of where they lived or the people with whom they lived, the schools they attended, or their achievements. Putting a Lifebook together for a young teen requires investigative work and perseverance. However, it may be the youngster's only link from a confusing and disjointed past to a more stable future. The Lifebook for the teen should include as much information from birth, medical, and developmental records as can be traced. It should include the information in Table 9.3, in addition to the information in Tables 9.1 and 9.2.[4]

Table 9.3.

What to Include	Where to Find It
Placement Information: Chronological listing of places where teen lived, with whom, reasons for moving, pictures of people and places that were important in the development of the teen	Previous caregivers, caseworkers, case record,

What to Include	Where to Find It
Educational Information: List schools attended with dates, names and addresses, and photos, if possible; pictures of classmates, teachers and other important adults; copies of report cards; samples of homework; special projects; pictures and mementos of special events; awards, achievements, and certificates	School personnel, teachers, yearbooks, school and community newspapers, coaches, school records, band/ music directors, drama teachers
Independent Living Information: Information and mementos gleaned from teen groups and classes; pictures of other teens in independent living; pictures of group leaders; pictures of graduating from group and moving into the new apartment	
Adoption Information: Tools used to prepare teen for adoption, date of finalization, adoption day pictures, any special mementos	

The Life Story Box

The Life Story Box supplements the Lifebook. It is a box or chest that will be the repository of all the child's mementos—everything from the first tooth, to sports or musical trophies, to report cards, heirlooms or special gifts from the birth family, and teachers' special notes. The older the child gets, the more important these mementos—samples of homework, special projects, pictures and souvenirs of special events, awards, achievements, and certificates—become.

Is It Worth the Effort?

Yes, making a Lifebook and continuing to use it as a tool of information, explanation, and even healing is worth the effort.[5] For perspective on the effectiveness of Lifebooks, see Appendix C, *Lifebooks—They Are Effective for Children in Understanding Their Story.*

TOOL 2: THE LIFE MAP

The Life Map is a tool useful primarily for children who have been in the foster care system prior to adoptive placement, or, in the case of international adoption, for children who have memories of life in an orphanage or foster home. It is helpful for children as young as four years through adolescence. Making a Life Map is helpful in reconstructing the child's placement history.

The Life Map can communicate a number of important life events that are often lost when children experience a number of moves. These life events include:

- Where the child has lived
- How long he lived there
- The people, pets, places that were important to him
- Why the child had to move
- How the child felt about the moves

Children should be active participants in the drawing of the map. They should be encouraged to draw it in any manner they choose. The key purpose of the Life Map is to generate open discussion about the children's history, to give the parents the opportunity to talk about and clarify any of the children's misconceptions, to provide support for painful feelings, and to provide reassurance about the children's new parents.[6] A creative way to draw a Life Map is to purchase white "butcher paper" from a grocery or meat market. Post a long sheet of the paper on a wall of the children's bedroom at their eye level. Allow the children to draw pictures or paste photographs on the Life Map, so they can visually see where they have lived and with whom. Pictures of the hospital where they were born, houses where they have lived, and pictures of people and pets are important components of the Life Map. It is likely that the children, depending on maturity level and attention span, will need several sessions to complete the life map.

Chad was born on June 15, 2004, and his brother, Logan, was born on January 15, 2005. Two months after Logan was born, the boys went to live with their grandmother. They eventually returned to live with their mother, Sandy. However, things did not work out at home, and both boys entered foster care. Chad went to the Brown foster home and Logan to another home. In January 2007, both Chad and Logan moved to the Smith foster home. Their sister, Krissy, was born and came to live with them at the Smith foster home when she was four months old. In April 2008, the Smiths adopted Chad, Logan, and Krissy (see Figure 9.1).

TOOL 3: THE CHILD'S ECO MAP[7]

The Eco Map is a valuable tool for a child in foster care and adoption. It was originally developed by the staff of Branch County Department of

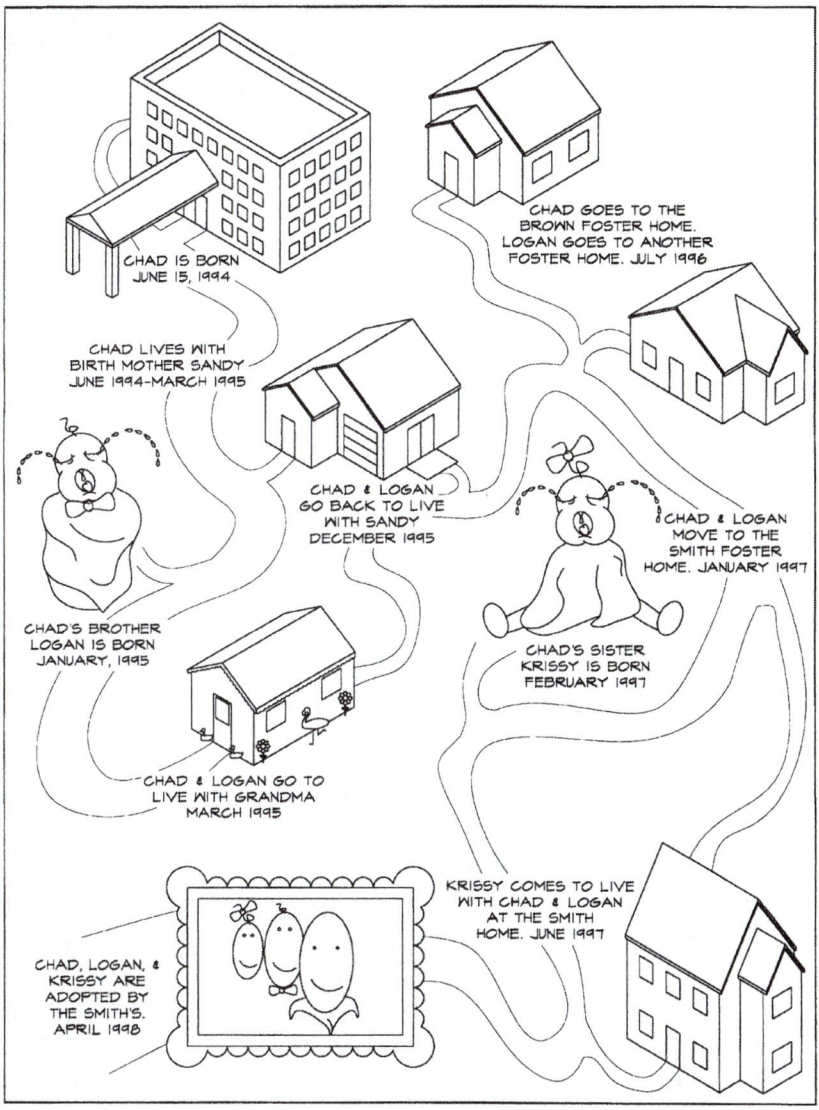

Figure 9.1 Life Map

Social Services, Coldwater, Michigan, as a tool to open communication between a child and his caseworker. It is used with foster and adopted children to guide them in understanding the reasons for their placement and to understand the role of different people in their lives. To use the concept, give children a copy of the Eco Map and crayons or markers. Encourage the children to do the writing and coloring themselves as the various areas of the map are discussed. The Eco Map is designed to alternate less psychologically loaded questions with ones that are more difficult.

1. *Why am I here?* Encourage children to share their own explanations to themselves about why they are not with their birth family. If the children say something like, "Well, you put me here; you answer the question," the parent or worker might respond by saying, "It is important for you to understand why the placement decision was made, but I'm also interested in your impressions. We will discuss both."
2. *Social worker:* Children are often confused about the agency people in their lives. Let them know what the worker's job is—that is, to work with them and their new parents toward building a happy adoptive family.
3. *Courthouse*: Briefly describe the hearing process and the role of the judge.
4. *Homes:* Encourage children to identify one of the homes as their birth home and one as the foster home, with pathways to both. A third home can be added when necessary (e.g., if the child has contact with two birth parents who do not live together). Encourage the children to talk about similarities and differences in the two homes and parenting styles. Although children commonly focus initially on the physical attributes, let them know that, through time, the two of you will be comparing them in terms of the interactions. Describe the roles of foster parents.
5. *Siblings:* Finding out about sibling relationships is important whether brothers and sisters are placed together or not. Many children find separation from siblings to be as painful, or even more so, than separation from birth parents.
6. *I feel . . .* Encourage spontaneous verbalization from children.
7. *Things that bug me:* Let children complete this. Younger children frequently respond to the visual cue by indicating "bugs" that bug them. Children will usually expand on their dislikes if encouraged to do so.
8. *School*: Encourage children to talk about previous school experiences and the feelings they have about going to a new school while they are in foster care.
9. *I worry about . . .* Encourage spontaneous responses.
10. *Things I like to do*: Let children talk both of the things they enjoy and things that others do that make them happy. The responses can be used to help foster parents initiate positive interactions with children.

11. *Dreams:* These can be either nighttime dreams or daydreams. The former frequently help identify fears and worries; the latter, hopes and dreams.
12. *Friends:* Talk with children about friends and how they might keep in contact with them, as well as discussing how they might go about making new friends in the new neighborhood and school.

Figure 9.2 Eco Map

TOOL 4: THE FAMILY TREE

The Family Tree, a modification of the more commonly known family tree, has a unique purpose. According to Dr. Fahlberg: The Family Tree can help children organize all the people who have been an important part of their lives. The biological family can be identified in the roots of the tree.

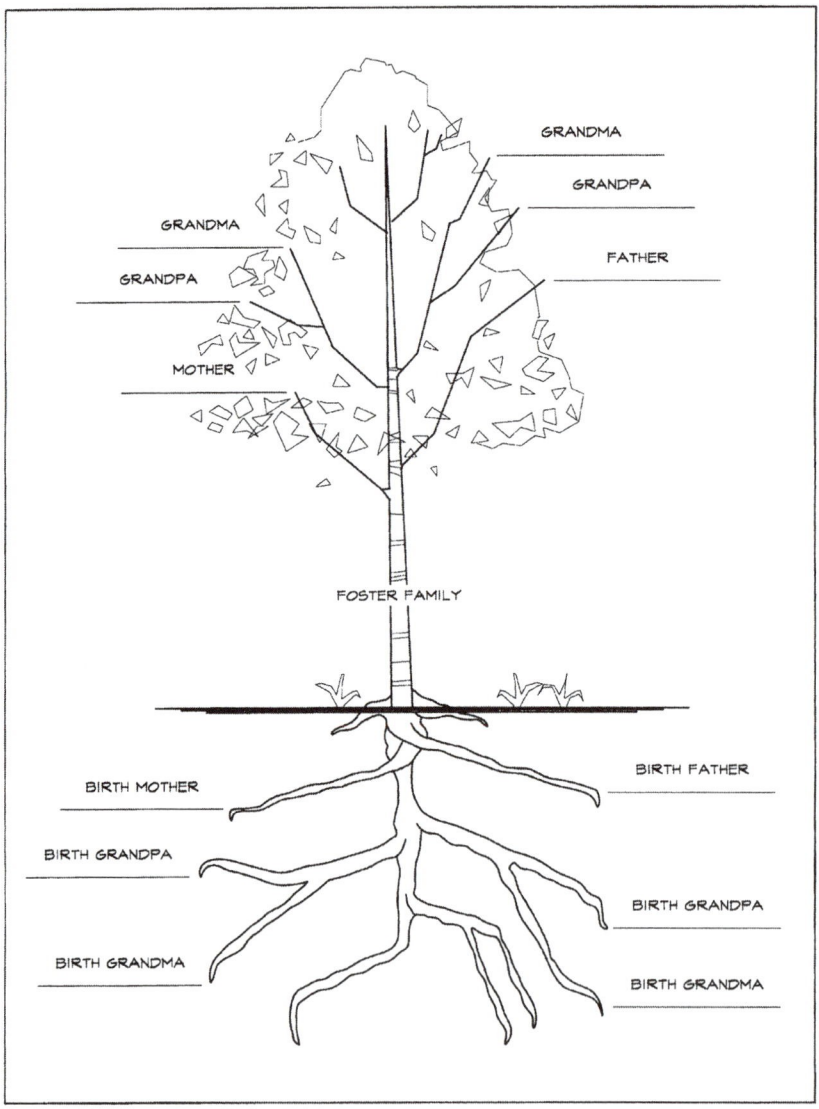

Figure 9.3 Family Tree

These "roots" (the biological family) cannot be seen, but they anchor the tree, just as the biological family provided the child with a genetic heritage, and will always be part of her. The children's foster or kinship families can be represented on the trunk of the tree, as they have helped them grow. The adoptive family may be represented on the upper trunk, branches, leaves, fruit, and flowers. Through this activity, children learn that they do not have to choose between families, and they can come to understand how each family played an important role in their growth and development.[8]

TOOL 5: THE FAMILY COLLAGE

The Family Collage can be a fun activity for a child and parent to assemble. A collage is a collection of pictures that are placed on a large piece of paper or cardboard. In adoption work, Goodman suggests gluing the pictures to a cutout of the body outline of the children. The collage is used to represent past, present, and future events in children's lives. Children are instructed to use photos, cut out pictures from magazines, or draw pictures that represent to them important people or events and their wishes for the future.[9]

TOOL 6: BIBLIOTHERAPY/FILMS

Bibliotherapy means "helping with books." Parents can broaden children's understanding of the circumstances of their adoption through the use of stories, other literature, and films. As children read the stories of others, they can see how other youngsters in similar circumstances confronted difficulties and overcame them. They can also see how children who had the same life experiences faced loss, disappointment, separation, and fear.

When selecting books for children, parents should consider the following:[10]

1. *Take into account developmental age as well as the child's reading level.* Preschoolers enjoy stories with colorful pictures and simple conversation. Older elementary school youngsters enjoy stories with mystery, plot, and intrigue. Teens usually pick books that are relevant to their concerns, such as identity, dating, decision making, and parent-teen struggles.
2. *Choose reading material or films that address a child's apprehensions.* Those apprehensions could include leaving a foster family, loss of birth parents or siblings, or living in a transcultural family. Dr. Vera Fahlberg points out that most G-rated movies for children deal with

loss.[11] Movies/films such as *Bambi*, *Tarzan*, or *Annie*, to cite just a few, can open up discussion between parents and children about feelings of separation and loss.

3. *Parents should learn how to explore feelings and attitudes by asking appropriate and timely questions.* Those personal questions can be couched by asking how children think the hero or heroine felt and how they would feel if they were in the same position.

Many books on this topic are available at

- Tapestry Books at www.tapestrybooks.com.
- Adoptive Families of America (1-800-372-3300) also provides an extensive reading list for children.

Parents can use the next five tools to encourage interactive communication from children ages 4 to 10:

- Let's Make a Phone Call
- Let's Tell a Story/Let's Write a Story
- Can You Tell Me What They Think? (Using dolls and puppets)
- Pick a Feeling Card
- Who Do You Go to for What?

TOOL 7: LET'S MAKE A PHONE CALL

The use of pretend and play is especially helpful for children who are developmentally between the ages of four and seven. One helpful game is playing telephone. Dr. Vera Fahlberg observes that very young children often do not respond to direct questioning. She suggests that using the toy telephone game, when combined with pictures of adults from whom the child is separated, can be helpful in gaining information that direct questioning would not elicit. It also helps parents to correct wrong information or wrong thinking.[12] The following example shows how to play the game:

> Casey, age six, had been in foster care for two years before being adopted by her foster parents. Her birth father had died, and her birth mother, who already had severe mental health issues, became totally dependent and was unable to parent a young child and keep her safe. Using the telephone, Casey pretended to call her birth mother. Before making the call, her adoptive mother asked her to think about questions that she wanted to ask her birth mother. When Casey "placed"

> the call, she asked her mother if she was still mad at her and why she couldn't come back to care for her. Casey's adoptive mom took on the role of her birth mother and said to her, "Casey, I was never angry at you. I was very upset that your daddy died. When he died, I became very sad. There were many days I didn't get out of bed. You weren't safe during those times. I couldn't take care of myself well, and I knew that I couldn't be the mommy that you needed. You now have a mommy and daddy who can take good care of you and keep you safe."

TOOL 8: LET'S TELL A STORY / LET'S WRITE A STORY

Stories can be powerful as they open the door to the heart. They allow us to feel without threat, to express without judgment. For the children who come into foster care or adoption from [as a result of maltreatment], their story is fragmented, damaged. This discontinuous personal narrative puts an individual child at risk.[13]

Dr. Bruce Perry says,

> A child that is lost within her own family, community and culture is neurodevelopmentally vulnerable. Without a life story, a child is adrift, disconnected and vulnerable—their neurobiology of reward, stress regulation and relational interactions are all altered—in negative ways—without a cortically mediated coherent personal narrative. Our conventional efforts to "treat" them will often be frustrated and ineffective. Sadly, most mental health interventions with maltreated children do not pay any attention to the child's story. The focus is the manifestation of pathology—the symptoms. Make Billy stop swearing, hitting, running away—make Billy pay attention, be respectful, comply. We lose sight of how disconnected Billy is, and often we actually contribute to the fragmentation and disconnection of his life story—a brief but telling story to illustrate how our efforts to "protect" maltreated children can add to their confusion and disconnection. We often make these children worse.[14]

A creative technique in using story telling as a healing technique is guiding children to communicate their thoughts and feelings about their life experience. Dr. Fahlberg calls this joint storytelling: "The child is asked to choose a favorite animal and name him. Then the adult starts telling a story about the animal that reflects the child's history. After several sentences, the adult asks the child to continue the story. In this way, the child has the opportunity to share emotional reactions to life events as well as his perceptions and desires for the future."[15]

Why is storytelling helpful? In *Working with Traumatized Children*, Kathryn Brohl notes that storytelling is "an effective way to address traumatic memories, [to monitor] responses and to teach problem solving. Storytelling also bypasses resistance by speaking to, as well as offering solutions to, overcoming a trauma without directly discussing the trauma."[16] The following example shows how to play "Let's Tell a Story."[17]

Benjamin, age four, had been living in interim care for close to a year because he had been severely physically abused by his mother's boyfriend. He had developed a close, loving relationship with his foster parents. Benjamin had weekly visits with his teenaged birth mother, who was no longer with the same boyfriend. The plan was for him to be returned to Mother's care shortly. His caseworker, Mrs. Shields, wanted to know more about how Benjamin viewed the past abuse and whether or not he perceived his mom as now able to provide adequate physical safety. She decided to use joint storytelling to facilitate her communications with Benjamin. She knew it is frequently necessary for the adult to ask a younger child some leading questions during the storytelling.

Mrs. S.: Once upon a time, there was a bunny named Ben. When he was just a baby, Bunny Ben lived with his mommy and his grandma. How do you think things went for Bunny Ben when he was a baby?

Ben: Bunny Ben was happy with his mommy and grandmother.

Mrs. S.: Then what do you think happened?

Ben: Then they moved.

Mrs. S.: One day Bunny Ben's mommy and grandmother had an argument, and Ben and his mommy moved. They moved in with some friends of Bunny Ben's mother. How do you think things went for Bunny Ben then?

Ben: Sad.

Mrs. S.: Was Ben sad a lot? Was he missing someone?

Ben: He was very sad for his grandma. There was a mean man.

Mrs. S.: When Bunny Ben was very sad or scared, he cried a lot. Mommy's friends did not like to hear crying. One of them would get so frustrated that he would spank Bunny Ben so hard that it really hurt him. It is not okay for adults to hurt children. One day some neighbors heard Bunny Ben crying very hard. They called some adults who help bunny families

> who are having problems. One of the adults came to visit Bunny Ben's family. Bunny Ben had lots of bruises on his bottom. The man who had spanked him was very angry at everyone. Bunny Ben needed to be in a safe place where he wouldn't be hurt. How do you think Bunny Ben felt when he moved to a new place?

By continuing the story, Mrs. Shields encouraged Benjamin to talk about his feelings in interim care and about his thoughts and feelings about the upcoming move back to Mother's care. She learned that he missed his mom and wanted to spend more time with her. However, Mrs. Shields also learned that he was less worried about physical harm in the future than sad about anticipating the separation from his foster family.

Like most children his age, the story solution he chose was for Mommy Bunny to move in with Bunny Ben and his foster family. Mrs. Shields then modified the ending to the story, acknowledging that Bunny Ben would like one ending, but that none of the adults thought it would work out for them. Instead, they decided that he should go live with Mommy Bunny but frequently visit with his foster family, so he wouldn't miss them so much. This same type of story can be used to help children verbalize their feelings about the adoption experience.

Older school-age children often enjoy writing their own story. The story that follows was written by a 10-year-old African American boy, Mike, after his adoption into the Caucasian family of his first grade schoolteacher.

Tom-Tom the Round Pumpkin

> Once upon a time, Tom-Tom the jack-o-lantern was born on a mountain. But he was abandoned by his mother. He felt sad when she couldn't take care of him anymore. He decided that he was too young to be alone, so he went to find a new family. He looked and looked. He was sad and lonely while he looked for a new family. It made him act bad. Everyone thought he was a bad-behaving pumpkin.
>
> Then one day when he had turned eight years old, he found a new family of pumpkins. They didn't exactly look like him because they were oval-shaped pumpkins and he was a round pumpkin. But they were still pumpkins anyway, even though they looked a little different on the outside. Now he is 10 years old and is a happy, good, silly, little pumpkin. He doesn't even notice their shapes anymore. Life is good for Tom-Tom.[18]

TOOL 9: CAN YOU TELL ME WHAT THEY THINK? DOLL AND PUPPET PLAY

This "play" technique is quite helpful to communicate about adoption with the preschool or young school-age children, ages three to seven. The activity has four purposes:

1. To teach or clearly illustrate the facts of the child's history
2. To elicit feelings and perceptions from the very young child
3. To correct misperceptions (often related to magical thinking of children in this age range) or fantasies
4. To express feelings, wishes, or dreams of the "characters" involved in the child's past or present

Parents can use small Fisher-Price figures, other small dolls, or puppets to represent important figures in children's past and present. Parents explain to the children that they are going to play out a story. Identify the characters, using the real names of the child, birth parent, adoptive parent, siblings, and others, or use fictitious names but actual circumstances of the children's adoption. Allow the children to control and speak for the "child" doll to elicit their perceptions and feelings.

Parents should never "correct" feelings, but they can "correct" the actual events in the story by saying, "Let's play the story this way—I think this is the way the story might have happened." This play technique allows learning through a visual, experiential activity that can be repeated many times over (children will thoroughly enjoy the attention and the activity as well as the ability to add more details and figures as they mature).

Children who have delayed language skills will especially benefit from seeing a reenactment of their life. This play therapy technique may provide a safe opportunity, for both the parents and children to express fears, anger, sadness, and good wishes for the future held naturally by all members of the adoption triad. Expression of these feelings occurs through a character, thereby creating an emotional comfort zone for all involved.

The number of figures or puppets used should be adjusted based on the child's age and developmental capacity to keep track of different characters in the story. A reasonable rule of thumb is to allow only as many characters as the child's age, plus one. That is, a four-year-old can accommodate a story with five characters.

Parents should not feel compelled to illustrate every detail in excruciating accuracy during the first play session. Initially, it is important only to understand the child's perception, "where the child is" in beginning to make sense of his adoption story. As the parent and child continue to "play the story" during subsequent sessions, the parent should address the following issues, one aspect at a time:

- Understanding what placements have occurred in the children's lives
- Answering questions about siblings, birth parents, and other attachment figures
- Understanding reasons for the children's separation from the birth family
- Exploring feelings about the children's separation from the birth family
- Understanding other separations that have occurred in the children's history (orphanages, kinship families, foster families, previous adoptive placements)
- Exploring feelings about the children's separation from these placements
- Understanding the reasons behind the adoption plan made by agencies and courts or by the birth parents
- Understanding why the adoptive parents wanted children and why they wanted these particular children
- Understanding the children's future with the adoptive family
- Exploring the children's wishes/dreams for the future in relation to siblings, birth parents, and other kinship or foster families with whom the child has connections
- Helping the children understand that their birth parents wish them to be happy and successful in their new family; they want the children to make them proud of them
- Helping the children to understand that they can love and be loyal to many persons and families at the same time

TOOL 10: PICK A FEELING CARD

A tool very familiar to therapists is also helpful for parents: the Feeling Faces. These cards can be purchased at educational stores or made at home. The cards reflect a variety of emotions that children may experience at various times in their lives. They can be used in conjunction with discussing the Life Map and in "Let's Tell a Story." A simplified sampling of common emotions that can be placed on the cards for younger children might include happy, sad, scared, angry, lonely, or confused.

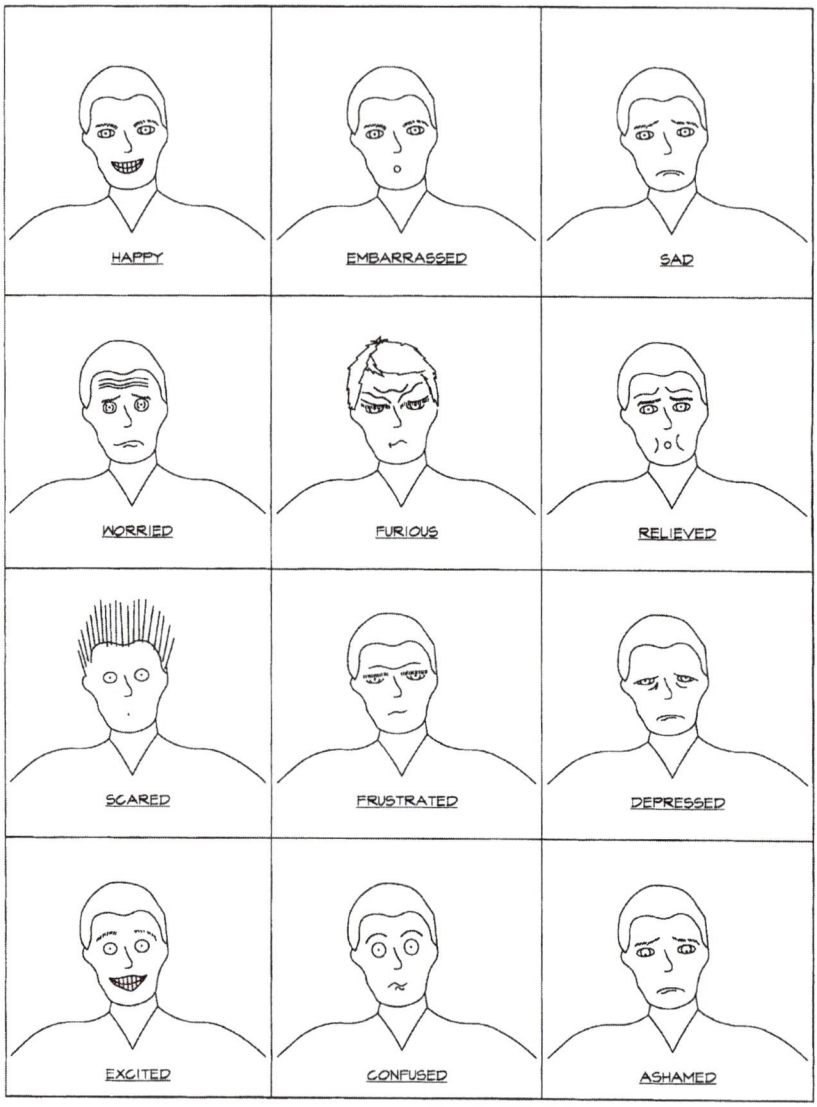

Figure 9.4 Feeling Faces

For older children, once they can read, a fuller range of emotions can be written on a single card:

- happy • ashamed • scared
- sad • relieved • confused
- frustrated • hopeful • angry
- guilty • rejected • lonely

- unloved • excited • powerless
- hopeless • furious • ignored
- worried • depressed • satisfied
- concerned • embarrassed • stubborn

Katherine's Story

Katherine, a nine-year-old foster child, had been in therapy for a number of months. Her therapist released her, informing her caseworker, Sue Pelleg, that the child no longer needed her services.[19] Sue wasn't convinced Katherine was healed due to the child's extensive background of abuse. Sue also knew that Katherine needed more work before her upcoming adoptive placement, as shown by the following incident:

> One afternoon, Katherine was in my office and started rummaging through my "goody bag." She pulled out my puppets and my face cards. She looked at me and said, "I am going to tell you a story about this bunny who is getting adopted. This card (the angry face) is the bunny's daddy. This card (the grumpy face) is the bunny's mommy. One day the bunny and her worker (holding up a smiling face) went to court. The baby bunny knew that today the judge would make a decision about her adoption. The mommy and daddy bunnies came crashing into court. They were yelling and screaming at each other. The baby bunny was really scared. Just like this (holding up the scared card). The bunny wanted her daddy and mommy to go to jail for all the things that they did to the baby bunny and so they couldn't come back and hurt her. The baby's worker (holding up the smiling face) asked the baby bunny how long should the bunny mom and dad go to jail. The baby bunny answered, 'until they get a heart.'"

For Sue, the use of the feeling cards revealed much anxiety and fear for Katherine, emotions another therapist said were not present. Sue was able to help Katherine deal with her concerns now that they were out in the open. She credits the use of feeling cards and the puppets for helping this youngster come to terms with emotions for which she couldn't find words.

TOOL 11: WHO DO YOU GO TO FOR WHAT?

Children, even young children who have been institutionalized, have been severely neglected or abused, or have experienced multiple moves, have developed a mental blueprint of themselves and the adults in their world. In *Troubled Transplants*, Richard Delaney and Frank Kunstal write that maltreated children often view themselves as unsafe, worthless, and weak. Those same children, according to Delaney and Kunstal, view the adults in their world as unresponsive, unreliable, and dangerous.

James Anthony developed a tool that is particularly helpful for parents (and caseworkers) in eliciting children's perceptions of the adults in their world.[20] It can be used early in placement for children ages 4 to 10 to help parents gain an understanding of the child's thoughts and feelings about adults important in the child's past and how those perceptions impact present and future relationships.

The parent develops three series of cards. The first series has stick figure drawings of family members: mother, father, grandmother, grandfather, older or younger siblings, aunts, uncles, foster parents, and so on. The last card in the first series, Mr. Nobody, should show a man's back. The cards should represent significant people in the child's past. On each card in the second and third series, the parent writes a single sentence. In the second series of cards, each begins with the words "This is who I go to when I . . . ." This set of cards is used to help the child initiate interaction. In the third series of cards, which addresses interactions initiated by others in the child's life, each sentence starts with the words "This is who comes to me when they . . ." The parent or child reads the card and places it on the appropriate person. This activity helps parents to develop an understanding of how children perceive others in their life—in a positive or negative manner.[21]

First Series of Cards: Significant People in the Child's Life

Second Series of Cards: "This is who I go to when . . ."

- This is who I go to when I am hungry.
- This is who I go to when I feel sick.
- This is who I go to when I fall down.
- This is who I go to when I want to share something happy.
- This is who I go to when I want to share something sad.
- This is who I go to when I am very scared.
- This is who I go to when I want a hug.
- This is who I go to when I need to share a happy secret.
- This is who I go to when I need to share a scary or sad secret.
- This is who I go to when I have a question about schoolwork.

Third Series of Cards: "This is who comes to me when . . ."

- This is who comes to me when they want to share something happy.
- This is who comes to me when they want to do something fun.

- This is who comes to me when they are mad.
- This is who comes to me when they are sad.
- This is who comes to me when they want a hug.
- This is who comes to me when they want me to do something (for example, chores, watch younger siblings).
- This is who comes to me when they want something from me.

Finally, along with the communication tools described above and adapted for use with older children, preteens and older teens can be encouraged to communicate their thoughts in writing.

TOOL 12: WRITE A LETTER OR JOURNAL

Teens often go underground with their feelings—at least in their willingness to talk with adults. Sometimes, the only way for an adolescent to communicate intense emotion is through letter writing or journaling. The following letter was written by a teen to her birth mother at the suggestion of her adoptive mom. The letter would never reach the birth parent in this particular case, but Tasha was willing to share it with her adoptive parents. It gave them tremendous insight into her feelings and perceptions about her earlier life experience.

> Dear Barbara,
>
> In just a few short days, I will be 16 years old. 16. Does that seem possible to you? It has been many, many years since I saw you. The last memory I have is at that agency. Mom and Dad have pictures of that last visit. I was around four. I hope now that you are happy. Are you? I'm not, not totally anyway. Happiness is what I wish for every year when I blow out my birthday candles. When you signed on that dotted line and gave me away, you blew out the candles. Why did you do that? Was it your wish for happiness? In these 12 years I have lived with a wonderful mom and dad. They have tended to and kissed my scrapes and scratches, helped me with homework, listened to my excited chatter (mostly about boys), taught me to drive the family car (I will be getting my license next week). I love them for what they mean to me. I know what I have done these years. I know what my parents have done. But, Mother, what have you done? Everyone tells me that 16 is too young to find you. They tell me that I am just not ready yet. I disagree. I have many questions that only you can answer. Why should such a large part of my life be missing? You blew out the candles? I had no choice. Why must I suffer?
>
> Your daughter, Tasha

Another helpful activity for teens is journaling. Keeping a running diary helps adolescents to formalize thoughts and feelings that are difficult to talk about. Carol, who was adopted as an infant, used her journal to chronicle her struggles with adoption issues. The following entries are in the form of a letter to her birth mother.

From Carol's Diary, December 30, 2012, Age Fifteen

today is my birthday. at 2:26 am you gave birth to me. does it mean anything to you that so many years ago you gave birth to a child? well, here i am thinking about you. are you thinking about me? it is only fair that you should be thinking of me, but how am i to know.

From Carol's Diary, December 30, 2013, Age Sixteen

it has been a difficult birthday to enjoy. thoughts of you dominated me all day. i feel like i walk around with a big label taped to my blouse. the label screams "ADOPTED," hushed voices whisper "given up," "thrown away" "adopted, adopted, adopted." i walk around, like today in the stores and it feels like everyone can see right through me and knows all about me.

SUMMARY

Knowing how to encourage a child to communicate about the issues of his past is a challenge for parents. Utilizing the tools discussed in this chapter will hopefully give parents a variety of developmentally appropriate tools to open doors to healthy family communication.

QUESTIONS

1. In what ways is a Lifebook valuable for an adopted child?
2. What challenges do you see in putting together a Lifebook for your child? How can you overcome these challenges?
3. What other tools do you see as particularly helpful?
4. Are there any tools that you do not completely understand how to use?
5. What other tools have you used that are not discussed in this chapter?

CHAPTER 10

Transracial or Transcultural Adoption: Talking about Adoption and Race

Just the other day our family walked into a large amusement park. My son looked around and then looked at me. "Mom, do you know why people are looking at us? It is because you are white." I loved that.

Brandy, an Adoptive Mom of Four Boys,
Adopted Transracially in Ohio

Race is one of those "forbidden" topics, much like politics or sex. We know it's there, but we feel uncomfortable talking about it.

Many families who adopt children of a different race or ethnicity struggle to find ways to help their kids develop a positive racial identity. Parents who may have only observed racism and discrimination now find themselves a "minority family" and must learn to deal with those issues themselves. Even more important, through effective communication about racial and cultural issues, they can help their children cope with unfairness, stereotyping, and discrimination. This chapter offers practical insights and describes tools needed by families as they face this unique adoptive experience.

OVERVIEW OF TRANSRACIAL AND TRANSCULTURAL ADOPTION

Race and culture are not synonyms. Race, on the one hand, refers to physical characteristics that are, of course, genetically transmitted. Culture, on the other hand, is created by people and is transmitted through socialization or learning. "Culture is a system of values, beliefs, attitudes, traditions, and standards of behavior that govern the organization of people into social groups and regulate both group and individual behavior."[1] Culture helps assure the survival of both the group and its members.

Transracial placement refers to the placement of children of one race with an adoptive or foster family of another race, for example, the placement of Asian or African American children with European American families. Transcultural placement is the placement of children from one cultural group with an adoptive or foster family whose cultural background is different. Examples of transcultural placements would include adoption of children of one religious culture or socioeconomic group into a family of a different religion or socioeconomic group. Transcultural placements would also include, for example, the placement of Eastern European children with American families. The children and families share the same race but have experienced different cultures. It can be argued that all adoptive and foster placements are, to a greater or lesser degree, transcultural in nature; virtually no foster or adoptive placements would be identical in culture to the practices, values, belief systems, and codes of conduct of the birth family. Statistics on transracial adoption are harder to nail down. According to the National Survey of Adoptive Parents (a survey of 2,089 adoptive parents with a child age 0 to 17 years) 40 percent of all adoptions in the United States are transracial.[2]

HISTORY OF TRANSRACIAL PLACEMENTS

During the first half of the twentieth century, most adoptive "matches" were based on physical characteristics, religious background, and ethnicity. Transracial placements were extremely rare. During the late 1950s and early 1960s, some agencies, particularly those based in large metropolitan areas, began transracial placements of children. Adopt-a-Child in New York City and Minority Adoption Recruitment of Children's Homes (MARCH) in San Francisco were both created in the 1950s to place waiting children of color in white adoptive homes. In 1961, Parents to Adopt Minority Youngsters (PAMY) was founded in Minneapolis.[3]

During the remainder of the 1960s and during the next decade, the incidence of transracial placement of children increased as the numbers of young white children available for adoption decreased. Lists of prospective parents waiting for young white children became longer and longer for a number of reasons. The stigma attached to unmarried parenthood was greatly diminished by the sexual revolution of the 1960s, and birth parents no longer felt social coercion to make adoption plans for children born out of wedlock. Further, abortion became legal with the Supreme Court decision *Roe v. Wade*, thereby providing an alternative way of dealing with untimely pregnancies. As the availability of young white children diminished, prospective adoptive families began to take another look at waiting children, often children of color. The number of African American children placed in white homes grew steadily through the 1960s and peaked in 1971 with over 2,500 such adoptions. Between 1960 and 1976, there were over 12,000 black/white adoptions recorded in the United States.[4]

In 1972, the National Association of Black Social Workers questioned the wisdom of placing children of color in white homes, fearing that white parents did not have the skills to prepare non-white children to cope with a racist society. In response to this criticism, numerous studies have been undertaken to validate or critique the practice of transracial placements. These research projects have come to conflicting conclusions, "proving" both that transracially adopted persons have well-developed racial identity and positive self-esteem, and transracially adopted persons have struggled with identity confusion, and they lack a sense of belonging in either the majority or minority cultures.

Choices made by transracial adoptive parents about where to live, educate their children, attend church, and so on, appear to make a difference in the adjustment of children of color adopted by white parents. "Transracially adopted black children who attended racially integrated schools and whose families resided in racially integrated communities and accepted their child's black racial identity tended to feel positive about themselves as black persons."[5] Conversely, those parents who isolated themselves and their children from the black community raised children who accepted, at least in part, negative stereotypes held by the majority culture about their own racial group. "These studies seem to imply that simply providing a child with a good home will not, by itself, lead to the child's identification and acceptance of their (sic) racial heritage."[6]

While social workers and parents remain widely and passionately divided on this controversial issue, the incidence of transracial placements has been steadily increasing. In 1994, the Multiethnic Placement Act (MEPA) was passed by the U.S. Congress. This act, amended in 1996 by the Interethnic Placement Act (IEPA), states that no foster or adoptive placement of a child can be denied or delayed based on race, color, or national origin. Likewise, no family can be denied the opportunity to adopt or foster based on race, color, or national origin. To discriminate in placement decisions based on these criteria is a criminal violation of an individual's civil rights. White infertile couples increasingly cross racial lines as they seek children to nurture. "Some applaud transracial adoption as a practice that challenges the traditional family form—a form that fosters sexism and racism.[7] For others, transracial adoption raises concerns. Critics see adoption policies, laws, and practices as benefiting White, middle-class couples at the expense of poor women of color."[8]

HISTORY OF INTERNATIONAL PLACEMENTS

World War II left thousands of European children orphaned, and American families provided homes for many of these children. In addition to European orphans, nearly 3,000 Japanese children were adopted by American parents between 1948 and 1962.[9] By the 1950s, the number of homeless European children had dwindled, but new conflicts in Korea created pools of children who needed families. An Oregon farmer, Harry Holt, began searching for permanent homes for Korean children orphaned by the war, and the largest international adoption, Holt International Children Services (website: http://www.holtinternational.org), was created. American families adopted over 38,000 children from Korea between 1953 and 1981.[10] The 1980s brought an increase in adoptions from Central and South America and India, while conflicts and political upheaval in Eastern Europe led to adoptions of children from Romania, Russia, and Bosnia during the 1990s. Further, social policies attempting to reduce population growth in China have limited families in that country to one child. Chinese families who wish to have male children care for them during old age have surrendered female children for adoption. As a result of all these social and political factors, the number of international adoptions has grown steadily over the past few years. In 2013, the number of children from other countries adopted by U.S. families reached 7,092. The mean age of internationally adopted children was between one and two years of age.[11]

Table 10.1 lists the primary sending countries for children adopted internationally by U.S. families from October 1, 2012, to September 30, 2013.[12]

As both transracial and international placements become more common, many adoptive families will need to learn to talk with their children about racial and cultural issues in addition to adoption issues. The work of Gail Stenberg and Beth Hall in their book, *An Insider's Guide to Transracial Adoption*

Table 10.1.

China	2,306
Ethiopia	993
Ukraine	438
Congo	311
Russia*	250
Philippines	178
Colombia	159
South Korea	138
India	119

**Note:* In December 2012, President Vladimir Putin placed a ban on American families adopting children from Russia, citing a number of incidents of abuse of Russian adoptees by American adoptive parents. It is assumed the US adoptions of 250 Russian children in 2013 were in process when the ban was initiated. At the time of this writing, that ban remains in effect.

(website: http://www.pactadopt.org/app/servlet/HomePage), stands out in addressing these issues and has informed many of the ideas presented here. The racial and cultural issues of identity formation and positive self-esteem add an additional layer to the task of parenting. Visualize the tasks of transracially parenting adopted children as an onion. The "heart" of the onion is the job of parenting any child, understanding normal child development, and responding appropriately to all the needs of the child. The next layer of the onion represents the generic adoption issues, involving separation from the birth family and the resulting grief, fear of abandonment, lack of trust and control, and so on. The final layer of the onion, for the transracial adoptive parent, is the layer of skill needed to parent a child of a different racial and/ or cultural background than one's own, helping the child understand and feel good about who he is, and helping the child cope with the baggage of living in a world that does not tolerate diversity well.

While it can be tempting to announce, "I don't see color, I only see the child," parents must remember that everyone else in the community will see both. Ignoring racial and cultural issues, like the proverbial ostrich with its head in the sand, leaves children ill equipped to build a positive racial and cultural identity and without the survival skills necessary to be successful adults.

BUILDING SELF-ESTEEM

Understanding Racial Identity Formation

One's sense of the world, as well as success in negotiating that world, is largely interpreted through the sense of self, through identity development. Identity can be defined as an individual's personal, coherent sense of self. Identity development involves the adoption of certain personal values, attitudes, feelings, characteristics, and behaviors in addition to identification with a larger group of people who share similar characteristics.[13]

Identity formation for all persons of difference (including, for example, persons with disabilities, persons of minority races or religions, persons who are gay or lesbian) becomes more complex. Persons of difference are often subject to prejudice and discrimination. Furthermore, they must learn to function within a bicultural context. That is, persons of difference must learn to adjust within the majority culture in school, work, and many daily living activities, and they are also expected to function easily within the culture reflected by their difference (deaf culture, racial or ethnic culture, Jewish culture, to name a few). The task of learning to cope with prejudice and discrimination and the task of forming a bicultural identity can lead to identity confusion, conflict, and various forms of anxiety and sociological dilemmas.

The challenge of living with a bicultural identity is documented in the work of the Institute for Human Services in Columbus, Ohio:

> This duality is difficult to comprehend by persons who have never experienced social oppression. Persons of difference struggle between their cultural norms and the norms of the majority. This is especially difficult for children of difference. This awareness doesn't occur all at once, but rather, gradually during school-aged, preadolescent, and adolescent years. Youth are confronted with being part of, yet apart from, in a larger social environment, but not of it, included at some level, and excluded at others. This duality is at the heart of the identity struggle and generates powerful feelings of rage and indignation.
>
> Parents and families of adolescents of color must be aware of this struggle. This insight will allow the parents and families to understand the nature of the youth's behaviors, attitudes and beliefs. Providing support and encouragement in a nurturing environment and multiple opportunities to model other youth and adults who have established healthy identities will facilitate the identity process for youth.[14]

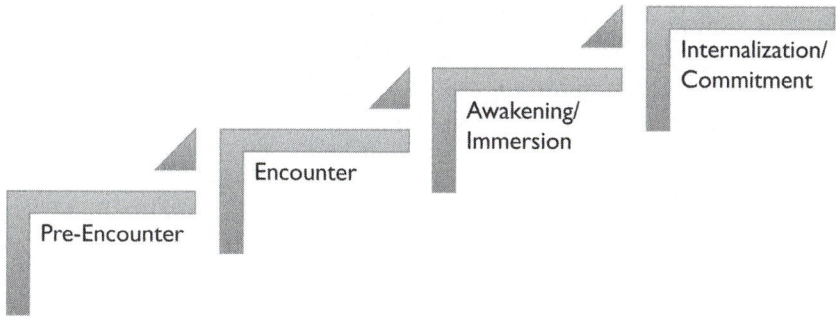

Figure 10.1

STAGES OF RACIAL IDENTITY FORMATION

All persons experience stages in the formation of their racial identity. Persons of color have an identity formation complicated by external factors. Incidents of prejudice, discrimination, and stereotyping create critical incidents during the process of identity formation. If, for example, children are confronted with discrimination, they will compare what they have been told to what they have experienced. This can trigger a deeper exploration of their racial identity and may challenge previously held beliefs. The model in Figure 10.1 was developed by Thomas Cross.[15] It describes four stages of racial identity formation for persons of color. The degree of discrimination experienced *and the level of contact and comfort with the culture of difference* will impact progress through these stages of identity formation.

RACIAL IDENTITY FORMATION

Stage One: Pre-encounter—I'm a Person of Color, but Who Cares?

Individuals in this stage of racial identity formation lack interest in the concept of race. Young persons are likely to interpret the world from the perspective of the majority culture, and they see no reason to challenge the views and codes of conduct of the majority culture. They may even think and behave in ways that communicate a devaluation of their own culture.

Stage Two: Encounter—Racism Hit Me Right between the Eyes, When I Wasn't Even Looking!

Individuals have experienced one or many critical incidents inconsistent with their earlier beliefs. A critical incident can be a single encounter with a racist or oppressive experience or an accumulation of more subtle experiences with racism. Some examples of critical incidents would be name calling, exclusion from groups or activities, or exposure to episodes of stereotyping. These critical incidents cause young people to question and re-examine previously held beliefs of the dominant culture. They may experience confusion about their own cultural group as well as the dominant culture. Youth may begin to develop new ideas and positive stereotypes about their own racial group as well as negative stereotypes about the dominant culture and/or other groups.

Stage Three—Awakening/Immersion. I Need to Know Where I Come From.

Youth in this stage have searched for their identity and are committed to their racial/ ethnic roots. This stage reflects the polar opposite of the pre-encounter stage. Youth at this stage of development are likely to reject the norms and practices of other groups and completely embrace the norms, values, and codes of conduct of their own racial group. Youth immerse themselves in the dress, language, friends, music, art, foods, and other manifestations of their cultural identification and reject those of other cultures. Confrontation and bluntness become the norm, and individuals in this stage may even decide that "all whites are devils." Immersed persons may avoid contact with those in the majority group. Persons in this stage of identity formation may also have confrontations with others in their cultural/racial group who are not thoroughly immersed or as confrontational with differences as they are themselves.

Stage Four—Internalization/Commitment. I Can Look beyond Myself.

Individuals in this stage are secure and self-confident about diversity. After the intensity of the immersion stage, individuals develop a more balanced, integrated perspective on racial identity. Persons in the final stage of identity formation can appreciate and even assimilate traits from other racial/ethnic groups. Still grounded in their own cultures, individuals in this stage move toward a more pluralistic perspective. Here is how James Baldwin described the internalization/commitment phase:

> Not one of us knows how to walk when we get here. Not one of us knows how to open a window, unlock a door. Not one of us can master a staircase. We are absolutely ignorant of the almost certain results of falling out of a five-story window. None of us comes here knowing

> enough not to play with fire. Nor can one of us drive a tank, fly a jet, hurl a bomb, or plant a tree.
>
> We must all be taught that. We have to learn all that. The irreducible price of learning is realizing that you do not know. One may go further and point out—as any scientist, or artist, will tell you—that the more you learn, the less you know, but that means that you have begun to accept, and are even able to rejoice in, the relentless conundrum of your life.[16]

Kevin's Story

In 1967, Kevin Hofmann, a biracial (white birth mother and African American birth father) was adopted at the age of three months by a white couple. Kevin was conceived following an affair between his birth parents, co-workers who were both married to other people. In 1967, Kevin was considered "difficult to place," due to his mixed racial heritage, even though he was a healthy infant. Kevin was born in Detroit at a time of extreme racial unrest, only two and a half weeks after explosive race riots in that city. His adoptive parents, a Protestant minister and his wife, had three children by birth: two sons and a daughter.

Kevin was one of the earliest adoptive placements of an African American child in a white family. Today, Kevin writes and trains about his experience in growing up as the only person of color in a white family. Kevin's insightful perspective is presented in his book entitled *Growing Up Black in White*, published in 2010. His long-range perspective is extremely valuable; Kevin's thoughtful ability to reflect on the impact of his multi-racial family on his life, both as a child and, today, as a mid-life adult, is instructive.

When Kevin joined his adoptive family, they lived in an all-white suburb of Detroit, and his father was assistant pastor of an all-white church. Even during Kevin's infancy, the family experienced racial incidents, including a burning cross on the family's front lawn as well as the congregation's attempt to remove Kevin's adoptive father from his position in the church. Kevin's parents decided to move to a predominantly African American neighborhood, and his father accepted a position as pastor of a largely African American church. This decision by his adoptive parents was life changing for Kevin. During all of his school years, he attended predominantly African American schools. From his school friends, he learned about black culture, racism, and survival skills. Kevin noted that he never remembers a time when he wanted to be white. In fact, he felt sorry for his siblings because they were not black! This attitude may have been quite different, however, if his family had remained in an all-white community.

Kevin's adoptive family liked to camp in rural areas of Michigan. During one camping trip when Kevin was four or five, he became quite sick and dehydrated with the flu. His parents took him to a local emergency room where he was refused treatment. (*Note:* Discrimination in this century is unlikely to be as overt as it was during the 1960s and 1970s. However, it would be naïve to assume discrimination is a thing of the past. A multiracial family should be prepared, through open dialogue, to cope with more subtle forms of discrimination in the community, school, church, and neighborhood.)

While the family certainly experienced critical incidents of racism almost immediately after placement, Kevin still feels the impact of a name-calling event that occurred when he was old enough to understand the shattering message. "When I was seven or eight, I was in a grocery store and exchanging eye contact, making faces and acting silly, with a little boy around my age. I thought we were having fun as friends. When we left the store, the other little boy was sitting on one of those mechanized ponies. He looked down at me and said one word . . . 'Nigger.' I was devastated."[17]

Kevin's maternal grandmother did not realize her newly adopted grandson was a child of color until he was placed in her arms. She worried about her daughter's decision, particularly after a cross was burned on the family's front lawn! This grandmother was consistently reserved and cool in her relationship with Kevin, very different from her response to her biological grandchildren. As a result of her cool response to their youngest child, Kevin's parents limited contact with the maternal grandparents to one or two visits per year.

Kevin remembers his adolescence as a time of moving through the third stage of racial identity formation: awakening and immersion. "My black friends and I used to sit at my dining room table and write rap songs that included a lot of anti-white lyrics. My mother would overhear us singing these songs, but she gave me the freedom to voice those feelings. She felt I had every right to be angry."[18] Kevin's mother did not attempt to interrupt his process of becoming a black man in a white culture.

Today, Kevin feels his transracial adoption has helped him learn to move comfortably in both white and black environments; he has entered the final stage of racial identity formation: internalization/commitment. His family was consciously instrumental in helping him to develop a bicultural world and identity by assuring Kevin had access to diverse racial environments.

Let's explore the experience of a more recent transracially adopted adult. Robin, a biracial toddler, was adopted in the late 1970s by her white foster parents. While growing up in a Midwest metropolitan city during the 1980s and 1990s, this young woman had somewhat different, but still challenging, experiences.

Robin's Story

Robin, 26 years old and the mother of three boys, was born to a Caucasian woman addicted to heroin. During the pregnancy, Robin's mother took methadone, a prescription drug used by treatment centers to "wean" addicts from heroin. Robin was born addicted to methadone and had to remain in the hospital for ten days following her birth. Her birth father was African American.

Robin was placed in the foster home of Dot and Bob, Caucasian parents who, for many years, fostered children with special needs. Dot and Bob had two children by birth, a daughter older than Robin, and a son who was younger. Her foster parents adopted Robin when she was only one and a half years old. They continued to foster children with special needs, including many children of color, over the next 25 years.

Today, Robin remarks, "I noticed I was darker than the others in my family when I was about three years old." She feels that her parents handled the racial issues well because "they were always open to questions and shared information honestly." As a young child, "I went to bed crying at night because I idolized my older sister and wanted to be white like her." As Robin got older, particularly during the middle school years, the racial issue became more significant because she felt different from her peers. "I was embarrassed, at times, when I was in public with my family because my parents and siblings were white." When with her family in the community, her adoption became public information to even the most casual observer. Dot recalls that Robin really did not understand until she was about 11 years old that her birth mother was white. This information had been shared with Robin when she was much younger, but she did not comprehend that information until she was in middle school. Dot commented on Robin's anger "that we hadn't told her," or at least hadn't told her in a way that could be absorbed by her.

Dot remembers that some of the African American girls rejected Robin when she was a middle school student because her choices for hair and clothing styles were not "appropriate" in their eyes. Robin wore her hair in an Afro and did not want her mother to touch it. The African American girls considered this hairstyle out of date and teased her about her appearance. Most of her friends during this time were white. Her most significant single critical incident occurred when a carload of teenage boys passed "me while I was walking on an isolated road in a white neighborhood. The boys yelled racial slurs at me, and I felt very angry and *very* afraid!" She considered responding, but felt outnumbered and powerless. She ran home and shared her feelings with her parents. During this time, Robin often fantasized about going to live with a black family, feeling that they would understand what she was going through. Her mother had an African American friend and coworker who became extremely important to both Robin and Dot.

When Robin was in high school, she became reacquainted with a grandfather who was married to an African American woman. Robin spent two summers with her grandparents, but she and her step-grandmother were not able to "connect." Robin was very outspoken, and she functioned very much as a white child. Her grandmother could not accept Robin's "white" behavior.

Dot believes the area where she was least proficient as a transracial adoptive parent was in understanding the importance of looking good in the African American community. Robin did not like to have her hair braided or relaxed, and Dot allowed Robin to wear her hair in a "natural" style. Dot believes now that Robin's journey through adolescence would have been easier if she had pushed the issue of hair care as a parenting issue and not a grooming issue. To what degree does a parent allow the child to be in control of hair, clothes, and behaviors, and when does the parent take charge of those decisions? "Our philosophies gave control of those issues to the kids in most situations. Our son's long hair and black leather jackets had one set of consequences, but Robin's 'Afro' had another. I believe hers was more damaging on a long-range basis because of the way the community dealt with it. The issues are more complex than knowledge about hair care, and, in my view, are not well understood across cultures. The senses of what puts our children at risk or in danger are different."

Dot does feel that her neighborhood was not as integrated as she would have liked, but the adoptive parents ensured that Robin attended integrated schools. In fact, they struggled with decisions about sending Robin to an excellent private school designed for learning disabled students, but chose to send Robin to the public school so that she would not be the only child of color in her classroom. The high school Robin attended was in a metropolitan community and was the magnet school for students who spoke English as a second language. As a result, Robin attended school with a very diverse group of students.

Dot also believes that fostering children of many different races was helpful for Robin, as she was not always the only person of color within the family. Further, routine interaction with several African American foster parents was profoundly important in helping Robin understand and feel good about African American families, and African American women in particular. In addition, these informal cultural consultants were helpful advisors to Dot and Bob as they marshaled Robin through critical incidents involving her schoolmates and others in the community.

Today, Robin identifies herself as a person of mixed racial heritage. She sees herself as neither black nor white, but as biracial. Her friends are almost exclusively African American. She lives in an African American neighborhood, and she does not feel comfortable dating white men. She sees herself becoming more "black" as she matures in many of her cultural practices—she has picked up African American mannerisms, styles of speaking, parenting practices, and so on.

Dr. Denise Goodman, adoption consultant and trainer, notes:

> Achieving identity congruence in the face of oppression and discrimination is a major challenge. Successfully navigating through these obstacles takes psychological and sociological stability, especially for children. Foster/adoptive families of persons of difference must first be aware of the struggle the youth faces. This will bring an understanding of the nature of the youth's behaviors, attitudes, and beliefs.[19]

COMMON THEMES THROUGHOUT DEVELOPMENT

Preschoolers

Children begin to notice racial differences as early as two years of age, and most often by the age of three. Transracial adoptive parents of preschoolers and early school-age children are often troubled when their child expresses the desire to be "white like you." Parents become concerned that this statement indicates a rejection of the child's racial or cultural identity. However, it is not unusual, in a society dominated by white people and images, for children of color, even those being raised in same race or birth families, to express a desire to be white or lighter skinned. It is important, however, that children of all ages (and children raised in all types of families) be exposed to diversity and be able to see people other than those in the media who look like they do.

School-Age Children

Transracially adopted children of school-age years may feel teased or excluded by their peers because of racial differences, or because they are different by virtue of transracial adoption: a child of color living with a white family. Children this age should be empowered to resolve their own problems as much as possible. Parents should ask a child about a critical incident, his or her feelings at the time, and possible responses that might have been used. Parents should help children explore both the immediate and long-term consequences of the potential responses. Children should be helped to explore whether it would be better to handle a similar situation differently in the future, or if they should respond in the same way if confronted with such a problem again. For example, in a dialogue with Robin about her critical incident (boys yelling racial slurs at her on an isolated road), Robin's potential responses might have included:

1. Engaging in a confrontation by yelling back at the boys
2. Responding through an obscene gesture
3. Running home without responding
4. Continuing to walk as if the encounter did not happen, without engaging in any verbal exchange

Robin and her parents could explore each of these alternatives, and any others that present themselves, to determine if she chose the most appropriate response at the time. The consequences of the first two alternatives might have been an escalation of the critical incident in an unsafe environment, jeopardizing Robin's safety. Running may also have led to escalation, prompting the boys to chase her, and the act of running may have sent a message to both the boys and Robin that she could not protect herself from verbal assaults. The final alternative, the one chosen by Robin at the time, seems to have the fewest negative consequences; therefore, her parents could support her in her ability to handle a difficult situation with both grace and good judgment. At the conclusion of such a teaching dialogue, parents should ask if the child feels there is anything the parents should do. The child should be secure in parental support, but allowed to handle unfairness without adult intervention whenever possible. Through these incidents and the "teachable moments" that follow, children can develop more sophisticated survival skills and a sense that they can cope with discrimination in the future.

Adolescents

Issues related to self-image and dating often surface for the transracially adopted teenager. "The development of body image and the successful assimilation of that body image into the psyche is an essential element of adolescent identity formation. It is critical for the development of positive body image that teens of color have role models that reflect body styles similar to their own. If a teen has no such personal experience, he will be at the mercy of the media's representations of people of the child's race or ethnicity."[20]

Dating can be problematic for transracially adopted teens, who may find barriers in dating others who are white, but may feel uncomfortable with, or lack access to, potential dating partners of color. Discussion and exploration of feelings about dating are critical for the transracially adopted teen. "The important thing in putting talk into the air is not whether the teenager responds or agrees, but that he or she hears the talk," Randolph Severson comments. "The psyche is such an extraordinary 'continuous learner' that it cannot help but assimilate every new datum of information in its lifelong quest for truth."[21]

STRATEGIES FOR PARENTS TO ENHANCE POSITIVE CULTURAL IDENTITY

Be a Bridge

Your child needs to belong to groups that you cannot belong to. "So when you can't be the direct provider of culture, be a bridge to the culture your child needs to be part of, a culture you can't be part of yourself. Please don't feel discouraged by his participation in a culture that does not include you. The connecting links you can forge will not only support him but will expand your family life in ways that will continue to unfold throughout your lives. Nothing could be more positive."[22]

> Remember the story of the ugly duckling? Could the mother duck who raised a swan have taught her baby to swim like a swan or to sound like a swan or to act like a swan? Of course not—she was a duck. She could certainly teach him everything she knew about how to act like a duck, but she couldn't know how to be a swan. Even if she had read 1,000 books about swan history and habits, she still wouldn't have been an authentic swan; she'd be a duck who knew a great deal about swans. That baby swan had to learn from other swans how to be a swan. In the same way, the foremost challenge you face as an adoptive parent is that you will not be able to provide directly for all your child's essential needs, no matter how hard you try and no matter how much you want to. You will not be able to provide personally for your child's need to belong to his culture. Culture is not something you learn about in books. Culture is something you live. You become part of it by living in the experience.

> And if you are parenting a child of a different race from your own, you will not be able to provide directly for your child's need to build a positive racial identity. You will never become a member of your child's race or genetic family, no matter how many books you read or how much soul food or chilies or dim sum you eat or how educated you become about the history of her race.[23]

Get Help from People from Your Child's Cultural Group

You cannot parent any child alone. When parenting a child of a different race or culture, you must aggressively seek help from persons of that child's culture.

Mary was sitting on a park bench, watching her biracial daughter play happily on the swings with several other children. Her daughter Crystal would periodically run back to Mary, "checking in," to be secure her mother was safely nearby. An attractive African American woman, a complete stranger, approached Mary and asked if she could come to her home that evening to fix Crystal's hair. Surprised, Mary accepted this offer of help. That evening, her newfound friend came to her home, put a tablespoon of Vaseline in Crystal's hair, and began to braid it. The following morning, Mary, as instructed, took out the braids, and she found that Crystal's hair looked more beautiful than it ever had before. Her friend continued to provide "cultural consultation" to the adoptive family as Crystal grew up. Crystal and other children of color in this large adoptive family benefited greatly from this woman's willingness and commitment to play a role in her development of self-esteem and positive racial identity.

Beth Hall and Gail Steinberg, authors of *An Insider's Guide to Transracial Adoption*, remind parents:

> The best tool you can develop as a parent of a child of another race is a healthy ability to challenge your own assumptions about what you need to do and about what your child faces. Even though, in every possible way, you are your child's parents and she is your child, she will be living in a different world than you do. You will not be able to provide for all her needs yourself. Once you give up that expectation, you can begin the process of providing.[24]

Make sure your child understands the "rules" of his birth culture as well as the rules of yours. All cultures have codes of conduct, styles of language and dress, and values that have served to foster the continuation of the culture and the survival of its members as well as a sense of group cohesiveness.

Your child, even more so than other children of color, lives in a bicultural world and must learn the skills to negotiate and navigate successfully in both cultures. Understand that you are not the best authority to teach the survival skills your child needs to navigate within his cultural milieu, but make sure that he has the opportunities to learn these skills at school, at church, in neighborhood groups, and with friends of the family.

STRATEGIES FOR TALKING WITH YOUR CHILD ABOUT RACE AND RACISM

Listen More, Talk Less

As the authorities in the family, parents often feel that they are appropriately providing guidance and instruction for their children only when they are doing the talking. Yet all effective leaders and teachers have learned the art of listening. Before teaching and guiding, parents must first understand where the child is in his experience, perception, and development. To understand those issues, parents must hear before they speak. Further, parents need to learn more about their child's reality to understand when they can provide help themselves, and when they need to seek help from others. "Parents may tell themselves they feel comfortable raising a child across racial lines, but when faced with issues that threaten their child's well-being, feelings of uncertainty, anger, and perhaps shame can arise. Don't assume your feelings are the same as your child's. Don't overload the situation with your input. If you bring race into every situation to the exclusion of everything else, your child may avoid talking about race with you at all costs. The best advice is: Listen More; Talk Less. You need to understand your child's experience, not direct the action."[25]

Ask Open-Ended Questions

To understand the child's perceptions, parents should not ask questions that can be answered with a monosyllable. Parents should ask, for example, "How did school go today? What happened?" instead of "Did you have a good day?" Use these open dialogues as a barometer to learn more about your child's experiences and stage of identity development.

Tolerate No Racially or Ethnically Biased Remarks

All parents should teach their children tolerance for diversity. This should include a lack of tolerance for bigotry. When biased remarks are made, these can be challenged in an assertive, but not aggressive, manner.

Even if the biased individual's attitudes are not impacted, an important message is sent to all children within the family.

> As adoptive parents in an interracial or intercultural family, you should refuse to tolerate any kind of racially or ethnically biased remark made in your presence. This includes remarks about your child's race or ethnic group, other races and ethnic groups, or any other characteristic such as gender, religion, age and physical or other disability. Make it clear that it is not okay to make fun of people who are different, and it is not okay to assume that all people of one group behave the same way. Teach your children how to handle these remarks, by saying, for instance, "I find your remark offensive. Please don't say that type of thing again," or "Surely you don't mean to be critical, you just don't have experience with . . ." or "You couldn't be deliberately saying such an inappropriate comment in front of a child. You must mean something else."[26]

There may be times individuals within your family or community of friends display harmful biases about your child's cultural group. Relationships with these individuals may become strained, limited, or, at the very least, changed.

Understand You Are a Family of Color

When your family includes children of color, your family becomes a "family of color." As such, you and your family members will be impacted by racism and discrimination. Majority race individuals may not have been consciously aware of "white privilege" (white privilege is the ability for whites to maintain an elevated status in society that masks racial inequality[27]), and they may be quite surprised and ill equipped to deal with discrimination, particularly subtle, hidden forms of discrimination prevalent today. In her essay, "White Privilege: Unpacking the Invisible Backpack," Peggy McIntosh writes, "As a white person, I realized I had been taught about racism as something which puts others at a disadvantage, but had been taught not to see one of its corollary aspects, white privilege, which puts me at an advantage. I think whites are carefully taught not to recognize white privilege, as males are taught not to recognize male privilege. So I have begun in an untutored way to ask what it is like to have white privilege. I have come to se white privilege as an invisible package of unearned assets which I can count on cashing in each day, but about which I was 'meant' to remain oblivious. White privilege is like a an invisible weightless backpack of special provisions, maps, passports, codebooks, visas, clothes, tools and blank checks."[28] When your family becomes a family of color, that oblivion regarding privilege will disappear, and individuals will come face-to-face with discrimination in a way they may find both surprising and disturbing.

Don't Create Problems Where None Exist

Parents should not constantly search the horizon for racial or cultural problems that do not exist for the child. It is possible to over-respond to the racial and cultural issues faced by adopted and foster children. Parents should not insist on the racial issue throughout every conversation with the child. "Encouraging your child to talk when she says, 'I'm okay, leave me alone,' may be overload. It's possible nothing is really wrong. We sometimes assume that superficial answers to our anxious questions mean the child is concealing painful emotions, but we may be looking for something that isn't here. On the other hand, don't assume that because there is no discussion, there are no problems. Trust your intuition and everything you know about your child, but don't overreact or invade your child's right to be the star of his or her personal drama by taking it over for yourself."[29]

Don't Ignore Adoption Issues and Over-Focus on Racial Issues

Identity is one of the issues impacting adopted children and adults. Transracial adoptive parents may be so concerned with addressing racial identity issues, they may overlook the need to address issues of loss, trust, divided loyalties, and so on.

Kevin's parents did not discuss issues of either race or adoption within the family. Kevin commented, "I always thought about my birth mother, but there was no space to talk about her." When questioned about why he did not ask his parents about his adoption history, he stated, "By not raising the issue with me, I received a silent message that it was not okay to talk about adoption or about race."[30] In the ensuing vacuum, Kevin wanted to know "why she gave me away" and assumed there was something inherently wrong with him. Interestingly, when as a young adult, Kevin decided to initiate a search for his birth family, his adoptive father gave him a large amount of information, "information he had been hanging onto for 20 years."

Be Sensitive to the Impact of Transracial Adoption on Your Birth Children

Your birth children will have experiences, both positive and negative as a result of being part of a family of color. Your children will be exposed to questions, at a minimum, and likely will also experience discrimination.

On the other hand, they will benefit from exposure to diversity and will learn much about the value of different cultural traditions.

Kevin's siblings, particularly his brothers, were impacted by being the "different" kids in a predominantly black school and neighborhood. The boys "struggled with being different;" they were no longer the majority group, but "the other."

Today, Kevin's adult siblings continue to live within diverse family structures. His sister married an African American man, divorced him, and remarried another African American man. His oldest brother married a Chinese American woman. And his other brother married and divorced a Chinese American woman and is now married to a woman of Japanese descent.

Create a Code Word or Gesture for Dealing with Rude Remarks in Public

When strangers or casual acquaintances make ridiculously rude remarks in the presence of the child, many families find it helpful to communicate their desire to terminate the encounter through use of a secret code word or gesture. Any member of the family experiencing discomfort can use the word or gesture to let others know that they can no longer abide the stranger's ignorance or rudeness. Children enjoy being a part of the "in group" that knows and uses these codes and can benefit from the camaraderie, implicit support, and fun of using these codes in public. These code words or cover stories can stop the escalation of an unpleasant encounter into a critical incident.

SUMMARY

Foster and adoptive parents should celebrate the rewards that diversity through transcultural and/or transracial parenting brings into their lives. Few persons of a majority race or culture have the tremendous opportunities for personal growth afforded to those individuals who benefit from this challenge. Robin's mother, Dot, has the following advice for a new generation of transracial adoptive parents:

- Be honest and open; it's the unknown that kids can't handle.
- Stay closely integrated in the child's culture. Seek out relationships and connections that will assist your child in maintaining an understanding of and attachment to his or her culture.

- Understand that you are not a white family with some members of other races. You are now a family of color. Remember that as you make choices about neighborhoods, schools, churches, and so on.
- It might be preferable, if adopting/fostering across racial lines, to adopt or foster more than one child of color.
- Don't isolate yourself. You need to socialize and interact with other foster/adoptive families, preferably those with racially mixed families. It is extremely helpful to have other parents to talk with about the issues of raising a child of color to have a positive self-esteem and racial identity.

QUESTIONS

1. In what ways does your family differ culturally from your child's birth family?
2. Do you see your family as a minority family? If yes, how has that affected your entire family?
3. At what stage of racial identity formation is my child? Why?
4. Has your child experienced critical incidents? How has he been affected? How have you been affected?
5. What kinds of discrimination might your child experience? Do you feel comfortable assisting your child in coping effectively with discrimination? Where can you find help?
6. Do you need to seek assistance from your child's birth culture to learn ways to enhance your child's self-esteem and positive racial identity? Where might you find that kind of assistance?

CHAPTER 11

Kinship Foster Care and Adoption: Telling the Truth When It's "All in the Family"

In the South Texas community where I was raised, there was an informal system of intra-family adoptions that undoubtedly evolved in response to family and community needs. Adoption was our way of distributing the burdens and benefits within a community.[1]

We have taken care of our granddaughter ever since she was born. When we refused to enable our drug-addicted daughter by giving her money, she would threaten to take our granddaughter and never allow us to see her again. Our granddaughter was traumatized by these threats. We finally decided to adopt her so we could all have peace of mind.

An Adoptive Mother

Many foster and adoptive families are created when a child is removed from the care of his parents and placed with close or extended family members. In fact, relative adoptions are historically the most common form of adoption since most cultures encourage the adoption (formal or informal) of orphaned children by extended family members.

While kinship care is not a new occurrence, the number of relatives caring for kin grew substantially during the early 1990s. It has since stabilized at a level approximately 50 percent higher than the steady rate of the 1980s.[2] Since 1994, the number of children in relative care (primarily with grandparents) has hovered around 2.2 million, or about 3 percent of children under age 18.[3] During the period from1991 through 2009, the change in the number of children living with relatives was relatively slow, compared with the pace of change from 1970 to 1990.[4]

In addition to those children adopted by relatives, approximately half a million children each year live with relatives in formal foster care.[5] A study conducted in 1994 found that almost one-fourth (24%) of foster children were in care with relatives.[6] These kinship parents have been licensed as foster caregivers to work with the agency toward the goal of reunification with the birth parents. If reunification efforts fail, these relative foster parents may choose to adopt.

Kinship care creates an unusual challenge for a family: telling the child the truth about the past when that truth involves a close family member. This chapter will discuss the joys and hazards unique to kinship care and ways to keep communication sensible, sensitive, and healthy.

HISTORY OF KINSHIP ADOPTION

> A study by Kari Sandven, PhD, of the Riverside Medical Center in Minneapolis, Minnesota, and Michael D. Resnick, PhD, of the School of Public Health at the University of Minnesota, found that the acceptance of informal adoption dates back to the kinship structures of ancient African cultures. It was customary then for aunts and uncles to help raise one another's children, creating the tradition of shared rather than exclusive parenting. Three generations of family lived together, and there were flexible boundaries that emphasized the clan over the nuclear family. The concept "It takes a village to raise a child" began here.[7]

While the numbers of kinship placements in the United States increased dramatically in recent years, the phenomenon of both formal and informal kinship placements has always existed in this country. A formal kinship adoption is one facilitated by an attorney and/or agency, with an adoption legalization in court. An informal kinship placement occurs when a relative or close family friend steps in during a family crisis to care for children who are orphaned or otherwise in need of nurture and stability.

An informal kinship placement, while statistically much more stable than agency foster placements, may or may not be permanent, and the placement does not involve institutions such as child protective services agencies, courts, and so on. Informal kinship placements have occurred often in minority cultures, where distrust of formal institutions is more prevalent and where family crisis might be precipitated due to higher levels of poverty. It is not uncommon in the African American community, for example, to see a grandmother or great-grandmother caring for children, or an aunt or close family friend assisting with care of children. Such informal networks also exist within many other cultures, including the Latino community.

Adoptive parents involved in either formal or informal kinship adoption share the same responsibilities as those in non-kinship adoption:

- They are to nurture and care for their kin children.
- They are to assure that the children's needs are met.
- They are to help establish a plan to connect the children to safe, stable, nurturing relationships intended to last a lifetime, when they cannot be reunited with their birth parents.

Many informal adoptive kinship families have strong reservations about a formal adoption of the children in their care. In fact, 85 percent of kinship foster families studied did not want to formally adopt the children.[8] Most of them believed that it wasn't necessary because "they are already family." Others thought that it would create conflict within the extended family and create problems with the birth parents of the children. Despite these reservations about formal adoption, most kinship families remain firmly committed to the care of their children. Seventy percent indicated that they would allow a child to remain with them either "as long as she wants to" or "until she is able to take care of herself."[9]

In 1997, the Adoption and Safe Families Act gave preference to relatives over non-relatives in foster care placement decisions.[10] In 2008, another piece of federal legislation, the Fostering Connections to Success and Increasing Adoptions Act, required child protection social workers to identify and notify relatives within 30 days whenever a child cannot safely remain with his birth parents.[11] "However, in four States (California, Missouri, New York, and Tennessee), if the child has been placed in foster care with a nonrelative and has been living with the same foster parent for significant period of time when he or she becomes available for adoption, the nonrelative foster parent may be given first preference to adopt."[12] For current information about regulations in your state, visit https://www.childwelfare.gov/systemwide/laws_policies/state.

Race and ethnicity have a significant impact on kinship adoption. For example, in 2000 almost one-third of Hispanic children (32%) were adopted by relatives. This number increased to 37 percent in 2001, and stabilized at 33 percent in 2003 and 2004. Between 2000 and 2004, the percentage of African American children adopted by relatives increased each year, reaching 25 percent in 2004. For White children, the percentage has remained relatively stable throughout this period at 18 percent in FY 2000, 20 percent in FY 2001, FY 2002, and FY 2003, and 21 percent in FY 2004.[13]

ADVANTAGES OF KINSHIP ADOPTION

There are powerful advantages for those children separated from birth parents who find permanency in kinship adoption. Whenever children must leave their birth parents, the trauma of separation is softened when they can remain with people, places, and cultures familiar to them. Further, research on kinship placements indicates that children who are placed with kin have fewer moves and more stability than children in the child welfare system usually experience. A study by the Child Welfare League of America concluded that only 23 percent of children placed with relatives were not able to continue living with them after three years, compared with 58 percent of children in nonrelative foster care. In New York City, where half of all children in foster care live with relatives, a task force on kinship care found that kinship parents were more likely than traditional foster parents to care for large sibling groups of children, further reducing the trauma of separation from the birth family.[14]

Research indicates adoption by relatives may promote improved child well-being over informal caregiving arrangements. Relative families who adopt legally likely have stronger commitments to the children in their care. Further, adoption provides legal protections that promote children's well-being, such as providing a defense if unfit birth parents seek to reassert parental rights. Adoption may also enable children to gain access to health insurance and other benefits unavailable to children with informal caregiving arrangements. In addition, adoption may provide enhanced emotional security for children, allowing them to thrive.[15]

Children in kinship adoptions may have more opportunity to stay in touch with their birth parents, particularly if birth parents continue to remain involved in functions with the extended family. As a result, children in kinship adoptions may not feel totally cut off from their past, may not, in other words, feel that much of their history is a mystery. And relatives may be less fearful than other adoptive parents of unknown factors within the child's genetic background.

COMMUNICATION CHALLENGES OF KINSHIP ADOPTION

Challenge 1: Familiarity Breeds . . .

One of the most significant advantages of kinship adoption, the relationship with the birth parents, can also present significant challenges to kinship adoptive parents. If adoptive parents know (and perhaps dislike or disrespect) the birth parents, will they be able to perceive the child as a person in his own right? Will they be constantly looking for evidence that he is "just like" his birth father? Will he have the same weaknesses as the birth mother? Furthermore, kinship adoption can include many of the same feelings and dynamics as an ugly, bitter divorce. Can, for example, kinship adoptive parents, who may have suffered themselves as a result of the behavior of these birth parents, present the birth parents in a positive light to the child? Can kinship adoptive parents, who have very strong feelings at times about the birth parents, talk with their children about the birth father without calling him "your *!?* /1* father?"

"This is an issue, of course, for all adoptive parents, even when they are not relatives," says Lois Melina, editor of *Adopted Child* newsletter. "But it's more complicated with family members. It's easier, for example, for a nonrelative to speak compassionately about a birth parent who is an alcoholic than for a family member who has experienced firsthand the birthparent's violence when drunk, inability to take responsibility for his actions, expectations that he will be forgiven (for his offenses) when he is sober, and refusal to seek help."[16]

Challenge 2: Change in the Extended Family Dynamics

Adopting a relative's child may set up stresses in relationships of family members. Other adult children of adopting grandparents, for example, may resent the fact their children could receive less attention from grandparents who are now busy parenting. Further, if the birth parents contested the adoption, they may have residual antagonism toward the adoptive parents; in other words, birth parents may feel their children have been "kidnapped" by adopting relatives. And the adoptive parents themselves may not be in complete agreement about the responsibility of providing a permanent family for one partner's children, increasing tension in the marital relationship.

"Adopting a close relative's child may be the best solution for the child, but it can cause a radical change in the dynamics of your relationship with that relative. These types of relationships have the potential to become strained or severely damaged due to questions of 'quasi co-parenting' and exactly who is the child's parent. The reality is that this dynamic will be different for everyone involved, including all family members, and extending to other children the biological parents may have now or in the future. You will be confronted with questions of relatedness (is your child their cousin? sibling? aunt? uncle?), among others. Can this be done? Yes. Will it be a snap? No."[17]

Challenge 3: Loss of the Dream of One's Child as a Parent

Beth Brindo, an adoption expert in Cleveland, Ohio, comments that grandparents who adopt must grieve the loss of the vision of their birth children as parents. They will not be able to enjoy watching their children raising children. The bitterness that might accompany this grief can spill over into their communications with their adopted children about their birth parents and the circumstances surrounding their birth, poisoning the children's understanding of their roots and their own self-esteem.

Kenneth and Claudia's 20-year-old daughter, Sandra, was their greatest joy and their greatest heartache. Right after high school, Sandra had become involved in an abusive relationship and refused to leave it. By the time she was 19, she was the mother of a beautiful son. However, the drugs and alcohol present in Sandra's apartment took precedence over her care of Mickey. Nothing other than the drugs would get her attention. Kenneth and Claudia made the heartbreaking decision of reporting their only daughter to the protective service agency in their town so that young Mickey would be safe. Sandra's live-in boyfriend talked her quickly into signing Mickey into the full and legal custody of her parents.

Challenge 4: Establishing Boundaries

Many kinship adoptions are also open adoptions. The birth parents often know where the children are, and they continue to relate, if not to the children, to the extended family. As in all open adoptions, adoptive parents must set some boundaries about the type of contact, timing of contacts, who holds parenting responsibility and decision-making authority, how and when information is to be shared, and so on. In kinship adoptions, setting boundaries can be even more difficult, creating increasingly complicated ripples, because the adoptive parent is functioning as the parent to the child as well as being the grandparent, aunt/uncle, niece, sibling, or other relative of the birth parent. The desire to "keep peace in the family" can sometimes interfere with creation of healthy boundaries so important in open adoption relationships.

Challenge 5: Family Gatherings

Some extended families can become fractured as members "choose sides" if and when adoption-related conflict occurs. In kinship adoptions where parental rights of birth parents were involuntarily terminated, this fracturing can become particularly problematic. Such fissures can present more than the usual family or holiday reunion stress. If disagreements exist about how to communicate with the child about the adoption, for example, the holiday gift exchange can become quite emotionally charged. Or if adoptive parents have tried to keep the adoption secret, it is highly likely that cousins or others within the family will use family gatherings to leak this information to the adopted child. This is hardly an ideal way to learn about one's adoption history.

Challenge 6: Keeping the Family Secret

Finally, one would expect kinship adoptions to be more open than adoptions arranged for nonrelated persons. However, according to Beth Brindo and other post-adoption specialists, the reverse seems to be the case, at least anecdotally.[18] Kinship adoptive parents seem *more* likely than nonrelated adopters to keep the facts of the adoption secret. Because the parties involved are "all in the family," there can be an increased tendency to withhold or distort information in an attempt to "protect" family members from shameful or painful scenarios.

Many individuals who grew up in kinship adoptions are surprised to learn, as adults, that they were adopted, and that "Aunt Susie" was really the birth mother. In other cases, while honest about the facts surrounding parentage, some kinship adopters avoid the topic of adoption altogether within the family. Many informal kinship adopters have had minimal contacts, or none at all, with adoptive parent support organizations, agency training programs, or social workers. Left to handle a delicate situation without support or knowledge, many resort to avoidance as the path of least resistance.

Darlene grew up with her aunt and uncle in an informal, privately arranged kinship adoption. She knew that she was adopted, and she regularly visited with her birth mother (the sister of the uncle raising her). However, she had never met her birth father, and she had no information about him. Whenever Darlene asked her adoptive mother or her birth mother about her birth father, she was told that she was "better off" to know nothing about him. In fact, she had never even seen a picture of him. The circumstances surrounding Darlene's birth (she was born out of wedlock, fathered by a man considered "beneath" the mother's family) were a matter of embarrassment to the mother's family; the subject of Darlene's father became a forbidden topic within the home. Darlene was left to imagine dreadful things about her father, and about herself. She spent a considerable amount of energy during her childhood and adolescence fantasizing and wondering about her birth father. She became fearful, as a young adult, of forming close relationships involving commitment and permanency with men.

PRINCIPLES OF TALKING ABOUT KINSHIP ADOPTION

Be the Parent.

"Adoption within families is not without its own unique challenges," says Sharon Kaplan Roszia, co-author of *The Open Adoption Experience* and a national expert on adoption. "In family adoption, everyone has two relationships to the child. The child's birth relatives are also his adoptive relatives. Adoptions within a family have 'strings attached' that reflect underlying issues in the family. Nonetheless, the child will not be confused about who his parents are as long as the adults are not confused and act accordingly."[19] That is, *the adoptive parent is the parent.* This is not a divorce situation, in which two parties who do not live together will be co-parenting the child. Children living in kinship adoption have *one set of parents*: the adoptive parents. Kinship adoption is not co-parenting!

Tom and Judy had adopted their niece and nephew. Tom's brother, Matt, was developmentally delayed and had a chaotic lifestyle. Matt was invited to stop by to visit the children in an "open door policy" as long as he would abide by a few simple rules. The most important of these rules was that Matt would respect the adoptive parents' authority as parents. One day, Matt visited and was playing board games in the living room with his school-age children. Tom stayed in the kitchen to give them some privacy, but remained within earshot. He heard Matt say to his birth son, "Don't you call him Dad! I'm your Dad!" Tom immediately invited Matt to join him on the front porch. He reiterated the rule and reminded Matt that he will always be birth dad, but he will not be "Dad" to these children in the future. Tom sensitively corrected Matt's communication outside the presence of the children. He effectively established a boundary. Due to Matt's developmental delay, it is likely this scenario and the resulting boundary setting will need to be repeated. However, Tom and Judy feel the relationship the children have with their birth dad is worth the effort of repeated communications with Matt.

Adopted People Have a Right to Know the Truth about Their Parentage. Be Honest.

Kinship adoptive parents may be reluctant to share information about a painful episode in the family's history, an episode that may have included drug addiction, criminal history, extramarital affairs, or other potentially embarrassing scenarios. And they may be particularly reluctant to share information with a child who developmentally lacks discretion about repeating this information outside the family or asking questions of other family members. Kinship adoptive parents have an unusually difficult balancing act on the tightrope of adoption communication. The parties involved in the troubling circumstances that led to the separation of their children from their birth parents are family members, people who will be a part of the children's future as well as their past. The principles of imparting the information, however, remain the same, regardless of the difficulties involved in the task (see Chapter 7). Honesty is paramount, and children are not "protected" by lies, omissions, or distortions. And if the adoptive parents try to protect the birth parents, or themselves, through untruths or half-truths, the children will suffer due to damaged trust, unrealistic fantasies, and anxieties about an unpredictable future.

Regularly Discuss with Birth Parents Ways in Which Communication Will Be Handled with the Child, and Adapt These Communications Appropriately as the Child Matures.

It is likely, in kinship adoptions, that birth parents will have some contact with the children. To ensure that communication given to the children is accurate and clear, make a plan with the birth parents, and review it regularly, on strategies to be used with the children in explaining the adoption situation to them. Birth parents will be more helpful in collaboration on clear communication if they have some degree of "buy-in" about the why's and how's of adoption communication. In discussing a communication plan with the birth parents, adoptive parents should regularly remind birth parents that they both have the same goal: healthy, well-adjusted children. There may be some disagreement about methods needed to achieve that goal, but communication will be much healthier, as well as more open and more effective, if parties have discussed those issues and come to some areas of agreement about what information will be shared, at what point, and using what language. Because the children's developmental stages, and therefore their ability to understand adoption-related circumstances (see Chapters 5 and 8), will change over time, these communication plans should be routinely re-addressed with birth parents.

Make Sure That Other Significant Persons in the Extended Family Are on the Same Page as the Adoptive Parents Regarding Adoption Communication.

Kinship adoptive parents must learn to communicate effectively with both the child and the birth parents. As in all open adoption situations, it is essential that communication philosophies and strategies are clear to both the birth and adoptive parents, so that a unified, clear message can be sent to the child. Differences of opinion about techniques or strategies will occur over time, as they invariably do with two parents living together and raising children together. However, kinship adoptive parents and birth parents should try to focus on the needs of the children and the shared purpose of both birth and adoptive parents: raising children who feel good about their family and themselves, who will be able to function as healthy, productive, and content adults.

Learn What Services and Supports Exist for the Child and Family, Regardless of the Association (or Lack of One) with an Agency.

Adoptive families are eligible for adoption subsidies, financial supports for families caring for children with special needs. When family members adopt formally, they too are eligible for these subsidies. Adoptive families should contact their local child protective services agency to learn more about the financial support available to them and their children. A Medicaid card to cover health care expenses for the children may be a part of the adoption subsidy.

When families adopt relatives informally, the child may be eligible for Temporary Assistance to Needy Families (TANF; also includes a Medicaid card) through the local Department of Human Services. Further, the nurturing family might be licensed to serve as foster parents through a child protective services agency and receive foster care board rates to assist with the cost of raising children. Children in the care of relatives may also be eligible for Supplemental Security Income (551) through the Social Security Administration.

Finally, 13 States (Arizona, Colorado, Connecticut, Delaware, Florida, Georgia, Iowa, Mississippi, Nevada, North Dakota, Ohio, Texas, and Wisconsin) have kinship care or relative caregiver programs to provide relatives with benefits and services to help them better care for a child placed in their home.[20] Under these programs, kinship adoptive parents do not have to meet state requirements for licensure as foster parents, but they receive a monthly payment for the support of the children. For current information, visit the following website: https://www.childwelfare.gov/systemwide/laws_policies/statutes/placement.cfm.

Kinship adoptive parents, formal and informal, should explore all avenues to support in their endeavor to provide a safe, permanent home for children. Certainly, all the support needed by families is not financial. Kinship adoptive parents also need help with special educational needs, counseling, parenting children with special needs, day care, health care, and so on. Many excellent support groups are forming for grandparents raising grandchildren, and adoptive parent support groups are a rich informational resource for families raising children with a wide variety of special needs. Local child protective services agencies can be contacted for more information about support groups, therapists, and resources within the community.

Jessica's Story

Eighteen-year-old Molly, a freshman in college, unexpectedly became pregnant. Her large Irish Catholic family was embarrassed by the pregnancy and strongly encouraged Molly to make an adoption plan for the baby. Molly's mother contacted her niece, Virginia, to ask if Molly could live with her during the remainder of the pregnancy. Virginia was 35 years old, single, and working as an attorney. Virginia, happy to help one of her favorite relatives, describes the five months with her pregnant cousin Molly as one of the best times in her life. Molly was planning, through her physician, an adoption for her unborn child with a young married couple. After several months of having young Molly live with her, Virginia began to think about adopting the baby herself. She had always wanted to adopt, but she felt reluctant to propose such a plan to Molly, fearing she would be pressuring the young woman to make a decision that might not be best for her. Just as the last trimester of the pregnancy was about to begin, however, Molly asked Virginia if she would consider adopting the baby. Virginia was thrilled and talked with her extended family about the plan. All agreed that Virginia made a good living, was ready to parent, and should proceed with the adoption. Virginia became the Lamaze coach for Molly and was present in the delivery room for the birth of a wonderful little girl, later named Jessica.

Even though Virginia knew the birth mother very well, contact between the adoptive mother and the birth mother was limited for several years. Molly needed time to grieve her loss, and Virginia needed time to become secure as the parent to little Jessica. Molly came to see the baby when Jessica was eight months old, and Virginia remembers feeling a strong connection to Molly. However, she felt some concern about a completely open adoption. Openness in adoption practice was relatively unusual in the mid-1980s, when Jessica's adoption occurred. Virginia was content to continue a "semi-closed" adoption, one in which she knew the birth mother but had very limited contact with her. When Jessica was two years old, Virginia married, and her husband adopted the baby. The family was ultimately expanded by the additions of a birth child and another adopted child.

All of Virginia's siblings knew about the adoption and the identity of the birth mother, and Molly's siblings also knew of the situation. Others in the extended family did not know that Jessica was the birth child of Molly. They were only aware that Virginia had adopted her oldest child. This secrecy had the effect of diminishing Virginia's contact with her aunt. Contact between them became somewhat uncomfortable. It seemed that the birth grandmother didn't know quite how to respond to a child who was both her great-niece (by adoption) and her grandchild (by birth). This distance in the relationship between Virginia and her aunt was difficult for Virginia to accept because they had always been close in the past. Virginia's mother had died when she was only twelve years old, and her aunt had stepped in to fill an empty space in her life. While the addition of Jessica to her home brought tremendous joy to Virginia's life, it brought with it a significant change in another important relationship.

While Jessica grew up knowing that she was adopted, she did not know the identity of her birth mother. By the time she was five years of age, questions about her birth mother began to emerge. She wanted to know why her birth mother had not kept her, what she looked like, and her name. Virginia felt uncomfortable withholding information from her bright, inquisitive youngster. She talked to two other parents who had open adoptions and was heavily influenced by one who commented, "After all, we don't own our children." After much soul-searching, she decided it was time to call Molly. The birth mother decided that, if a more open relationship between birth mother and child would help Jessica, she would consent to risk revealing the family "secret" by opening the adoption.

Molly and Virginia met to consider the decision they were making; if they openly told Jessica about her birth mother's identity, the information could not later be retracted. Jessica remembers meeting her birth mother for the first time when she was six and one half years old. Virginia, Molly, and Jessica all baked cookies together, and, not surprisingly, the cookies did not come out very well!

Since the original meeting, Jessica and Molly have had sporadic contact. Jessica was nine years old when she last saw her birth mother at a family reunion. At that time, Molly promised to stop by the family home and see Jessica before the night ended. Molly did not keep her promise. Jessica was extremely angry and felt that Molly chose to be with her boyfriend instead of with her.

Jessica was later upset by another comment made by her birth mother, who told her, "If I could take back my decision to surrender, I would. If I could do it all over again, I would have kept you." Jessica was very troubled to hear her birth mother express feelings that Jessica should not be with her adoptive family; it made her feel that perhaps she was not where she was meant to be.

Jessica began experiencing tremendous anger toward her birth mother. Due to Jessie's feelings of confusion and anger, the adoptive family sought the help of a post-adoption support group. Jessica acknowledged that the group experience was very helpful in sorting out her feelings about adoption and her birth mother.

As a result of Jessica's rage, the adoptive family decided to avoid the next reunion. Jessica, however, talked her parents into attending the family get-together. Molly did not attend this reunion, and the situation was not uncomfortable for any of the adoptive family members.

Virginia acknowledges that her kinship relationship with Molly has sometimes made it difficult to establish boundaries with her. The birth and adoptive mothers have been able to talk candidly about their feelings, and have successfully resolved many of these issues. The birth and adoptive mothers have always shared a positive relationship. In fact, as she emphasized when confronted with Jessica's anger toward her birth mother, Virginia would always have strong affection and respect for Molly. Molly is still single (marriage plans did not materialize) and currently has a master's degree. She works with adolescents as a school guidance counselor.

When asked about the pros and cons of kinship adoption, Jessica stated that if her birth mother and birth grandparents were not part of the family, she would not always see them and feel uncomfortable. She would not have worries about family loyalties, and she would not wonder how it would feel to have her picture taken with the "birth" branch of the family tree at reunions instead of with her adoptive branch of the family. Virginia commented on the changes in her close relationship with her aunt, also Jessica's birth grandparent. On the other hand, Jessica is able to get most of her questions answered (though she still has little information about her birth father), and it is comforting to know that she can locate and see her birth mother whenever she chooses to do so.

SUMMARY

Virginia has the following advice for other kinship adoptive parents:

- Be honest with the child. Don't withhold or distort information.
- Open the adoption from the time of the placement.
- Know where boundaries are and keep them clear to all involved.
- Remember that you are the parent.
- Be sure that you have the support of the extended family.

QUESTIONS

1. What are some advantages of kinship adoption to your child?
2. What have been some of the communication challenges you have faced in talking about the adoption with your child? With the birth parents? With the extended family?
3. What are some boundaries you have had to maintain? Are there others you need to develop for the health of your child or your family?
4. Do you feel that you are the parent? Does the birth parent understand you are the parent?
5. Do you need additional support or services in raising your kinship child? Do you know where to get this support or service? If not, whom can you ask to find out?

CHAPTER 12

Adolescence: Parents Matter—Keeping Lines of Communication Open

CARRIE'S STORY

Carrie, age 15, had been placed with her adoptive family at the age of six. She was placed by a public child protective services agency, and her three biological sisters were placed in three different adoptive homes. Carrie's story is typical of children who experience early life trauma and loss. While the girls maintained some telephone contact, they were rarely able to visit one another. The children had been removed from two alcoholic parents who neglected the girls over several years. Carrie had adjusted remarkably well with her empathetic, supportive adoptive parents until she was 13 years old.

As she was entering adolescence and middle school, Carrie began to underachieve in school, to select "low-life" friends and to experiment with numerous bizarre identities, to reject her adoptive parents' attempts at affection and support (interpreting these as attempts at controlling her), and to display alarming anger toward her birth parents. Her behavior had meaning, and her trauma-competent parents understood that.

The adoptive family wisely sought the assistance of post-adoption professionals who assisted Carrie in understanding, if not accepting, her birth parents' addictions and poor parenting skills. Carrie confronted things from her past that she did not like and could not change. Those things were overwhelming to this growing adolescent, but she developed coping strategies to ease her pain.

Carrie returned, with the help of her adoptive parents and therapist, to the placing agency, gaining additional information about her history. This information helped her to sort through her identity confusion without constant, and often self-destructive, fantasies and experimentation. While Carrie continued to be preoccupied with concern about her sisters, she made progress in grieving for the life they would have shared together if the birth parents had been stable enough to provide for their care. The assistance Carrie and her parents received in communicating about the past enabled Carrie to cope with her history in less destructive ways. She could directly address her anger, experience sadness for her lost life with her birth family, and emancipate several years later as a young woman who had endured significant losses and was able to anticipate a promising future.

Adolescence is difficult for all children, regardless of how they joined their families. The circumstances surrounding adoption add another layer of adjustment to two tumultuous developmental tasks for adolescents: identity formation and separation from the family. Both of these critical tasks are especially challenging for adopted teens. In this chapter, we are going to explore what studies explain about adopted teens, what is happening inside the adolescent brain, and how to continue to build connection and relationship that will keep lines of communication open.

TWO ADOLESCENT TASKS: IDENTITY AND SEPARATION

In searching for an identity, most adolescents experiment with a variety of personas. They alternately shun and embrace family values, codes of conduct, career choices, and expectations of themselves. When children have more than one family (and multiple fantasy families) on which to base their self-concept, the struggle to form an identity becomes much more complicated. "*Adopted teens* may question who they are more deeply than non-adopted peers, as the questions they face are more complex. Although both biology and environment shape all of us, forming an identity is complicated for adopted teens because they have two sets of parents/families. They must consider birth family members as they figure out who they are like and who they are different from. Adopted teens may feel that parts of their identity are missing. Unknown or missing information may prevent them from knowing where certain characteristics, abilities, or talents come from. They may worry that they will take on undesirable characteristics or repeat behaviors, tendencies, or mistakes of a birth parent. Teens whose race or ethnic background is unknown (completely or to some degree) or whose race or ethnicity is different from their adoptive parents may feel that they do not fully belong in their family or community."[1]

"The process of adoptive identity development may involve a period of time when adoption issues are particularly salient, involving intense reflection and emotional engagement, perhaps preoccupation on the part of the adolescent. When this occurs, it may be accompanied by the adolescent's temporary emotional withdrawal from the adoptive family. On average, girls' levels of preoccupation (measured by the Adoption Dynamics Questionnaire) were higher than boys'. Differences in degree of preoccupation with adoption were not related to the level of openness in the adolescent's adoption. *Adoptive identity, the sense of oneself as an adopted person, emerges during adolescence and is related to qualities of relationships within the adolescent's family.*"[2]

Further, children who have already lost families may find emancipation from their port in the storm, the adoptive family, extremely difficult. The last time this young person lost a family, it was forever. According to Dr. Gordon Neufeld, the greatest need for children and teens with a trauma and loss history is attachment. Their greatest fear is separation.[3] When one thinks of about the task of leaving the nest for any adolescent, it is the loss of the familiar and safe attachments and the addition of an unknown and frightening world outside the family. For adopted young people this separation is huge.

Adopted youth may loudly assert they plan to move far, far away from the adoptive family as soon as they graduate from high school or that they may even return to live with the birth family. This form of *defensive detachment*[4] is evidence of the anxiety adopted teens feel about losing the only source of security they have had. They may wonder if they will still be considered part of the family if they move out of the adoptive family home.

WHAT RESEARCH SHOWS ABOUT ADOPTED ADOLESCENTS

Over the last two decades, researchers have explored critical questions regarding adopted adolescents and their non-adopted peers. "Do adopted adolescents display more difficult and challenging behavior than their non-adopted peers? Do they have a more complicated adolescence than their non-adopted peers?" Some studies have indicated yes to both questions, yet others "did not observe significant behavioral differences between adopted adolescents and those who grew up with their biological families."[5]

What We Do Know

Some studies report that adopted adolescents fare at least as well as, if not better than, their non-adopted counterparts. For example, 715 adoptive families with adolescents adopted as infants were studied in 1994 by Benson, Sharma, and Roehlkepartain to determine the level of success in key developmental tasks of adoption-formation of identity, attachment to family and others, quality of family life, and psychological well-being. Adopted adolescents in this study were as likely as their non-adopted siblings to express high self-esteem and positive concepts of identity. A little more than half of the sample wanted to know more about their birth parents, and two-thirds of the sample expressed the desire to meet their birth parents. Infants placed before one month of age showed the highest indicators of attachment. The adopted adolescents in this study demonstrated successful adjustment at a rate that equals that of other adolescents. On some indicators, the adopted adolescents ranked slightly higher than a comparison sample of public school adolescents.[6]

Other studies report that adopted children engage in delinquent and dysfunctional behavior at significantly higher rates than do children who were not adopted. This may be in large part due to the long-term impact of early chronic trauma and neglect, not just being an adopted teen. J. Lynn Rhodes found, in a study done in 1993 of 380 adopted children and 290 birth children, a strong pattern of dysfunctional behavior in approximately one out of every four of the adopted children. While all the problem behaviors existed in both birth and adopted children, they occurred with much greater frequency and intensity in adopted children.

The behaviors reported most frequently by the adoptive parents were rejection of authority, lying, cruelty to other people, refusal to accept responsibility for or consequences of actions, school performance below ability, lack of long-term friends, manipulation, difficulty with eye contact, stealing, refusal to follow parental guidelines, and self-control problems. Other behaviors seen more frequently in adopted children than in birth children were inability to give or receive affection; self-destructive behavior; phoniness; problems with food; thinking about fire, blood, or gore; superficial attraction to and friendliness with strangers; substance abuse; and promiscuous sexual activity. It is important to note that children studied were primarily adopted as newborns, with 44 percent being adopted by 30 days of age, and 87 percent adopted by 180 days of age.[7]

Another study, completed by Illinois State University, focused on adoptive families at risk of dissolution. It found that the serious problems of many adopted children with special needs "endure long after adoptive placements become legal, and despite traditional therapeutic efforts to ameliorate them. For many children, these problems escalate with age."[8]

"Research has consistently shown that adopted children are overrepresented in both outpatient and inpatient mental health settings Individual studies from the United States, Canada, and Great Britain suggested that the proportion of adopted children in outpatient clinical settings is between 3 and 13%—at least twice what one would expect given their representation in the general population. Record review research on inpatient mental health populations indicates an even greater percentage of adoptees in these facilities—between 9 and 21%. The latter figures suggest that adoptees appear to be at least five to eight times as likely to be referred to an inpatient mental health facility compared with their nonadopted counterparts."[9]

In reading many research studies on the adjustment of adopted adolescents, parents and professionals have difficulty making sense of conflicting results. All should agree, however, with Victor Groza, who observes, "For the most part, adoption has been a very successful social arrangement. . . . Most studies support the notion that adoption outcomes are overwhelmingly positive."[10]

However, we are aware that adopted children are particularly vulnerable to the stresses of adolescence. They frequently experience trauma related to separation from birth parents and other caretakers, early abuse and neglect, stressed attachment and lack of trust, identity confusion, transcultural assimilation (or lack of it), poor self-esteem, and struggles for control. The adoptive family can be equally stressed through disappointment, inappropriate guilt, unmet and/or unrealistic expectations for themselves as parents and for their child, helplessness, and lack of understanding of the child's grief and anger.

UNDERSTANDING THE ADOLESCENT BRAIN

Is it "hormones" that propel our adolescents into challenging circumstances? According to Dr. Daniel Siegel in *Brainstorm: The Power and Purpose of the Teenage Brain,* the answer is no. Although they of course, play a part of the equation, "we now know that the adolescent experience is primarily the result of changes in the development of the brain," says

Dr. Siegel.[11] He says that during this period of growth, the teen brain is actually experiencing a "remodeling" and describes it as important a time of development as the earlier first years. Those brain changes emerging during early adolescence, set up what Dr. Siegel calls "the **ESSENCE** of Adolescence":

ES – Emotional spark – An intense and enhanced vitality to life that often looks like impulsivity and moodiness, yet gives the adolescent a zest for being alive. There are upsides to this emotional spark, because we envy the energy and enthusiasm of youth. The downside, however, this emotional spark can lead to impulsive decisions and behavior.

SE – Social Engagement – A time in life where teens gravitate to peer relationships and new friends. This gravitating toward peers is such an important part of development for teens. Dr. Siegel notes that this distancing from parents is normal, but a total disconnection is not.

N – "Novelty-seeking emerges from an increased drive for rewards in the circuits of the adolescent brain that creates the inner motivation to try something new, take risks"[12] and live life with passion and pursuit. This is a part of teen development that causes parents most concern. Teens make decisions based on the "thrill quotient," not the safe quotient.

CE – Creative Exploration develops as conceptual thinking and abstract reasoning begin to emerge. This creates "a gateway to seeing the world through new lenses."[13]

Why is it important to have an understanding of what is driving teen behavior? If a parent understands the "remodeling process," this awareness will guide their own response to the teen's behavior. It helps them look for meaning in behavior instead of continually just responding to behavior. It will lead to better lines of communication between the teen and parent. Knowing about the "Essence of Adolescence" opens the door to critical understanding of what is actually going on in the life of a teen. How parents navigate those waters of their emerging young adult with the additional challenges of adoption, trauma and loss is crucial. Parents can choose to resist and push against their teen, or they can choose to journey alongside him.

COMMUNICATING WITH ADOLESCENTS—PARENTS MATTER

Many parents of teenagers find communication and conversation to be trying, at the very least. Some adolescent boys often grunt in monosyllables, seeming more unable to complete a sentence than they have been since they were two years old. Adolescent girls, while certainly able to talk for hours with their peers, find it impossible and exasperating to converse with parents, who "don't understand *anything*!"

Deborah Clark writes about communication with adolescents on a parent-to-parent forum. "It is during this period that communication seems to consist more of the slamming of doors, tears, sulks and angry outbursts than of actual rational talk. Parents and professionals know that this is the most difficult time for parents and children alike."[14]

Haim Ginott, who wrote *Between Parent and Teenager* remarks:

"Our only consolation (or perhaps half a consolation) is that here is a method to his madness. His behavior fits his developmental phase. The purpose of adolescence is to loosen personality. His personality is undergoing the required changes: From organization (childhood) through disorganization (adolescence) to reorganization (adulthood). Adolescence is a period of curative madness, in which every teenager has to remake his personality."[15] It is during this difficult period that parents need to understand their presence matters to their teen children, although at times it doesn't appear that way. When parents understand the dynamics of the Essence of Adolescence,[16] and with compassion understand the impact of every life trauma and loss on their teen, they will learn to respond to their teenagers from a relational perspective, not a behavioral one.

The following principles will assist any parent in communicating with adolescents.

Understand That There Is Meaning Behind the Behavior.

> Behavior is the language of children (and teens) who have lost their voice.[17]

For all of us, there is meaning behind the behavior; all behavior is purposeful. For adopted teens, struggling to find their voice in the midst of their circumstances, their behavior may be their only way to express a need. Unfortunately, parents can easily get caught in a negative spiral of only responding to behavior instead of the need.

Adoptive parents have often seen the attachment cycle in their preparation classes. Figure 12.1 looks at this in a different way. A teen has a need. The teen lets the parent know he has a need (arousal) that often looks like bad behavior. Parents can get caught in a negative reaction cycle to the behavior and totally miss the meaning behind the behavior.

Parents can find themselves driven by the rules of the household—or the failure to comply at the high cost of the relationship. Teen's behavior,

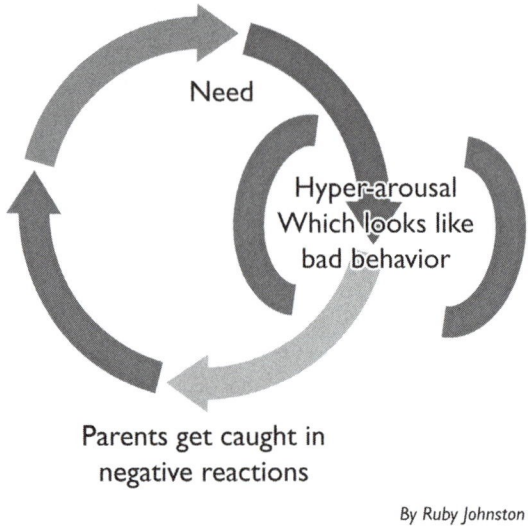

Figure 12.1

often tested by the challenge to a sense of connection we once felt, becomes like sandpaper, everything is irritating.[18]

R + R – R = R & R

Rules + Regulations – Relationship = Resentment and Rebellion[19]

The good news, according to Dr. Siegel is that this state of teen development does not have to set up a war between parents and teen. If parents focus on the rules and behavioral failure and forget the relationship, "disconnection, secrecy, isolation and many other negative and hurtful social responses can emerge."[20] Keeping communication open with a teen is vital, and the task of preserving the relationship must be of highest priority.

Choose Your Battles Wisely—You May Have to Lose Some Battles to Win the War.

A teenager's job description is to challenge authority, test values, and create their own credibility/competence, often by belittling that of their previously accepted experts: their parents. They will create conflict in the process of these endeavors, and the wise, secure adult knows when to engage in conflict and when to let it slide. If their "baiting" behavior does not endanger the youths or others, adults may wisely allow natural consequences of poor choices (if you don't turn in your homework, you have to attend summer school) serve as the most effective teachers. When adults are forced by circumstances to intervene with guidance and protection, they should cool off so that instruction and limits are not given in anger. It is hard to learn from someone who is enraged. Ginott cautions "wise parents know that fighting a teenager, like fighting a riptide, is inviting doom. When caught in [a] crosscurrent, expert swimmers stop struggling. They know that they cannot fight their way to shore. They float and let the tide carry them, until they find a firm footing. Likewise, parents of teenagers must flow with life, alert to opportunities for safe contact."[21]

Avoid Criticism—Focus on Positives.

Some parents make a career of criticizing their children, believing that such criticism will enable their teenagers to achieve a level of perfection that the parents were unable to accomplish themselves. "For their own good," they remind their teenagers of imperfections. It is natural for all parents to focus attention on behaviors that need to improve and ignore those that are acceptable. How many parents open a report card full of A's and B's, with one C–, and remark, "Why did you get that C–?" Any animal behaviorist can assure us that positive reward and praise are much more effective in shaping behavior than constant rebuke and punishment. If you want your teenager to talk with you, don't bombard him with "helpful" suggestions for improvement. Instead, look for opportunities to give him positive feedback, not only when he has done a perfect job, but also when he has improved over his last performance.

Encourage and Respect Independence—Allow Your Teenager to Make Some Mistakes Without Creating Dependency Through Parental Intervention.

Resist the temptation to "help" your teenager too often. The wise parent can tell the difference between a youth who is about to make an insignificant mistake that can be corrected easily and a youth who is about to plunge headlong into a disaster that cannot be remedied. Help should be available, but given only when really needed. Repeated "rescues" can become enabling for continued dysfunctional behavior. "Helicopter parents" who are always hovering to assure their teens don't ever make a mistake also assure their kids never learn to make a decision or develop effective problem-solving skills (other than calling Mom for help). Child psychologist Ginott explains:

> In adolescence, dependency creates hostility. Parents who foster dependence invite unavoidable resentment. Teenagers crave independence. The more self-sufficient we make them feel, the less hostile

> they are toward us. A wise parent makes himself increasingly dispensable to his teenagers. He sympathetically watches the drama of growth, but resists the desire to intervene too often.[22]

Respect the Teen's Privacy.

Teenagers begin to emancipate from their families years before they actually move out of the home. Teenagers accomplish this distancing behavior by drawing very firm, clear boundaries around their privacy. They place signs on their bedroom doors, informing siblings and parents that they are no longer welcome. They write poetry, make entries in diaries, and have long conversations with friends, all of which are inviolate from family intrusion. Teenagers may even resent casual, caring questions from concerned parents such as "How was school today?" as an intrusion into their privacy, their personhood. These boundaries are a normal part of adolescence and should be treated with reasonable respect, not interpreted by parents as indicators of rejection.

Keep Guidance Short and to the Point—Focus on the Present, Not the Past.

Parents communicating with teenagers should avoid the temptation to preach incessantly during long lectures about problem behaviors. In his book *The One Minute Manager*, Kenneth Blanchard recommends that supervisors in a work setting tell employees in one minute or less what they have done wrong and what needs to be done to correct the problem. Parents could learn much from this book about talking with teenagers about problematic behaviors. When approaching your adolescent about a behavior that needs to change, think about your willingness to talk about your own deficiencies for extended periods of time. Keep it brief and end the discussion with a positive expectation for improvement.

As in marital relationships, healthy communication depends on keeping the present problem in perspective. Avoid a tendency to bring up past "sins"—they will not add any power to your position. A focus on the past only makes you appear unreasonable and ridiculous, someone who can be much more easily ignored by a recalcitrant teen.

Don't Catastrophize or Label.

When children make poor choices, it can be a short leap for many parents to make dire predictions about their future: "You will never get into college." "You will never get a good job." "You will be living under the freeway overpass in a refrigerator box." While parents may experience many of these fears and firmly believe in the imminent realization of them, such anxiety almost always reflects a gross exaggeration, and the situation is never improved by sharing these viewpoints with the child. More appropriate messages that will help teens improve their behavior and learn to be self-sufficient are: "That was a mistake. I know you will do better next time." "Let me know if I can help you solve this problem. We may be able to talk it through together and come up with a solution that makes sense." These messages keep the focus on the problem (and its solution) and don't label the child as a failure.

Don't Overreact.

"Although it's tempting to blurt out they're grounded for life when they've done something outrageous, sometimes it's best to take a moment to cool down. Overreacting tells your teen not to come to you when they have a problem because they fear your anger or unfair punishment."[23] Talk with your parenting partner, an understanding grandparent, or a friend with children of a similar age. They may be able to help you see your parenting problem from a new perspective.

Don't Minimize the Teenager's Pain.

Adolescents experience life in extremes. Daily life for them is a roller-coaster ride of the highest highs and the lowest lows. When they are in pain, the pain is extreme. While parents with greater experience and maturity recognize that sibling squabbles, invasions of privacy, slights from friends, disappointments, or rejections from the current "significant other" are not as life altering as they seem to the adolescent, parents can provide significant support and can enhance communication through *reflective listening*, a technique of listening intently to another's story or problem and responding only with a summary of the situation and the reflected feelings. Solutions to, or evaluations of, the problem (or, even worse, a denial of the problem) are *not* offered. The following interchange is an example of reflective listening:

> *Teen*: I hate Stacy!! I told her a secret, and she blabbed it to everyone else! I can't ever go to school again. Everyone there thinks I am an idiot.
>
> *Parent*: You must be angry and embarrassed that Stacy did not keep your confidence. It's really disappointing when someone lets you down.

Adoptive parents should become particularly adept at the skill of reflective listening. Adopted teens need empathy about feelings related to adoption and can rarely find it among their non-adopted friends. Adoptive parents should allow children to express their feelings of rage or grief and respond only with understanding and support, without judgment by either their parents or themselves. They are entitled to their feelings, and their experience of the adoption is real to them, regardless of whether his perceptions match those of the adoptive parents. Reflective listening is not an easy art because we want to "fix" the pain felt by people we love.

Timing Is Everything.

When limits must be set or parental "correction" is required, the timing of the correction is critical to its success. Remember that the role of the parent is to teach independence, and the function of discipline is in teaching, not in punishment. When emotions run strong in either the teenager or the parent, conditions for a teachable moment are hardly optimal. When teens are overwhelmed with difficulties, they are not open to learning. When parents are enraged or panic stricken, they cannot serve as teachers and mentors. Sometimes, the most important part of communication is the ability to defer discussion until everyone is rational. The most mature comment to the teenager who finally comes home two hours after his midnight curfew to face a worried, sleep-deprived and angry parent might be: "I am too worried, exhausted, and upset to talk about this now. In the morning, we will talk about the consequences of your lack of consideration for me and your lack of respect for family rules. Right now, we are all going to bed."

HOW TO TALK ABOUT ADOPTION WITH AN ADOLESCENT

As adoption adds a layer of complexity to the tasks of adolescence, it adds a similar layer of complexity to parenting a teen. The adoptive parent has more sensitive information to communicate and needs an even higher level of skill to keep communication open and productive.

Share Full History Prior to Adolescence.

Again, timing is important in communication. If teenagers are adopted, they need all the facts about their history *before* they enter adolescence. Parents can withhold some facts for a time until children are sophisticated enough to hear them (see Chapters 7 and 8), but too long a delay in withholding information erodes trust and sets up teenagers for self-destructive fantasies.

Assist Teens in an Information Search.

Adolescents struggling with identity formation may need to revisit either the agency that facilitated the placement or their country of origin, if the adoption was international, to get as many facts about their history as possible. Sometimes, these interviews or trips can do little more than assure the teenager that information is really not available and that the adoptive parents are not withholding information.

Assess the Need for More Openness in the Adoption Relationship.

Some teens may need more openness in their adoptions as they become more mature. They may wish to correspond, without identifying information, through an agency intermediary, with their birth family members. They may benefit from asking directly for answers to their questions. Some teens may need to see pictures of their birth parents and/or siblings so that they can see someone who looks like them. And some teens may need to meet their birth parents to ask questions, be sure that birth parents or siblings are safe, and express their feelings directly about the adoption. Decisions about opening the adoption should be made with the help of a post-adoption counselor and should be made slowly. Chapter 13 addresses how to manage openness communication for both young children and adolescents. Today's teens are adept at using social media; in the absence of parental communication about adoption, they may decide to open a closed adoption through the use of media such as Facebook.

Don't Overreact to Overacting.

Remember that adolescence is a time of high drama, and the "players" (adolescents) frequently overact, making extremist statements. The "directors" (parents) must not overreact to these histrionics, and they must learn to translate the extremist language into dialogue that makes sense. It is much easier for parents to respond appropriately to hurtful comments made by their adopted teens if they understand that all teenagers are very dramatic, and that much of this drama masks feelings of rejection and fear of future abandonment (remember *defensive detachment*). Table 12.1 includes some common examples of statements made by adopted adolescents (with appropriate translations).

Table 12.1.

Dramatic Overacting	Possible Translation
I hate you! I wish you had never adopted me!	Are you going to keep me, no matter what?
I want to go live with my birth family.	I want more information about my birth family. Can you help me find out more?
I can't wait until I'm eighteen. I am out of here as soon as I am old enough!	I am afraid to leave home. Does adoption end when I turn eighteen? If I leave, can I come back?
I don't want to talk about adoption. Why do you always bring that up? I never even think about it!	I need to know if you love me as much as a child who was born into this family. I'm afraid you don't love me, and neither does anyone else, including my birth family.
You can't tell me what to do! You're not even my real mother!	Are you really my mother?

Adoptive parents must learn to respond to the translations, the "real" dialogue beneath the words used by an angry adolescent. Note that the teen's dramatic assertions are really questions that express a need for reassurance and security.

Honor Their Roots to Enhance Their Self-Esteem.

Remember that one's need to feel good about one's identity is based largely on one's roots and heritage. Help adopted teens to discover the positives in their history as well as the negative aspects that may have led to their separation from the birth family.

Recognize Teens' Fantasies, but Tell the Truth.

When your teens share with you a belief about their history that you know to be untrue, ask them where and how they got their information. Their beliefs may be embedded in a cloudy memory or may have no basis other than their wish for a history that is more dramatic and appealing than the real one. Offer to share the information the agency has already given you, or ask if the teenagers would like to begin an information search with your assistance. Adolescents needs to have an accurate history, but need to get this information gently and with parental support.

Help Teens Construct a Realistic Vision of Their Adoption If Facts Are Unavailable.

If adoptive parents don't know all the facts and cannot get answers due to the nature of the circumstances around the adoption, look for "most likely scenarios" to share with the teenager. That is, if children are abandoned or come from a country that collects limited social history from the birth family, try to get information about the situation in that country or at the period of history surrounding their separation from the birth family. Children needs assistance in building a "fantasy" that is as close to the reality of their adoption as possible.

Use Support Groups for Adopted Youth as a Springboard to Assist Teens in Talking about Adoption.

Remember that adopted youth often have difficulty talking about adoption with their parents. They may assume that the adoptive parents will be hurt if they know how much the child thinks about the birth family. Support groups for adopted youth can be an extremely helpful tool, as teenagers will talk and listen to other kids when they will not communicate openly with adults. Further, teenagers do not like to be different, and they may not have access to other adopted teens within their peer group at school. Finding a group of kids with similar life experiences helps in making the adopted teen feel less like an outsider.

PARENTING STRATEGIES FOR THE ADOPTED ADOLESCENT

Develop a Short List of Non-Negotiable Rules.

Just as adoptive parents need to choose their battles, they also need to prioritize rules. That is, adoptive parents should think about what is most valued in the family and develop a small number of inviolate rules that support those values and principles. Examples are: "We value education. Therefore, in our family, the rule is that you must go to school until you graduate from something." "We value your safety. Therefore, in our family, all members must inform the family where they are at all times and when they are expected home. If your plans change, you must call home to inform us of the change. Between the ages of 16 and 18, you have a 12:30 P.M. curfew on the weekend and a 10:30 P.M. curfew on weeknights." Parents should keep rules to a minimum (three to five is a reasonable number) but let teens know that the few rules that do exist are *not* negotiable. Consequences for violation of these rules should be predetermined and automatic (again, *no* negotiation).

Beyond the Nonnegotiable Rules, Allow Teens to Exercise Control and Decision Making Whenever Reasonable.

Adopted children and youth often struggle with issues of control, as significant decisions regarding their lives have been left to birth and adoptive parents, social workers, judges, government bureaucrats, and so on. Adoptive parents should allow their older adopted children to exercise as much control as possible. Adopted teens can exercise control when given freedom to make choices within guidelines provided by the parents. Demanding compliance with parental time frames, dress codes, standards of academic performance, and so on only creates conflict and reduces the likelihood of appropriate behaviors.

Don't Personalize Teens' Anger.

Adoptive parents should try to understand that their children's anger is directed toward the separation from the birth family and is not aimed at them. Children may express rage toward the adoptive parents because they are available and because they are "safe" targets. Human nature compels us to feel anger when confronted with the anger of others, and parents may be tempted to respond with more anger to the rage felt by adopted teens due to grief, loss of control and trust, and fear of future abandonment. The wise adoptive parent must be able to withdraw from teens' angry outbursts, physically and/or emotionally. These outbursts must become tornados that parents learn to sidestep, allowing them to pass by and dissipate. Adoptive parents cannot allow their teen to create havoc within the family by accepting the adoption-related rage personally and responding in kind.

Remember Teens' Need to Be Different from the Adoptive Family.

The need for teens to create an identity separate from that of the adoptive family will likely be stronger than the need for individuation among non-adopted children. Don't panic if teens experiment with identities that are similar to those of the birth family. Modeling after the birth family is normal and to be expected; don't begin to catastrophize and predict that the child "will wind up in prison like his father or pregnant at age 14 like her mother."

Be Alert for Signs of Distress in the Child Following Losses and Transitions.

Adolescence is a time of tremendous change. School transitions occur as the child moves into middle school, on to high school, and perhaps even on to college or emancipation. All of these transitions can prove particularly difficult for a teenager who has experienced little permanency or security. Furthermore, adolescence can bring many real or imagined rejections (abandonments): a boy is dumped by his girlfriend, a girl is not accepted into the most popular clique at school, a boy or girl does not make the team. These rejections can be devastating to young people who already believe that they are not worthy of love because their own birth parents could not or would not keep (love) them. Adoptive parents must be aware of the intense impact of these blows to their self-esteem and must *initiate* conversation and show support for shaken youth. When such rejections occur, youth need to feel the unconditional support and love of their parents. Greg Louganis, the Olympic diving champion and adoptee, once commented that he used to get very nervous before a dive until he remembered, "No matter how I dive, I know my mom will always love me."

Be Sensitive to the Adopted Child's Challenge with Intimacy.

Adolescence is a time when many young people have their first serious romantic involvements. "*Adopted teens* may think a lot about their birth parents as they begin to explore romantic relationships, although some of this may be at a subconscious level . . . . If their past relationships were inconsistent or abusive, some adolescents (whether adopted or not) will have difficulty trusting others. Some will use sexual activity to ease painful memories or to fill feelings of emptiness."[24]

Parents of adolescents should have frank conversations about healthy and respectful relationships, appropriate boundaries, family and cultural values around sexual activity, and information regarding safe sex and contraception.

Prepare for Search and Reunion.

Many adopted youth begin thinking about searching for birth relatives, and with the help of social media, some may even begin an active search during their teen years. The wise adoptive parent will include as part of his ongoing adoption communication questions about how the young person feels about finding or reconnecting with birth family members. Perhaps youth need additional information from their parents or from the placing agency. Open communication regarding search issues may help adoptive parents remain "in the loop," thereby avoiding unexpected contacts with birth family members. Talking about search within the adoptive family, as well as perhaps finding post-adoption services to explore questions about adoption, help youth have a compassionate sounding board to consider the pros and cons of such an endeavor.

Maintain Your Commitment.

Perhaps the most significant thing adoptive parents offer their children is maintenance of commitment and permanency. Children and teens can be angry, too preoccupied with adoption issues to achieve success in school, too afraid of failure to achieve success in sports or other endeavors. They may experiment with bizarre identities or even proclaim their strong desire to leave the adoptive family. The steady, enduring commitment of parents to children and adoption can yield unimaginable healing during the turbulent years of adolescence. Remember that adolescence is chronic, but not terminal, both for you and your children.

CONCLUSION

Adolescence can be a difficult time for any family. Having an adolescent in the family creates a period of imbalance for all family members, not just for the adolescent whose identity is emerging. Many parents with adult children assure us that nothing challenged them to grow more as individuals and as parents than mentoring their child during adolescence. While navigating the turbulent waters of parenting teens, it is easy to forget that there is, indeed, light at the end of the tunnel . . . that adolescence is, fortunately, time limited. The reward in survival as the parent of an adolescent (and very happily, the vast majority do) is that survivors will experience one of the greatest joys of the life span: watching your child blossom into a young adult. The surprises and joys that accompany this blossoming are well worth the struggles necessary to the "pruning" and "shaping."

QUESTIONS

1. What questions has your teenager asked about her adoption? Birth family?
2. Do you sense that your teens might be asking in nonverbal ways for more information about their history? In what ways do your teens "act out" the need to know more?
3. Do you feel you need additional information to respond appropriately to your teens' need for information? If so, what plan do you have

to get that information? How can you involve your teens or young adults in getting it?

4. What have you communicated well with your teens regarding their history? Where would you like to improve?
5. What are three ways you can improve communication with your adolescents?

CHAPTER 13

Managing Communication with Openness in Adoption: Questions Most Asked by Parents

In the last two decades, adoptive relationships have changed. Many adoptions, even those within the child welfare system share some degree of openness. A national study of adoptive families in the United States found that in approximately one-third of all adoptive families, the adoptive parents or the adopted child or youth had some contact with the birth family after the adoption. Post adoption contact occurred more often in private domestic adoption (68%) as compared with adoption from foster care (39%) and international adoption (6%). A more recent study among U.S. adoption agencies reported that almost all (95%) of their domestic infant adoptions were open.[1]

Even the definition of those impacted by adoption has evolved. The meaning of what was once called the *adoption triad*, (child, birth parents, and adoptive parents) has evolved into a something that encompasses much more. Author Michael Grand first coined the phrase adoption constellation in 1994 to broaden our understanding of who is affected by adoption and thus affected by openness relationships. The term *adoption constellation* "allows for the consideration of adoptees, birth parents and adoptive parents, but also incorporates birth and adoptive extended families, service providers, teachers, physicians, the courts, social service workers, legislators and the clergy. In fact, anyone whose life is entwined with adoption is a member of the constellation."[2] Openness relationships do impact many people. In this chapter, we are going to look at what openness adoption is. What is meant by open adoption? How does a parent decide what type of openness would work within the family? We are going to examine what makes a healthy openness adoption relationship and key principles that should go into forming that relationship. Finally, we are going to then look at the most asked questions in opening a closed adoption and how to manage challenges once the adoption is open.

UNDERSTANDING THE CONTINUUM OF COMMUNICATION

Managing openness communication can be challenging for adoptive families. It is important that parents clearly understand the different degrees of openness possible within adoptive relationships:

What Closed Adoption Means

No identifying information is shared between the birth family and the adoptive family. This is also called *confidential* or *traditional* adoption. Information may be given to the agency to update the records, but is not intended for transmission to either party.

What Openness in Adoption Means

Openness in adoption refers to a continuum of openness within relationships that may exist between members of the birth family and the adoptive family of a child. Openness may include knowledge about the "other" family of the child, the birth parent's selection of an adoptive family for the child, contact through a third party, or ongoing visitation. The relationships may exist among the child, the adoptive family, and the birth parents, or among the child, the adoptive parents and birth siblings, and the grandparents, other relatives, or kinship figures (including former foster parents).

What Open Adoption Means

Open adoption means that everyone involved in the process, whether adoptive or birth parent, is open to meeting and talking with each other both prior to and subsequent to the placement. How much communication and contact will occur is impossible to say. But in an open adoption, the assumption exists that there will be as much communication as possible within the limits of courage, compassion, and common sense.[3]

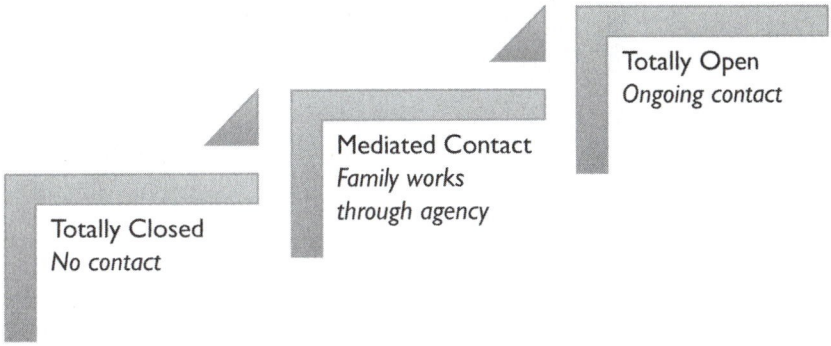

Figure 13.1 Continuum of Contact *(examples of each in text)*

Totally Closed: No Contact

John, a three-year-old child, is placed with his adoptive family. Only non-identifying social/medical information is given to the family. The adoptive family plans no contact with the birth family.

Mediated Contact—Family Works through Agency

Cassie is eight years old. She has a lot of questions that her adoptive parents cannot answer. When she joined her adoptive family as a one-year-old, they were given very little information. Her adoptive family contacts the agency to ask social workers to work with the birth family in exchanging information, pictures, and so on. The social worker will serve as an intermediary at the present time. No last names are exchanged.

Totally Open

Betsy and Kenneth are 10-year-old twins. Victims of child abuse, they were adopted at age four from the local protective services agency. They have had no contact with their birth family since that time, although the families had contact with each other when the children were in foster care. Each family knows the names of the other. About six months ago, the adoptive family received word that the abuser (their father) had died and their birth mother has stabilized. Their agency worker felt that the mother had a clear understanding why she would never be able to parent her children. The family begins writing letters to her and will eventually plan for phone calls. Within a year, they hope the children can visit with their birth mother.

MAKING A DECISION REGARDING OPENNESS

How does a family choose an appropriate level of openness? In an article entitled "Openness in Adoption: Building Relationships Between Adoptive and Birth Families," the authors suggest:[4]

> In exploring open adoption, it is important to thoroughly consider what is best for your child and family and to think not just about current needs and preferences but also those that may emerge in the future. For an adoption to be truly open, the relationship with the birth family must be shared with the adopted child. As such, an adoptive parent must consider how and when this relationship will be shared with the child or youth and how it may change as the child gets older. Some of the questions that adoptive parents may want to consider include:
>
> - What would contact between our family and our child's birth family mean to our child?
> - Do I want my child to know about his or her family background and related information?
> - What forms of communication (letters, emails, videos, Facebook, phone calls, visits) am I comfortable with?
> - At what age should our child be included in contact with his or her birth family?
> - What role will our child's birth parents (and/or other birth relatives) play in our child's life?
> - How will openness with one child's birth family affect adopted siblings who have different levels of openness in their adoptions?
> - How will we react if we choose a closed adoption and our child and birth parents later establish contact through social media or other avenues?[5]

MANAGING COMMUNICATION

Often in the practice of open adoption, the research has explored the family structure of openness. Questions like "What has been the family's level of satisfaction with openness?" or "How often do the two families communicate?" or "What does that communication look like?" have dominated the research. However, Dr. David Brodzinsky and Dr. James Gritter suggest that, before there can be a *healthy family structure of openness,* the deeper issues of openness in adoption communication must be addressed.

When discussing openness in adoption, Dr. Gritter views it from a much broader perspective. Openness in adoption reflects the attitudes, emotions, and expectations of all those touched by the adoption experience. Gritter explains adoption communication is not just about the content—the dissemination of information—but it is about "the sharing and supporting of adoption-related emotions both within the adoptive family and between the adoptive and birth families." It has much more to do with how all the parties touched by the adoption experience manage intrapersonal emotions, and interpersonal emotions, rather than a specific type of family or systemic structure. Its emphasis is on the adoption communication process, both informational and emotional with the individual, between adoptive family members, and for those involved in a structurally open arrangement, between members of the two family systems.[6] The two examples that follow help to illustrate both open communication and openness in adoption.

Micah's Experience in Openness in Adoption

Micah, a handsome, sensitive 12-year-old joined his family as an infant. Much is known about his birth parents and his extended birth family. Before Micah was born, his adoptive parents met his birth mother and birth father and the extended family members of both. They exchanged identifying information and unique family highlights, and they set up a plan for contact.

Over the years, Micah has grown up visiting his birth family members three times a year. He always receives birthday cards from both sets of birth grandparents, as well as gifts on special occasions. He sees them usually over the Christmas holidays each year. If one would ask Micah who he looks like, he readily responds, "My birth dad! And we even like the same sports team."

Although Micah has experienced a very open adoption, it has not been the ideal arrangement. On the outside, it looks beneficial for Micah, but there are struggles within that relationship. His adoptive parents kept their promise for an open adoption but admit that "we felt pressured to do it in the first place. If we didn't agree, Micah's birth mother would never have selected us as parents for Micah." They kept the promised contacts, but when Micah returns from visits, they do not talk to him about his birth family or his thoughts and feelings about the activities they shared. Whenever he raises a question about his adoption experience, his parents change the subject or provide some superficial response. They are not emotionally attuned to his needs.

"Because I don't really know how my parents feel about my contact with my birth family, I never talk about it. I am frustrated about their silence, and I can only talk about this stuff with my closest friend."

Elizabeth's Experience in Openness in Adoption

Beautiful, articulate, bubbly 10-year-old Elizabeth smiles widely as she talks about her relationship with her adoptive and birth parents. Elizabeth has known only complete openness in adoption—not only physical openness, but emotional openness as well. Elizabeth's parents, David and Ann, made a conscious decision while pursuing adoption that the birth family had to be open to contact. "We knew it would be a road less traveled as many families maintain a distance from their child's birth family," said Ann, "but it has been the best decision we made right after adopting Elizabeth."

What they created with Elizabeth's birth parents, Bob and Kelley, is just what they desired—complete openness. Elizabeth has grown up in an environment where she can freely express her needs and feelings regarding her birth dad and birth mom to her parents.

Elizabeth visits her birth family members usually twice a year. "She initiates the need for the visit," said Ann, "and with our busy schedules, it usually takes a month to get it all coordinated."

Is this openness arrangement beneficial? The answer is a resounding yes from David, Ann, and Elizabeth.

"One of the greatest factors for me," commented David, "is the confidence I have in talking to Elizabeth about adoption. There are no secrets. Also, I know from our times together with the birth parents, who Elizabeth really perceives to be her parents. She calls her birth parents by their first names, and we are Dad and Mom in every way. I don't know if I would have the confidence that this was true in a closed adoption experience."

For Ann, a great benefit is that Elizabeth sees who she looks like, whose likes and dislikes she has, whose talents she has. She not only knows her birth parents, but her birth grandparents on both sides and a great-grandparent as well.

Elizabeth, although only 10 years old, can articulate what openness means to her. "I feel a sense of connection to Bob and Kelley when I see them. I know what they look like. I can talk to them. I know I can trust what they say to me."

These two examples give a clear illustration of openness: the first has no healthy family communication about the relationship or adoption, while the second has openness with open family communication. Before any suggestion of openness arrangements with the birth family can be considered, the foundation for a psychologically well-adjusted adoptive child is "the creation of an open, honest, non-defensive and emotionally attuned family dialogue not only about adoption issues, but any issue that impacts the child."[7]

Key Principles in Building a Healthy Openness Relationship with Birth Family Members

For any relationship to be and continue to be healthy, it takes each person to be intentional about it. Here are some key principles that can keep an open adoption agreement continuing, even through the challenges that will come.

- Stay focused on what is in the best interests of the child, which may not always be the same as the preferences of the birth and adoptive parents.
- Show respect for and acceptance of the other family members.
- Set clear boundaries of what is and what is not acceptable in terms of contact and communication, and respect the limits requested by the other parties.
- Maintain open communication that reflects a genuine commitment to maintaining connection.
- Be flexible and recognize that needs may change over time.[8]

OPENNESS IN ADOPTION: QUESTIONS AND ANSWERS

One of the critical questions asked by adoptive parents around the lifelong impact of adoption and openness is this: Will children growing up in an open adoption face the issues of adoption such as loss, identity, trust, and so on, found in those who grew up in closed adoption?

Developing some level of openness and contact with the birth family does not erase the pain adopted children sometimes experience in relation to issues of loss, rejection, abandonment, shame, or guilt. What it does do for the child and his adoptive parents, according to Roszia, is move the work to the front end of the child's life, instead of waiting until the time of search and reunion. "It is short-term pain for long-term gain," Roszia asserts.

Abby's Story

Abby just turned 16. She is the daughter of Don and Martha Kammer and the younger sister of Elizabeth. The Kammers live in central Idaho. Abby is bright, inquisitive, and her parents' joy. She is quite the typical adolescent, interested in dancing, talking on the phone, gymnastics, talking on the phone, getting her hair to look just right, and talking on the phone.

Abby entered her adoptive home at the age of four months. Martha and Don first met her when they visited the foster home where Abby lived and felt an immediate connection. Abby is biracial. Her birth mother is Caucasian. Her birth father is African American. Throughout Abby's life, the Kammers have been open and honest about Abby's racial, cultural, and social history.

The family's journey into openness in adoption began when Abby was three and a half years old. They made the decision to begin contact with her birth mother. Opening the closed adoption has indeed been a journey, a process. The following scenarios walk through different seasons in Abby's open adoption experience. By observing Abby, her adoptive parents, and her birth mother, other adoptive parents can gain a perspective on the issues and concerns that arise. They can also recognize the opportunity some level of openness affords in creating an atmosphere of open and honest communication around the issues of adoption.

Abby: At Age Four

Event: Bubbly, energetic Abby is excited. Today is her birthday. She will finally be four. Also, something else is about to happen. Today, her birth mother, Allison, will be coming to her party. Abby has heard of Allison all of her young life. Abby has talked with Allison on the phone, and now she is coming in person.

The day goes exactly as planned. Allison, rather nervous and shy, comes in quietly and gives Abby a hug. She stays long enough to have cake and ice cream and then slips out. The next day, Allison stops by the house to ask a question. "May I take Abby out to lunch at McDonald's by myself?" Martha, Abby's adoptive mother, responds, "Let me think about it. Give me a call on Friday morning."

After Allison leaves, Abby approaches her mother. She has overheard Allison's request. She quietly asks her mother, "If I go to McDonald's with Allison, can you and Beth [Abby's older sister] come, too?"

What might be Abby's anticipated feelings? Abby, at four, does have a budding understanding about adoption. Why? Because it is concrete. Allison is there in person, and they meet. Abby can understand that Allison is her birth mother. Her hesitation about going with Allison, however, is probably more a developmental issue than an adoption issue. Very few children her age would go with a stranger—even to McDonald's. Other feelings or questions might be sprouting in her mind, but at four, she may not be able to verbalize them. These questions, related to her racial and cultural heritage, may arise because Abby may recognize and acknowledge:

- Her birth mother is not the same color as she is.
- Her birth mother and her adoptive mother are the same color.
- Her birth mother may talk and act very differently than her adoptive family, and those differences make talking to her awkward and difficult.

Abby: At Age Nine

Event: Allison, Abby's birth mother, has been part of her life now for over five years. Abby sees her about once a month. On this particular occasion, the whole family is camping, and Allison is invited out to the campsite for dinner. After dinner, Allison and Abby take a walk around the campground. During the walk, Abby asks her birth mother a question. "Allison," she says, "why did you give me away?" Allison responds, "Abby, no one can just give a child away. There were a lot of things wrong in my life at that time." "I know, that is what my mom told me," Abby counters. "But why did you give me away?" What might be Abby's anticipated feelings?

By the time many adopted children reach the age of nine, they have moved developmentally in their thinking to conclude that their adoption means that they were given away. Children who experience openness in adoption encounter many of the same feelings. Abby is dealing with issues of rejection at an early stage. The benefit of now having openness is that Abby can direct that question to the person who is the best one to answer it—her birth mother. Other feelings or questions simultaneously developing in her thinking are connected to her racial and cultural background. These lingering questions, which she can now verbalize, may arise because she is able to:

- Recognize her different racial identity
- Wonder if she was "given away" because she does not look like her birth mother.

Abby: At Age 12

Event: Beth, Allison, and Abby enjoy doing things together occasionally. Allison has been part of Abby's life for eight years. On this particular evening, the three of them have just returned from the movies. When they reach home, Beth jumps out of the car and scoots into the house. Abby lingers a few moments. "Allison, I need to ask you a question. Is my birth father black? When can I meet him? Does he want to see me? Why doesn't he ever call? Who else in your family is black?"

Allison has avoided any reference to, or conversation about, Abby's birth father. She has been dreading the moment this question would come up because she will have to tell Abby that her birth father died. Allison never shared that piece of information with Abby's adoptive parents. "Yes, Abby, your birth father was black. He came from a big family with lots of brothers and sisters. They don't live around here. The reason that he doesn't call is that he died a few years ago."

Abby grows quiet and opens the door to get out of the car. "Oh," she whispers. "1 just wanted to see someone I looked like." Abby never tells her mother about this conversation. Allison mentions it a few days later, in a casual conversation with Martha, Abby's adoptive mom. What might be Abby's anticipated feelings?

As Abby matures, questions related to the pain of adoption continue to emerge. She is feeling a sense of loss related to the fact that she doesn't know anyone that looks like her. The birth father, now dead, was never a memory for her. She perhaps is also struggling with rejection from her absent birth father as well as budding issues of identity development. A curious issue is the fact that she asked her birth mother a question even though she has grown up knowing the answer: "Is my birth father black?" This feeling is possibly related to trust; Abby is just checking to see if the story her parents told her was the truth.

Questions connected to her racial and cultural background are far more obvious. They emerge because:

- She is entering a normal stage of identity development, which for her includes her racial and ethnic identity.
- She is perhaps struggling to integrate her black and white identities—she doesn't look like anyone in her birth mother's or adoptive family.
- She may be subjected to teasing at school or in the neighborhood because she is biracial.
- She may perceive that she was "given away" because she is "different."

The fact that Abby now experiences a level of openness in her adoption doesn't erase questions and feelings. It moves them to the front end of her life, where she and her parents can deal with them openly and concretely.[9]

A second major question often voiced by adoptive parents is this: What happens if, after living within an open adoption relationship, the birth family backs away? Won't the child face another layer of rejection?

- **In a perfect world, this wouldn't be an issue; it wouldn't happen. However, we do not live in a perfect world. Parents can use this painful opportunity to talk about the feelings birth families may encounter when facing the issues of opening up an adoption.**
- Birth parents may have trouble dealing with their feelings around the adoption, especially when the adoption occurs as a result of involuntary surrender through the public system. There still may be a lot of blame directed at the agency, and responsibility for the birth parents' part in the circumstance is denied.
- Members of the birth family may not support opening the adoption. The birth parents would have little or no support for opening the adoption when discouraged from doing so by relatives.
- Birth parents may find questions from the child too difficult and too painful to answer. It would be much easier to avoid the relationship altogether than to try and work through the varied emotions encountered by all parties.
- The sense of guilt for "failing" one's child may be too overwhelming to process.
- Not continuing the relationship would help the birth parents to put the guilt on a back burner.

We have spent the first portion of this chapter looking at adoption from the lens of openness. We are now going to explore the challenges of opening a closed adoption after finalization through questions asked by many adoptive parents.

OPENING A CLOSED ADOPTION: QUESTIONS AND ANSWERS

QUESTION 1: How do I know my child is ready?

When a family decides to open a closed adoption, managing openness communication issues may surface later. For Sharon Kaplan Roszia, an expert in the field of adoption, the question isn't simply about the child. "When assessing readiness to open an adoption, the question is not about the child's readiness, but the readiness of the adoptive parents," Roszia asserts. "Children take their cues from their parents. When the parents think it is a good idea to grow up knowing all of life's connections, most children will follow suit. In my opinion, the earlier those connections are made, the better for the child."[10]

QUESTION 2: My child has asked to make contact for a number of years, and we are finally doing it. How can we address his expectations and concerns?

Adults who have searched for their birth parents often have high expectations for the experience. Some youngsters hoping to have contact with birth parents share those high expectations. When a closed adoption is opened, communication challenges require that the adoptive parents gently and wisely address the child's expectations. The following questions can be used to explore your child's expectations.

1. How do you expect that you will feel when you hear from your birth mother (or father) the first time?
2. How do you expect that you will feel when you see your birth mother (or father) for the first time?
3. What do you expect your birth mother (or father) to say to you?
4. What do you expect will happen in the future with them? Do you expect to see them regularly? Never see them again?
5. What do you want to ask him/her?
6. Who do you want to be there when you meet her/him the first time?
7. Where do you want to meet her/him the first time?
8. How do you think you are going to feel after meeting her/him?

QUESTION 3: Are a parent's fears and apprehensions a normal part of the process?

Yes, opening a closed adoption can be a fearful, uncertain step for families. "Adoptive parents do have fears related to opening an adoption," Roszia states. "One fear comes when birth fathers who were out of the picture suddenly reach out for contact. The adoptive parents remember the terrible things they heard about the father and want nothing to do with him. They are left with remnants of an old image. What I tell my families is that they must update the image. Engage in honest conversation with those who know him and if possible with the birth father himself. Make a decision as to what level of openness is appropriate for the child after this."[11]

QUESTION 4: What if the updated story of the birth mother or birth father is no different from before?

People can change, but sometimes they don't. Even if the circumstances of the birth father or birth mother remain the same as at the time of the adoption, Roszia suggests that adoptive parents generally have new tools to deal with some degree of openness. "Adoptive parents have themselves grown and have come to a better understanding of people: why addictions happen, or even how to deal with mental illness. They find themselves better equipped to talk with their child, who is now older and [to] help the child with understanding and expectations for the birth family contact. Life experiences and maturity generally provide those new tools of managing birth family issues and contacts."[12]

QUESTION 5: Once the birth and adoptive families have been involved in an ongoing relationship, what other concerns do adoptive families express?

Another concern parents have for opening the adoption is the influence of the birth family on the child. As Roszia points out, "There may be a vast difference in lifestyle and values that will conflict with those of the adoptive family. Families must keep lines of communication open-not in a judgmental sense, but as an opportunity for the child to see and express the differences he witnesses."

Not only is the influence of the birth family a question for the adoptive parents, but the child may be confused by lifestyle differences her two families. Roszia comments that, if there is some level of contact with the birth family, the child in the adoptive home may experience sadness or survivor's guilt when in contact with siblings in less desirable circumstances.

Working with an old image, fearing influence, and worrying about guilt are three matters that confront adoptive parents. Roszia cites one more: "The bottom line for many adoptive parents in hesitation about any level of openness, especially in older child adoptions, is the fear there will be damage to their child's relationship with them. They fear that the child will feel less a part of the family and that they will feel less a parent."[13]

In their excellent book, *The Open Adoption Experience*, Lois Melina and Sharon Kaplan Roszia point out significant gains rather than losses for the adoptive parent and child relationship:

- "For some children, having contact with the birth parent forces them to confront extremely painful events they experienced at their birth family's hands." By facing those issues, fantasies are dispelled, grief work begins, and the child eventually is able to move on in forming other significant relationships.

- After removal from the traumatic experiences in the birth home, children can more easily move to a level of forgiveness for their birth parents. Once that happens, they can also see good things about them. With some level of contact, children often are able to see ways they are different from their birth families. The understanding that their lives are changed for the better frees them to make more positive choices.
- Resisting attachment to a family for a child adopted at an older age can create a powerful block to positive relationships or attachment in the adoptive home. One reason for that resistance is the loyalty they feel compelled to keep for their birth parents. When parents encourage some level of contact, even if it is very occasional, and even if it is just a letter, children receive the message that it is still okay to love their birth parents-that they can learn to love both sets of parents.[14]

QUESTION 6: What are some questions that parents can explore to assess where they are emotionally in this process?

Some of the following questions will guide parents in talking about openness with a trusted, supportive friend. These will help parents assess their own expectations and worries for opening up their child's closed adoption.

1. What are my objectives for my child in opening up this adoption?
2. What are my worries about contacting this birth parent?
3. What are my expectations for this relationship?
4. Do I have the ability to perceive the needs of my child in order to set boundaries for the birth parent?
5. Do I have the ability as the adoptive parent to assess the capacity of the birth-family members to respect boundaries?
6. Do I have the ability to set boundaries?
7. Do I have a supportive, objective person to help guide us through this?
8. Do I have the ability as the adoptive parent to maintain a sense of entitlement, even though the birth family is involved?[15]

QUESTION 7: What about internationally adopted children? What options are available to them? How should this subject be approached?

Susan Soonkeum Cox, Vice President of Public Policy and External Affairs for Holt International Children Services, feels strongly that opening up an adoption for an internationally adopted child can be very difficult emotionally for that child. The reality of search and reunion (opening a closed adoption) is extremely complex and intense. Many international adult adoptees who have searched believe search is generally positive and the right of every adoptee. Yet those who search should be emotionally mature and prepared. The feelings and emotions experienced during the search process are so powerful, complicated, and overwhelming, they can be difficult to understand and process.[16]

What issues make opening a closed international adoption far more complex than domestic adoption? Cox cites two:

1. *Language:* Every communication must go through a translator. There is always a filter. Countries where international search is taking place do not share English as a first language. It is necessary to locate a resource who can translate communications and is also competent in sometimes reading between the lines of answers that are given, or perhaps withheld. Finding someone sympathetic to the objective of search, who does not have their own political or ideological agenda, and can objectively present information and facts is critical.
2. *Culture:* There is a huge cultural component when communicating with the birth family of another culture. People in different cultures do not process things in the same way. People in different cultures do not express feelings and emotions the same way. In some cultures, dealing with issues such as those involved in opening up an adoption is far too personal.

Cox favors opening adoption for internationally adopted children, but feels that timing is critical. She suggests that opening up an adoption for a minor child should be done only when there are special circumstances. Cox, however, is a strong advocate for homeland tours—a return to the child's birth country—for minor children. A trip to the homeland will give children an opportunity to visit important places, such as the sending orphanage or child care center, and perhaps even to meet people such as caregivers or care center staff who knew them as babies. Some children, even if unable to meet birth relatives, experience a feeling of connection and "wholeness" if they are able to visit the place they lived prior to joining the adoptive family. The following areas can be explored as families prepare their child for a homeland tour:

1. Sit down and talk about what information the family already has about their child, the birth circumstances, and the birth family.
2. Ask questions about the child's expectations. (Questions used earlier in the chapter can be adapted here.) Additional questions might include:
   a. How do you think you will feel when everyone you see looks like you?
   b. How do you think you will feel when you return to the orphanage?
   c. How do you think you will feel when all you hear is your birth language, yet you don't understand it?
3. Talk to the child about cultural differences they may encounter—from food to sleeping arrangements. For an older child, this can be a fun research project to do before going.

Is a homeland tour helpful for an internationally adopted child? Ask Josh Barr, now a young adult, who experienced this at age 11.

Josh's Story—An 11-Year-Old Perspective on His Homeland Tour

Joshua Barr, a delightful, inquisitive 11-year-old, was adopted from Korea when he was just a few months old. No information about his family was in the file. From the time Josh was an infant, the Barrs have created an environment that would tie him to his culture and homeland. However, they knew that someday their inquiring son would need to connect to his homeland in hopes of finding answers to questions that they couldn't give him. On June 27, 1998, Josh and his father, Jim, joined a homeland tour group for a two-week trip to Korea. The following is a brief look at the trip from Josh's perspective.

Q. How did you prepare to go to Korea?
A. I spent a lot of time reading about the country from books at the library.

Q. How did you picture the country before you went?
A. I thought it would be very, very big and it was! [Josh lives in a small rural county in southeastern Ohio.]

Q. What surprised you most about Korea?
A. It was so crowded. My town isn't crowded at all. It was kinda scary, because everyone looked like me and if I got lost, how would I be found? I couldn't believe how fast the subways were. They were so

crowded. One thing I wondered about when I got on the subways was if one of those people is my birth mom or dad.

Q. What was your most enjoyable memory?

A. One of the first nights we were there, we had a real Korean meal. It was at the Holt agency where I was adopted. I got to meet the doctor who gave me my shots when I was just a baby. Another neat memory was a trip up Mt. Sorak. We first went on a trail and then it got real steep and we had to use a cable built into the side of the mountain. It was awesome!

Q. What do you remember about Korean housing and food?

A. Most of the houses we saw were one-story houses. The food was different, for sure. For breakfast, we ate garlic bread and salad. I tried all the neat foods. I ate a whole cup of charcoaled silkworms. I ate the eyeballs of fish—raw—and squid with soy sauce dumped all over it. I tried snails at one meal for an appetizer. They were good!

Q. A trip like this can be emotionally difficult for anyone. What was difficult for you?

A. All the time before I went, I thought a lot about meeting my birth parents. I had really hoped I would get to do that. But that didn't happen. We went one afternoon to a home where girls stay that are having a baby and placing that baby for adoption. Those mothers talked about how impossible it was to keep a child as an unwed mother in Korea. That helped.

Q. What else happened that was meaningful for you?

A. Some kids did get to meet their birth mothers, and I was happy for them. One of the girls was nineteen, and she met her birth mother at a hotel where we were staying. She introduced her to us. That was awesome for us!

Q. How do you think this trip helped you?

A. It made me very proud of Korea. I understand more about the history of the country. I do understand now why my birth mother made an adoption plan for me. I also got to meet some other kids my age and a little older that were adopted from Korea, too. I do hope that when I get a little older, I can go back there again.

QUESTION 8: What about social media? A good thing or a challenge?

Social media, like Facebook, Twitter, and so on, have opened up the world. It has dramatically changed the way in which people connect with each other. In recent years, it has also greatly impacted adoption openness.

"While exact numbers are not known, anecdotal evidence suggests that increasing numbers of adopted people and their birth families are finding each other through social networking sites, such as Facebook. In adoptions that are already open, social media is creating new questions for adoptive and birth parents. For example, adoptive parents may wonder if they should 'friend' their child's adoptive birth parent on Facebook or other social networks. Will they be comfortable if their child's birth mother reads their blogs with stories of the adoption journey?"[17] The greatest challenge for adoptive parents is the opening of an adoption "by accident" through social media without any previous preparation or conversation with their child.

"She Found Me on Facebook" Managing Birth Family Contacts on Social Networking Sites

Marisa walked slowly down the stairs and sat down at the kitchen table where her mother was preparing super. "Mom," she said, "I think my birth sister found me on Facebook. She wants my phone number and wants to know where I live. What should I do?"

Since that day, things have been different for Marisa. Adopted at the age of seven, separated from two older sisters, she has been managing her adoption issues well, talking openly when questions or concerns arise. But now, at 14, it has all changed. She is confused and upset. Why? She was totally unprepared for birth family contact. Her birth sister's contact has sent her into a wilderness of emotions she hadn't yet experienced.

Although the names have changed, this is a true story. During an adoptive parent training recently in Dayton, Ohio, one of the adoptive moms shared this experience; it had just happened to their family. Sensing a growing concern for adoptive and foster families, we decided to spend some time developing social networking guidelines for their children. Being intentional and proactive may help prevent or at least alleviate some of the challenges and confusion Marisa and her parents are struggling through now.

Guidelines for Social Networking Site: Facebook, Twitter, and So On

There are a number of things parents can help their children and teens understand about Facebook contacts in general, and more specifically those related to birth family contact. It is also important to set some guidelines in place so the tween or teen will be ready for such contact. In this day of such readily accessible knowledge, closed contact in adoption is a thing of the past.

Many families choose to have some level of openness contact in the early years through letters and perhaps pictures., but this may have faded away, only to be reactivated by a simple Facebook post. Some families, due to safety issues, choose to have completely closed adoptions, but, again, this can all be uprooted by a simple Facebook post.

Ages 10 to 12

- What do tweens need to know and understand about social networking?
  - No privacy: Once you post information, you have given away much of your privacy. Once you are on, you are searchable. Anyone can find you.
  - Any picture that you post can be used in ways that may not be appropriate, so make sure it is a picture that would look great on the living room wall as well.
  - You may want to immediately respond to a birth family contact, but resist the temptation to "friend them."
  - You can/must inform us if you have been contacted by birth family and are feeling uncomfortable, frightened.
  - You can always come to us with any concerns.
- Guidelines—Have tweens help develop these rules:
  - Communicate with us first before responding to a birth family "friend request."
  - Keep us informed if the birth family contacts you.
  - We will need your password/access to Facebook, and we will always be monitoring your Facebook pages.
  - Never arrange to meet someone who contacted you on Facebook, including a birth family member.
  - Do not post identifying information, such as your full name, address, phone number, name of your school, or other activities that could be used to locate you.

Ages 13 to 15 (All of the above, plus the following)

- What do teens need to know and understand about social networking?
  - What is public/what is private
    - Know the rights to say no/reject
    - Know privacy settings
  - What's appropriate to tell/say
  - What do predators/pfishing look like

- Guidelines
  - Don't keep birth family contacts a secret . . . we will work with you.
  - Content awareness
  - What information you can share
  - Let us know if you are contacted before you "friend" a birth family member.

Ages 16 and Older

- You may learn things you don't like
- You may need help processing it all
- You have the power to control the conversation
- Guidelines
  - Never set up a meeting without our knowledge.
  - Let's keep conversation open.

QUESTION 9: What characteristics are found in parents who either begin their adoptions with openness or later choose to make contact with the birth family for the child's sake?

"One of the primary characteristics is that adoptive parents have confidence in their own parenting abilities and styles," says Martha Nabor, an adoptive parent and an adoption professional with International Adoption Services Center in Maine. "They do not need to always second-guess themselves about discipline or boundary setting." Another characteristic Nabor cites that is helpful is that these parents need to be able to take risks: Open adoption relationships require risk taking. Adoptive parents with these ongoing relationships need to be able to function without all the answers up front and clear. You don't know all the answers when it comes to working out these types of arrangements.

A final characteristic is that these adoptive parents are aware of and sensitive to the core issues of adoption that impact not only their child, but the birth mother as well. Open adoption does not eradicate the grief, loneliness, and guilt for these birth mothers. It eases these issues but does not erase them.[18]

SUMMARY

When opening up a closed adoption, it is critical that both adoptive parents and the adopted child have the opportunity to assess the following with an objective, supportive person:

1. What are the expectations?
2. What are the fears?
3. What are the wishes and worries?
4. How will we handle disappointments and setbacks?
5. How have we handled discussions focusing on social media and birth family contacts? Is this a discussion we haven't yet had and need to?

QUESTIONS

1. How would you describe the current level of openness in your adoption?
2. What are some of the questions you can use to address your child's expectation about opening up the closed adoption?
3. What are your own wishes and worries for this experience?
4. What type of support do you have from your extended family, friends, or adoption agency?
5. Discuss why you agree or disagree with the recognition that opening up a closed adoption does not completely erase some of a child's pain regarding adoption?

CHAPTER 14

Communication about Adoption Outside the Family

Which ones are your real children? What a nice thing to adopt a child like that. What do you know about her background? Why couldn't Jason's real mother keep him?

Communicating about adoption and the unique challenges within the child's history is not just something between parent and child. It involves a wider set of people who touch the life of the child. The former meaning of "the adoption triad" (adoptee, birth parents, and adoptive parents) has evolved into a something that encompasses much more. Author Michael Grand first coined the term *adoption constellation* in 1994 to broaden our understanding of the impact of adoption on a much larger group of people. The term adoption constellation "allows for the consideration of adoptees, birth parents and adoptive parents, but also incorporates birth and adoptive families, close family friends, service providers, teachers, physicians, the courts, social service workers, legislators and the clergy. In fact, anyone whose life is entwined with adoption is a member of the constellation."[1]

Most challenging for adoptive parents are the following major questions:

1. Who should know our child is adopted?
2. Who should know about our child's difficult history?

3. How much should they know? And can they be trusted with confidentiality?
4. If I share my children's story with those within the "constellation," what are the ramifications for my children? Will they be labeled as "something that will always follow them? Will that affect how others see them and treat them?"

ADOPTION COMMUNICATION WITH EXTENDED FAMILY AND CLOSE FRIENDS

Building a Supportive Communicative Environment

Developing a supportive environment within the extended family and with close friends is a high priority for adoptive parents. It is not only learning how to talk about adoption with the family, but being proactive along the way in helping parents gain a better understanding of how to build a relationship with an adopted child, especially a child who enters the home at an older age. That comes with intentional, ongoing conversations throughout a lifetime.

One of the first steps adoptive families can take is to provide their extended family an opportunity to learn. Rick and Christina were brand new adoptive parents and they felt that couldn't answer some of the questions and concerns raised by family members. They made a decision to do something very creative and helpful. They invited their adoption worker and two other prospective adoptive families and their family members to a casual informational meeting. During the meeting, the worker shared with the families the process of adoption, what would be the unique needs of the child, and how to develop relationships with an adopted child. Just this small event eased many of the apprehensions of extended family members.

Addressing Concerns

A second step in addressing adoption communication is to understand what fears or concerns extended family members might have. Establishing a loving relationship with an infant or toddler is not as challenging to grandparents as building a relationship with an older child.[2] Adoptive grandparents may wonder how and where they fit in with an older adopted child.

David and Jody Miller communicated with their relatives that they understood that building a family connection with an older child is a process that grows with "love actions," such as affirming conversation, kindness and sensitivity. They also suggested the following strategies to help other adoptive parents bridge any gap:

1. Take pictures of the new child and display them with those of other family members.
2. Establish a new tradition that is special just for the grandparents.
3. Choose the name they want the child to call them.
4. Encourage extended family members to treat all children the same (bio and adopted) at gift giving time and with claiming behaviors such as "my grandchildren" when talking about all the children in the home.

Occasionally, extended family members remain lukewarm in their acceptance of adopted children, or if preferences are shown to non-adopted children within the family, adoptive parents may need to have a frank discussion with those family members who cannot demonstrate full acceptance of adopted children. It is possible the extended family member may not realize how clearly their behavior reflects their lack of acceptance. As children mature, the adoptive parents may want to also discuss family favoritism with adopted children, allowing them to see that their parents acknowledge the unfairness of such differential treatment and empathize with the pain that must cause them. It may even be necessary to limit, but not necessarily terminate, contact with family members who cannot accept the children's position as other members of the family.

Communication about Openness in Adoption

While the adoptive parents have had training and experience regarding openness in adoption, close friends and members of the extended family have not. These individuals may have some anxiety about "interference" from the birth family or confusion on the part of the child. An adoptive grandmother may even feel threatened about her own status as the child's grandparent if the birth grandmother continues to be part of the child's life.

Donna and Martin had two gorgeous adopted children: Briana, age four, and David, age two. Both had been adopted as newborns, and both adoptions were completely open. Briana's birth mother was planning to marry and wanted Briana to be the flower girl in her wedding. Donna and Martin had a positive relationship with Briana's mother and were quite enthusiastic about Briana participating in her birth mother's wedding. However, virtually every person in the extended family was unnerved about the upcoming wedding. They feared the birth mother, now an adult with a husband, would try to "reclaim" Briana, taking her away from her adoring adoptive family. Donna and Martin had more work to do in explaining openness in adoption to their relatives than in getting Briana fitted for her dress and prepared for her role in the wedding!

Many adoptive parents may remember their own concerns when initially considering openness in adoption. Family members and close friends can be helped to learn the child's adoption cannot be reversed following legalization. And parents can help friends and relatives learn more about openness:

- The child is able to love many individuals and should not be forced to choose.
- The child has one or two parents. The adoptive parent is the parent. Period.
- The child has birth relatives (birth mother, birth father, birth grandparents, birth siblings) who may continue to have some level of contact with the child IF that contact meets the long-range needs of the adopted child.
- The adoptive parents are capable of assuring appropriate emotional boundaries are maintained in the relationship with birth family.

Communication about the Child's History

While many adoptive parents might consider complete openness in adoption communication with close friends and family, it would be wise to exercise caution in sharing information about the details of the child's history. First, the child's history belongs to the child, and it should be the child's decision about what details of that story should be shared and with whom. Second, information shared with a sister or close friend could become a topic during the family's dinner table conversation. This exposes the adopted child to insensitive comments made by the sister's children—for example, "My mom said your REAL dad is in jail and doesn't even care about you."

ADOPTION COMMUNICATION WITH THE SCHOOL

Greg, age 15, was a tenth grade biology student. He and his brother, not biologically related, were both adopted by the same family as infants. They had one sister, much younger, who was born into their family. Greg's biology teacher, Mr. Sparks, was teaching about heredity and eugenics. He had explained the concepts of dominant and recessive genes, and, to illustrate these concepts, he told the students to make a chart of all the members of their families. The students were instructed to chart which family members had earlobes and which did not. Mr. Sparks would then use these charts to show the students the principles of heredity. When Greg went home to complete the assignment, he discovered that he was the only person in his adoptive family who had earlobes. He charted his family's ears, as instructed. The following day, Mr. Sparks held up Greg's paper for the entire class to see how miserably he had failed at the assignment. "Look at Greg's homework! This is absolutely impossible! You obviously weren't paying attention yesterday!" Mr. Sparks was the one who had not been paying attention. While Greg's chart was not biologically possible, the teacher overlooked the fact that many families are created by social, not biological, ties. Mr. Sparks ignored the existence of blended families, adoptive families, foster families, and kinship families.

Not surprisingly, this embarrassing episode for Greg resulted in a critical incident that ignited anger and confusion about his identity as an adopted person. The assignment, by itself, caused Greg to acknowledge that he was different from everyone else in his family. The public ridicule by the teacher added insult to injury. The insensitivity of this teacher created several difficult months for Greg and his adoptive family.

Many adoptive families can tell similar stories about problems created by teachers who do not understand adoption and do not know how to address the topic in a sensitive way in the classroom. Teachers are hardly malicious people who seek to harm children. The harm occurs out of ignorance.

This section presents information that adoptive and foster parents can share with educators in their communities. After all, children spend a significant part of their lives at school, and the messages given at school about adoption can have a tremendous impact on children's attitudes toward, and understanding of, their histories. In any discussion about adoption communication, teachers cannot be overlooked as a powerful resource to help children better understand adoption, develop positive attitudes toward both birth and adoptive parents, and further self-esteem and positive self-identity.

Adoptive and foster parents may present information about adoption-sensitive communication to teachers on an individual basis or through in-service training workshops with entire schools or districts. Adoptive or foster parents may wish to address the issue as a single concerned parent, or they may wish to use an adoptive parent support group to develop a workshop to be presented at teachers' meetings or conferences. The goal is to help educators understand ways to better communicate about adoption and foster care with all of the children in their classrooms.

Sharing Adoption History with the School

Many adoptive parents struggle with the issue of telling the school/teacher that their child has been adopted into the family. They struggle with such questions as:

- Should we tell the school/teacher that our child is adopted?
- If so, when should we tell it and to whom?
- How much history should we disclose and to whom?

A concern about adopted children being labeled as problem children has some basis in research. In 1987, Freidman-Kessler of the Fielding Institute (Santa Barbara, California) asked 121 Caucasian female teachers to evaluate the behavior, personality, and intentionality of a child described in a vignette. Half of the children were identified as being adopted. The study found that the severity of the wrongdoing of the child in the vignette was the most important factor affecting the teacher's judgment of the child's behavior, personality traits, intentionality, and the designated punishment. However, the researcher found adoption affected, to varying degrees, the teachers' determination of the child's attractiveness, aggressiveness, callousness, disagreeableness, and how intense the punishment should be. Nineteen graduate students in education were asked to give their first impressions of adopted children. The responses were overwhelmingly negative.[3]

Of course, many families have adopted transracially or internationally, have adopted older school-age children, or live in small communities where the adoption is common knowledge. None of these families will struggle with the decision to share adoption information with the school. The adoption is obvious to everyone in the community. In these situations, adoption information must instead be managed in a positive way. This chapter will provide parents with some resources to help teachers learn more-effective ways of addressing the issue of adoption and foster care.

Other families who adopt younger children of the same race wonder if the teacher should be informed at all that their child joined the family through adoption. This issue is a thorny one because, once the school is told of the adoption, the information cannot be retrieved. When adoption history is not obvious, the decision to share the information is final, and made when the child is only a few years old and unable to make an informed choice. Some of the arguments for and against sharing adoption history with the school are listed in Table 14.1.

Table 14.1.

Parents Should Share Adoption History Because:	**Parents Should *Not* Share Adoption History Because:**
The child should not be "ashamed" that he is adopted. Secrecy implies and reinforces shame.	The child will be identified and labeled in a negative way.
Educators and other children need to learn more positive attitudes about adoption and foster care. If these circumstances are hidden, others have no opportunity to become more aware and sensitive. If educators have not learned about adoption, they are more likely to thoughtlessly give assignments or make remarks that could be hurtful to adopted children.	The child owns his history, and that history should not be shared outside the family before he can make an informed decision about doing so. To share his past is a violation of his rights.
If educators are unaware of issues, they cannot possibly cope effectively with behaviors related to adoption. An educator would be unaware that a child is angry or sad because of grief or identity confusion related to adoption.	The other children in the class will learn about the child's adoptive history and will torment him with insensitive comments.
	Adopted children already feel "different." Making an issue of the adoption reinforces that sense of being different. It is possible to insist *too much* on the issue of adoption.

Clearly, the arguments on both sides of this issue are compelling. Adoptive parents should make decisions about sharing adoption history with their eyes open, aware of the ramifications of their choice. If parents decide that adoption information should be shared, the teacher should be explicitly reminded that adoption information is to be held in professional confidence and not shared with anyone who does not have a need to know. While parents might make different, situation-specific decisions about what information to share with the school, *all* parents must inform the school of any special academic, behavioral, medical, or psychological needs the child has. It is important not to tell all your child's history of early harm, but to tell teachers and others what your child needs. Finally, if parents decide to share adoption history with the school, information in this section may be helpful to the teachers who instruct their children.

Creating Professional Awareness: Address Common Pitfalls for Teachers

The Family Tree

Experienced adoptive parents can assure educators that the single most dreaded school assignment made by teachers is the family tree, often assigned in the third grade. The family tree assignment often occurs at about the time children are developmentally able to understand what adoption means, what it means to be born to one set of parents, but raised by another set. Concerns and fears about the "real parents" crop up at this time, and the family tree assignment throws many an adopted eight-year-old into feelings of confusion, anxiety, and divided loyalties. While a family tree assignment can be very difficult for adopted or foster children, if handled with sensitivity and creativity, the assignment can be helpful to them in understanding all the important persons in their histories (the most significant point of the assignment for all children).

When making the family tree assignment, for example, teachers can acknowledge that trees, and families, have many branches. All of the children should be given the flexibility to represent their important "branches" in ways that make sense to them. For example, some adopted children benefit from drawing a tree that represents the birth family in the roots, foster families in the trunk, and the adoptive family in the leaves (see Chapter 9).

This type of flexibility and sensitivity helps not only adopted and foster children, but children who live with stepparents, grandparents or other kin, and single parents. In fact, the assignment itself is not problematic unless it is given with an expectation of rigidity, of a "right and wrong" way to represent families. Adopted and foster children given an opportunity to represent only one family on their tree will, of course, struggle with which family to draw. The struggle leads to an entirely unnecessary loyalty conflict. Messages to foster and adopted children, both at home and at school, need to clarify for the children that they are allowed to love, and feel good about, all of the families in their histories.

The Baby Picture

Other children or teens have difficulty when they are asked to bring baby pictures to display for an assignment or for the high school yearbook. Teachers or yearbook editors find it fun to have students guess whose baby pictures are included in a class or school collage. Some adopted and foster children have no baby pictures, and such an assignment can emphasize this gaping wound in their histories.

Writing a Family History

Elementary teachers often assign children to write family or "backyard" histories. These autobiographies may be challenging for children who are uncertain about their histories or who have histories they do not want to share in a public forum. Children who find themselves with a difficult family history to write will need sensitivity from both parents and teachers in better understanding their histories, making appropriate decisions about information to be shared, and making decisions about shortened "cover stories" to be used, when necessary to help a child tell the truth in a way that does not compromise his ability to keep some of his history confidential from other children or from teachers.

Adopting a Whale (Highway, Park)

Some elementary or middle school teachers may attempt to increase community involvement through programs to adopt a zoo animal (or street, park, etc.). Such an assignment can be problematic for young, concrete thinkers who believe that adoption involves only signing up and paying money annually. "Do their parents have to pay more money every year to keep them? And if their parents do not pay the money, will they be thrown out?"[4] An exercise to increase the children's responsibility for their environment is a great idea, but it should not be tied to adoption by using that language.

Using the Most Appropriate Language

Finally, teachers need help learning appropriate language and terminology associated with adoption. As part of the larger community, teachers have sometimes developed attitudes and beliefs about adoption that are inaccurate and even potentially harmful to children who live in adoptive families. Teachers and guidance counselors need to learn from adoptive parents what terminology to use in talking with children about adoption and foster care. Appropriate language should be used in discussing adoption with a single child who expresses feelings about adoption, with two or three children who have had a conflict involving name calling at recess, or with the entire class in thinking about ways families are formed. Parents should use the information presented in Chapter 7 to help educators understand appropriate language to use in discussing adoption with children and teens.

Creating Professional Awareness: Do's and Don'ts for Educators

Table 14.2 presents some do's and don'ts for educators as they seek to improve their sensitivity to the issues of adopted children.

Table 14.2.

Do	Don't
Ensure that books about adoption and foster care are available for all children in the classroom and in the school library. Check with a local adoptive parent association or agency for recommendations.	Assume that all children in your classrooms are living in two-parent, biological families. Children living with both biological parents are now a minority, and nontraditional families are becoming the norm.
Learn and use appropriate adoption language.	Talk about "real" parents, siblings, etc., in reference to birth family members. Insist that assignments related to family issues be done in a prescribed, rigid manner with little or no room for flexibility or creativity. Publicly display family-related assignments for the entire class to view and question.
Consider the potential impact of any assignments made on all children who live in non-traditional families. Think about ways to minimize any potential negative consequences for those children who have multiple families and attachments.	Expect that education can be a "one size fits all" experience. Refuse to address or "benevolently" ignore the special needs brought to school by children.
Talk with adoptive parents and guidance counselors about the need for a support group series for children who live in non-traditional families.	Stereotype adopted or foster children as "problem children." Refuse to see children as individuals who have experienced trauma.

Do	Don't
Explore resources such as post-adoption service providers, the North American Council for Adoptable Children, and the Child Welfare Information Gateway for potential curricula for such groups.	
Talk with parents about potential anniversary reactions, anxieties, and fears related to a particular child's adoption. Learn about the developmental awareness of adoption typical of children in your classrooms to understand common questions and concerns of children in your particular age range.	Create expectations that children who have experienced trauma and separation will be developmentally unaffected by their histories.
Assure that other children in the classroom become more aware of and sensitive to issues related to adoption.	Ignore comments or conflicts of children related to family or adoption issues. Neglect to teach *and model* values of understanding and respect for feelings of others, diversity in families, and the worthiness of all persons.
Be alert for signs that the child is experiencing grief or depression. Report concerns to adoptive parents for intervention and support.	Assume that misbehavior is an indication that a child is a "bad" kid whose problem behavior can be resolved by additional punishment.

Tips for Parents Addressing Groups of Students or Teachers

If adoptive parents speak with students or teachers to help them overcome media images of adoptive families, they should speak about adoption in general terms. They should *not* share their own children's personal histories. Those personal histories belong to the children and are not open for public examination.

Talks with students will, of course, need to be directed at the developmental level of the children. Even very young children can understand, however, that families are formed in many ways. Patricia Irwin Johnston, adoption author and expert, wrote in *Adoptive Families Magazine:*

> You might begin by helping children understand that families come together and their members are "connected" in more than one way. Blood and genes (e.g., a birthmother and her birth daughter) relate some family members to one another. Law (e.g., a husband and wife) forges some family members' connections. Still other family members share no genetic ties or legal connections but are members of the same family by social custom (e.g., a man and his mother-in-law). Sometimes what binds together a group of people as members of the same family is neither genes nor law, but the love they feel for one another (a stepparent's mother, who serves as a "Grandma" or a parent's close friend who becomes "Aunt Sally"). Families expanded by adoption may not share genes, but they are connected by love, by social custom, and by law.[5]

If a child is uncomfortable with his or her own parent making a presentation to his school (either to peers or teachers), the parent might consider asking another adoptive parent (from another school or district) to make a presentation on adoption. However, children or teens old enough to make informed decisions about the subject of adoption can be involved in designing either a presentation or a panel discussion of peers whose lives are touched by adoption for teachers and/or students.

Helping Non-Adopted Children Become More Aware

Even children born into adoptive families who grow up as siblings to adopted children have difficulty understanding the feelings and behaviors of their adopted brothers and sisters. It is not surprising, then, that children who have had little experience with adoption would have many misconceptions and would lack empathy.

Adopted youth have suffered from schoolyard taunts, name calling (Cabbage-Patch Kid, bastard, etc.), and comments about being unwanted, unworthy, and without "real" parents. Transracially adopted children may also suffer from acts of discrimination from both majority and minority groups because their family is so different. As a result of the insensitivity of their peers, many adopted children feel embarrassed or shamed about their status as an adopted person, "go underground," and want to share very little about their adoptions outside the family.

Matt, age 16, was a biracial young man attending high school. He had been adopted at birth by two Caucasian parents. For years, Matt had tried to hide from his friends the fact that he was adopted. He did not invite friends to his home, and he repeatedly found excuses to keep both parents from attending conferences, sporting events, or other special events at school. Matt believed that his friends would not suspect that he was adopted if they did not see that both of his parents were white. Matt was ashamed of being adopted because, when in elementary school, other children had told him that his "real" mother did not want him. Some of his schoolmates had lorded over him the fact that they were wanted and kept by their real mothers, taunting Matt that there was something wrong with him because his own mother did not want him. Matt had never shared these experiences with his adoptive parents, not wanting to hurt their feelings because they were not his "real" parents. He suffered quietly with feelings of being unlovable and unworthy. He tried to hide his adoption as he grew older and more sophisticated in his relationships with peers. He tried to blend in with the other children who understood little or nothing about his history. His feelings of shame about his lack of worth were expressed through a fear of failure (and therefore a fear of trying to be successful in spite of considerable natural gifts of intellect, art and creativity, and sports) and a fear of close relationships/friendships with others.

Children do not like to feel different from their peers, and they do not tolerate differences in others well. Children must be taught to have sensitivity and respect for others. Such teaching can occur most effectively through modeling, use of proper adoption language, access to resources and learning about adoption, and perhaps special bulletin boards with information about adoption (famous adopted people and characters: Moses, Superman, Dave Thomas, former President Gerald Ford, Olympic diver Greg Louganis), or class discussion about various ways families are formed.

Teachers should remember that about 2 percent of all U.S. children were adopted. Among all adopted children—with the exclusion of those living with at least one biological parent (i.e., in stepfamilies)—one out of four was adopted from other nations; of the remaining children adopted domestically, half were adopted from foster care and half from private sources.[6] The 2010 U.S. Census found that 1.5 million children in the United States are adopted.[7] Further, 6 out of 10 Americans have had a personal experience with adoption. Either they have a family member, close friend, or they themselves have been adopted.[8] Further, at the end of 2012, there were 397,091 children in the United States living in foster care.[9] Adoption and foster care touch many more lives than has been widely perceived. Learning about non-traditional families can benefit all children within the school system.

The Role of Guidance Counselors

Guidance counselors, as professionals who address the emotional needs of children that can interfere with learning, should become educated about the issues that are faced by adopted and foster children and about resources available within the community to address the needs of those children. It has been widely estimated that 33 to 40 percent of adopted children have attention deficit disorder (ADD) or attention deficit hyperactivity disorder (ADHD). It is likely that a disproportionate number of children not raised by their birth families is affected with these and other neurological problems, largely due to substance abuse in utero, child maltreatment, multiple moves, genetics, institutionalization, and lack of stimulation. However, it is also likely that adopted and foster children are sometimes mistakenly diagnosed as having ADD, ADHD, or other learning disorders because they are *preoccupied* with the emotional work of resolving loss, identity development, anger, lack of trust, and so on. Such preoccupation gets in the way of learning because it funnels the child's available energy and attention away from the cognitive domain, the learning domain, of human development. Instead of placing angry, frightened, insecure children in time-out, we need to place them with counselors, therapists, and/or support groups that address their issues and allow them to concentrate and engage in learning.

Guidance counselors should provide the school system's leadership in learning about the dynamics of growing up adopted. They must understand completely the impact of child maltreatment and separation from the birth family on child development. And they must find or create programs to assist adopted children and youth in addressing anxiety, anger, and confusion. Guidance counselors can consult with post adoption service providers, adoption agencies, adoptive parent support groups, the North American Council for Adoptable Children (651-644-3036), or adoption-related websites on the Internet to learn about resources for adopted children.

Resources for Educators

Additional resources of particular interest for schools and adoptive parents include the following:

- *Adoption Awareness in School Assignments: A Guide for Parents and Educators*. Christine Mitchell. http://www.adoptionpolicy.org/Adoption_Awareness_Schools.pdf.

- *Back to School: A Guide to Making Schools and School Assignments More Adoption-Friendly.* Mitchell, Christine. *Adoption Advocate.* National Council for Adoption. 2010. http://www.adoptioncouncil.org/images/stories/NCFA_ADOPTION_ADVOCATE_NO27.pdf.
- *Adoption Basics for Educators: How Adoption Impacts Children & How Educators Can Help.* Iowa Foster and Adoptive Parents Association. Provides educators with basic information about adoption. http://www.ifapa.org/pdf_docs/AdoptionBasicsforEducators.pdf.
- *Teacher's Guide To Adoption.* Robin Hilborn. 2005. http://www.familyhelper.net/ad/adteach.html.
- *Help for Billy.* Heather Forbes.

Summary of Adoption Communication with the Schools

The school system has a tremendous impact on children. To assure that the impact on adopted children is one that helps them learn and ultimately mature into productive adults, the school system must become more aggressive in learning about and meeting the needs of this growing segment of the population.

- Parents must consider their own child and school setting in making a decision about sharing adoption history with the school, considering carefully the ramifications and "hidden messages" of sharing and not sharing.
- Parents may decide to educate the educators individually, through group presentations to teachers and guidance counselors and/or students.
- Parents must seek ways to involve their own child in decision making about the design of any educational presentation (either individual or group). The child's particular history should never be shared in a public forum.
- Parents should be alert to the impact of school assignments or interactions with peers at school on their children's understanding of adoption and their feelings about themselves, their birth family and/or culture, and adoption in general.

ADOPTION COMMUNICATION WITHIN THE LARGER COMMUNITY

Sometimes, complete strangers feel compelled to comment on your family, particularly when the children look very different than the adoptive parents. These comments can be irritating for parents and potentially hurtful to the adopted children. How does a parent respond to unsolicited comments or questions from strangers or very casual acquaintances?

Occasionally, a stranger is genuinely interested in foster care or adoption and would like to get more information about your experience. If you sense this is the case, you might ask for that individual's contact information and phone or email them at a later time to share information about how to adopt or foster.

Other times, strangers may be intrigued by your multi-cultural family, particularly when it is obvious you are not biologically related to the children. These strangers may not intend to be hurtful, but they may not know appropriate terminology or they might blurt a question or comment without realizing how this impacts you or your child. The following guidelines were suggested by Deborah McCurdy, an adoptive mother and Adoption Supervisor at Beacon Adoption Center in Great Barrington, Massachusetts:[10]

Q. Where did you get this dear little one? Where is she from?

A. *She was born in Korea, and her brother here was born in Albany. (Most people will pick up on your inclusion of the older child and start including him, too, if you furnish answers about both to EACH question asked about the adopted child.)*

We can start early to practice answers that will AFFIRM THE CHILDREN, preparing for the day when they will be old enough to understand:

Q. Isn't she a lucky little girl? What wonderful people you are!

A. *We're the lucky ones, to have such a wonderful child!*

Q. And do you also have children of your own?

A. *Just these two. (This affirms adopted kids as our own.)*

Q. Are they REAL brother and sister?

A. *They are NOW! (This clarifies that adopted kids as our own.)*

Q. How could the mother have given up such a lovely child?

A. *It was very hard for the birth mother, but she just couldn't take care of ANY baby. (This reassures the child that there was nothing wrong with him or her.)*

Q. What do you know about the real parents?

A. *Well, we're his real parents, actually, since we're bringing him up.*

Q. Oh, of course—I meant the natural parents.

A. *We don't know very much about the birth parents. How have you been? How was your summer?*

If all else fails when confronted with an insensitive stranger, adoptive parents may always respond with, "That's my son's story, and I don't feel comfortable sharing his story outside the family."

Finally, remember that after an incident regarding awkward or hurtful questions, the incident does not end until parents have "closed the circle" by privately communicating with their child about the incident.

Molly was the only adopted child in her family, but, ironically, she looked much more like the adoptive mother than her two biological children. Strangers often commented on how much Molly looked like her mother. The adoptive mother, in an effort to be respectful of Molly's privacy, never shared with the strangers that Molly was an adopted child. The adoptive mother's decision was absolutely correct; Molly did indeed look very much like her mother, and her adoption did not change that fact at all. Further, Molly's story should be shared by her, not by her mother. And finally, personal family information should not be shared with complete strangers! However, Molly, now an adult, shared that she often felt uncomfortable during these exchanges with strangers. She felt her mother was ignoring "the elephant in the living room." While Molly was pleased her mother did not casually share her personal information, she wished her mother would have said to her with a wink in private, "Isn't it funny how everyone notices we look just alike? I bet they think your brothers are adopted!" or "We must have been destined to be part of the same family since we look so much alike!"

The following questions might be helpful in an "after-the-fact" conversation with your adopted child:

1. How did you feel when that woman asked about our family? (Share how you yourself felt about the intrusive questions or comments.)
2. How did you feel about how I responded to the question or comment?
3. If that happens again, how would you like to have it handled?
4. Would you like to develop a secret sign to show me you want a conversation ended right away? Maybe you could pull on your ear, scratch your head, or take my hand?

Finally, the child can be helped to understand many people do not understand adoption and foster care, and many have misconceptions or are simply curious. While interactions with uninformed people can be irritating or offensive, these exchanges provide opportunities for others to learn proper adoption or foster care etiquette!

SUMMARY

Healthy communication about adoption helps others to be sensitive to the feelings and needs of adopted children and youth. It also sends a powerful message of advocacy when that communication occurs in the presence of your adopted child.

QUESTIONS

1. What information will be shared with relatives and close family friends?
2. Do you feel you should share your child's adoption history with the school? Why or why not?
3. What critical incidents regarding adoption has your child dealt with at school? How did your child respond? How did you respond?
4. How do you intend to prevent future critical incidents at school?
5. Are you interested in forming a support group for adopted children in your child's school? What would be the necessary steps to implement such a plan?
6. Have you experienced insensitive questions or comments while in the community? How will you handle these in the future?

APPENDIX A

Information Needed to Prepare a Case for Adoption

CHILD-SPECIFIC DESCRIPTIVE INFORMATION

- Photographs, videos
- Personality, including positive characteristics
- Cultural, ethnic, and racial background
- Religious experiences and preferences
- Likes and dislikes
- Special hobbies, skills, and interests
- Readiness for adoption (understanding, feelings, preparation)

PRENATAL AND NEONATAL INFORMATION

- Course of pregnancy and delivery, including any complications
- Drugs, medications, or alcohol taken by the biological mother during pregnancy
- Results of any testing and screening completed after birth for either child or mother, including drug toxicology, PKU, and so on
- Neonatal development, including complications and treatment

CHILD'S MEDICAL HISTORY

- Findings from most recent physical exam
- Immunizations
- Childhood illnesses
- Serious illnesses
- Surgeries
- Hospitalizations
- Chronic medical conditions or risk factors (e.g., diabetes, Sickle Cell Anemia)
- Handicapping conditions or risk factors (e.g., mental retardation, spina bifada, cerebral palsy, etc.)
- Genetic influences
- Identification of medical professionals/facilities involved with care and treatment
- Resources for further information

CHILD'S DEVELOPMENTAL HISTORY

- Early milestones and subsequent development: motor, speech and language, toilet training, feeding
- Developmental testing results, if any
- Identification of developmental services/professionals involved
- Resources for further information

CHILD'S HISTORY OF ABUSE AND NEGLECT

- Incidents of physical or sexual abuse, neglect, or emotional maltreatment experienced by the child prior to placement
- Abuse or neglect experienced while in placement
- Reason for initial placement
- Listing of all out-of-home placements, dates
- Significant events in each placement
- Adjustment in each placement
- Reasons for moves from one placement to another

CHILD'S RELATIONSHIPS

- Identification of past and current significant relationships
- Attachment history (primary attachment figures)
- Information regarding capacity to attach

CHILD'S PSYCHOLOGICAL AND/OR PSYCHIATRIC HISTORY

- Temperament
- Response to stress
- Emotional or behavior problems, current and past
- Behavior that has been harmful or dangerous to others or to self
- Counseling or mental health treatment received
- Psychological or psychiatric evaluations, results
- Mental health, psychological, and psychiatric professionals who have provided evaluation or treatment
- Resources for further information

CHILD'S EDUCATIONAL HISTORY

- Current school attendance, grade
- Schools previously attended
- Special education services, current or previous
- Current and previous IEP or 504 documents, if applicable
- Academic performance
- Behavior issues
- Extracurricular activities, interests, and awards
- Teacher comments
- Identification of schools/teachers or other professionals involved
- Resources for further information

SIBLINGS

- Names, ages
- Current living situation
- Significant conditions or issues
- Special abilities and strengths
- History of relationship/frequency of contact
- Plans for continuing contact

BIRTH FAMILY INFORMATION

- Photographs (provided only with permission of birth parents in voluntary surrender cases, unless child had pictures in a lifebook prior to the surrender; in cases of involuntary termination of parental rights, pictures do not require permission of birth parents for release to adoptive family)

- Non-identifying descriptive information
- Physical characteristics
- Marital status
- Cultural background, including race and ethnicity
- Religious background and preferences
- Extended family information and involvement
- Special abilities, talents, and interests
- Education, including any special education services
- Employment
- Social problems
- Medical history
- Chronic illness
- Handicaps
- Emotional/psychiatric problems
- Drug/alcohol/tobacco usage
- View of adoption, including preferences regarding openness and future contact

KNOWN GAPS IN INFORMATION

- Unknown parents
- Missing agency documentation
- History of many moves by family and multiple agency involvement

BIBLIOGRAPHY

Gathering and Documenting Background Information – A training curriculum written by the Institute for Human Services for the Ohio Child Welfare Training Program (March 2011). http://www.ocwtp.net/PDFs/Trainee%20Resources/Assessor%20Resources/All%20Gathering%20Documenting%20handouts.pdf

APPENDIX B

Triggers for Adoption Issues

Adoption Issue	Possible triggers
Loss	Child's birthday Anniversaries of prior separations Holidays Adoptive family moves Any loss (pet dies, friend moves away) Transition from one school level to another High school graduation
Abandonment	First day of school Going to sleep-over camp Being "dumped" by significant other High school graduation Divorce of adoptive parents Adoptive family moves Anniversaries of prior separations
Identity	Adolescence Insensitive remarks from family, friends, and strangers School assignments (family tree) Critical incidents involving racism for a transracially adopted child Pregnancy Midlife crisis

(*Continued*)

Adoption Issue	Possible triggers
Divided Loyalties	Mother's Day Engagement or marriage Visits or contact with birth siblings or other birth relatives Holidays
Trust	Felt betrayal in a relationship Being "dumped" by significant other Discovery of information that had not been shared honestly
Control	Adolescence School Parental limits
Shame/Guilt	Failures (not making the team or winning in sports; school failures) Rejection experiences (being excluded by peers; feeling as though birth children in the adoptive home are loved or valued more)

Preservice Training for Foster, Adoptive, and Kinship Parents – A training curriculum written by the Institute for Human Services for the Ohio Child Welfare Training Program (June 2015). http://www.ocwtp.net/PDFs/Trainee%20Resources/Preservice/Session11ho.pdf

APPENDIX C

Lifebooks—They Are Effective for Children in Understanding Their Story

By Monica Johnson, M.S.W.
Lifebook Program Supervisor
Lutheran Social Services of Illinois

Children in the child welfare system often have fragmented life stories. Important elements that represent the child's identity become scattered or missing. Consequently, children are left with blurred memories, unanswered questions and gaps in the timelines of their lives, leaving them to answer their own "why" questions and to fill in gaps with fantasy and misinterpretation. To heal from losses, trauma and transitions, foster children must be able to make sense of their life stories. Too many are left alone, confused, and angry, without accurate, honest information and guidance to help them truly understand and find meaning in painful, difficult changes, transitions, and trauma.

"The ability to make meaning of one's life, to put the pieces together in a logical, coherent narrative that acknowledges difficulty as well as growth and change is the essence of mental health" (Howard & Johnson, 2007). Children who experience multiple moves in the foster care system are especially vulnerable. With every move, they lose or have significant risk for losing crucial records, important documentation, treasured possessions, and valuable information about their histories. In contrast, children in nurturing families have histories that are kept and told by adult family members who love them. Birth family medical history, cultural background information, birth certificates, baby pictures, developmental milestones, report cards, awards, and other mementos, as well as someone to continue the story as the child grows, are important aspects of the child's identity. Long after children leave the home of their family of origin, the family continues to keep these important artifacts and stories safe and coherent (Howard & Johnson, 2007). Children in the child welfare system often do not have reliable historians to help them keep, understand, make meaning of and tell their life stories as they grow. They lack a coherent life narrative.

For foster children, it is the lifebook that gives them a complete and meaningful life narrative that can prevent blurred memories, dark holes of time, and loss of birth family history, information, pictures, and mementos important for identity and understanding. The lifebook is organized with writing prompts and spaces for pictures and messages giving children, foster parents, social workers, therapists, birth parents, and adoptive parents the ability to record crucial information children need about their lives. "A lifebook is a tangible, chronological and evolving record of a child's life" (Howard & Johnson, 2007). It assists children in processing and understanding the losses and difficulties of their lives, as well as celebrates their strengths to support them in developing a positive sense of self as they grow. "Lifebook work is a path to memory, to reinterpretation, and to understanding" (Howard & Johnson, 2012). When considering the painful and devastating losses foster children experience, lifebook work with children is highly valuable and necessary.

The benefits of Lifebook work for foster and adopted children are many, as are the consequences of not doing this work. Lifebook work not only benefits the child, but also those who assist the child in the work. It is imperative that adults understand children's past histories so they can support them in the present and into the future, given that children view and interpret their past experiences differently at various developmental stages. Lifebooks are a catalyst to important conversations between children and adults, building rapport and strengthening relationships (Jajko & Johnson, 2012).

Through writing prompts on various topics, lifebooks allow children to learn the truth about their lives and their histories. They are given the opportunity to express their feelings, ask unanswered questions about events or people in their lives, and share their perspectives. In turn, learning children's perspectives gives adults a better basis for how to help and support them. For example, providing accurate and honest, age-appropriate information and offering gentle, alternative explanations to self-blaming ones will help children better understand why they were placed in foster care or why they could not return home to their parents. Other significant benefits include bringing difficult feelings to the surface that youth may otherwise act out, building rapport between the child and the foster or adoptive parents and using the lifebook in a therapeutic manner for trauma recovery as children work through the abuse and neglect they've experienced (Jajko & Johnson, 2012).

Honesty is essential to lifebook work. This builds trust and children will learn that they can talk to their caregiver about difficult topics along with the pleasant ones. The consequence of not discussing difficult topics with children, not answering or addressing their questions, and denying information vital for identity formation such as aspects involving birth family connection is that children will learn they cannot talk to their foster or adoptive parent about things that matter to them. They may seek support and information from undesired or unreliable sources (Jajko & Johnson, 2012). In addition, "when children do not have the opportunities to discuss their experiences, especially traumatic ones, they may develop distorted views about why they are in foster care, how people feel about them, and how they feel about themselves" (Dorow & Clark, 2013, p. 2). Children often blame themselves for their family being separated, creating serious risks for negative self-perception and low self-esteem. Children who are not assisted in expressing their points of view, their story, thoughts, and feelings in a positive way may externalize or internalize their feelings in unhealthy or disruptive ways (Jajko & Johnson, 2012).

The concept of lifebook work and life histories for children in the child welfare system and adopted children is not new. The benefits have been acknowledged in the social work field for many years. There are websites that advocate lifebook work, offering education and guidance on how to help children create meaningful lifebooks. Former foster children and adoptees are speaking out about how the work has positively impacted their lives. There are lifebooks available for social workers, foster parents, therapists, and adoptive parents to purchase for children, and professionals in the field write about how their work with lifebooks and children has a had a positive impact that continues to validate its significant value. Yet, there is an absence of research literature supporting efficacy of lifebook work.

Understanding how crucial completed lifebooks are for children in foster care and those exiting the system, Lutheran Social Services of Illinois (LSSI), a statewide agency serving 2,000 children in its foster care program, developed a program that specifically assists children and their caregivers in creating meaningful lifebooks. As Lifebook Specialists in this program worked with children and their caregivers on lifebooks, the positive impact of this work was observed. Children seemed to learn more about their histories, seemed to gain more insight and understanding of difficult events, shared their thoughts and feelings, and had opportunities for their questions to be answered or at least acknowledged. Although there was no clinical research to support the efficacy, the actual work appeared to easily validate it. Generously grant supported by the Christopher Family Foundation and others, LSSI chose to formally evaluate their program and measure the effects of lifebook work with children and foster parents through an applied research study in collaboration with researchers Tina Dorow, MSW, LCSW, and Courtney Clark, MA, LCSW. In this 2013 study, LSSI and the researchers identified the following research questions: (1) Does children's functioning improve after participation in the LSSI Lifebook Program? (2) Are there differences in functioning between children who worked with an LSSI Lifebook Specialist and children who did not work with an LSSI Lifebook Specialist? (3) Do children who participate in the LSSI Program gain additional knowledge of their histories? (4) Are children and foster parents who participate in the LSSI Lifebook Program better able to talk about children's past experiences and relationships? (5) Are children and foster parents satisfied with LSSI Lifebook Program services that they received? The methods of measuring these research questions involved pre- and post-questionnaires administered to foster children ages 8 through 18 and their foster parents who worked one on one with a Lifebook Specialist. Lifebooks used in research were books created by LSSI titled "My Awesome Life™." A control group was identified from a large statewide agency comparable to LSSI in size and services offered. The control group had not been exposed to LSSI's lifebook, "My Awesome Life™," nor the services offered by LSSI's program.

Prior to their participation in Lifebook program services, pre-knowledge questionnaires were completed by foster caregivers and children and completed again at the end of their Lifebook Program services. The pre- and post-knowledge questionnaires explored children and foster parents' comfort levels in discussing children's histories before and after services as well as what information children and families have about children's histories, what they would like to have, and what was gathered during Lifebook Program intervention. Pre- and post-knowledge questionnaires were also administered to the control group in which there was no LSSI Lifebook intervention.

The Strengths and Difficulties Questionnaire (SDQ), a standardized behavioral screening questionnaire was also administered to children and their foster parents prior to services and following Lifebook intervention. The SDQ questions identified children's strengths and challenges in regards to their behaviors in six areas: emotional symptoms, conduct problems, hyperactivity/inattention, peer relationship problems, and prosocial behaviors. Foster parents completed the SDQ for all children, but only children ages 11 to 18 completed one for themselves.

Data collection occurred for six months with an intervention group of 60 foster children and foster parents and 14 control group participants. (The control group agency experienced difficulty with obtaining consent from the state agency in one of their regions.) Overall, the results from the study were positive and supported the research questions, demonstrating how lifebooks are valuable tools in fostering important conversations with children. After intervention, foster parents reported feeling more comfortable talking with children about previous placements and birth family histories. Children's comfort level also increased. Eighty-two percent of the intervention group children reported knowing more about why they were in foster care, and 73 percent reported they knew more about their birth families, showing that lifebook work does help children learn more about their histories and answering "why" questions about difficult topics such as the reason they were placed in foster care. For the control group, there was no change between pre- and post-knowledge questionnaires.

Results supported improvement in children's functioning after participation with LSSI's Lifebook Program. Intervention group foster parents reported positive changes for children in four of the six areas of functioning, a decrease in stress and attention and an increase in relating and helpfulness. Children reported positive changes in the same five areas identified by the foster parents above but also in emotional symptoms. Finally, the vast majority of children and foster parents receiving LSSI's Lifebook services were satisfied with the services and would recommend them to others. They felt listened to and supported.

Results of this study show that LSSI's Lifebook work is an important catalyst for conversations between children and foster parents/caregivers about transitions and birth families. Early in this article, it was discussed that children who do not have opportunities to express their feelings may internalize or externalize them resulting in behavior difficulties. In LSSI's Lifebook Program, children have these opportunities for self-expression, thus their "functioning seems to improve in key areas, such as experiencing less stress, better attention skills, increased ability to relate to others, and improved social skills" (Dorow & Clark, p. 12). Overall, LSSI's Lifebook Program and the observed effects of direct lifebook work with children demonstrates how this work is extremely valuable in helping children and foster and adoptive parents learn more about children's histories, aiding in the development of coherent life narratives. Ultimately, lifebook work offers foster and adoptive children the necessary, essential opportunities for expression, understanding, and healing.

BIBLIOGRAPHY

Dorow, T., and C. Clark, Lutheran Social Services of Illinois Lifebook Program *Research Summary* (2012).

Howard, J., and M. Johnson, *Putting the Pieces Together: Lifebook Work with Children*, training DVD. The Center for Adoption Studies at Illinois State University & Lutheran Social Services of Illinois (2007).

Jajko, R., and M. Johnson, M. *Putting the Pieces Together: Lifebook Work with Children,* a training curriculum. Lutheran Social Services of Illinois (2012).

Notes

CHAPTER 1

1. Schooler, Jayne Elizabeth. *Searching for a Past* (Colorado Springs, CO: Pinon Press, 1995), 105–6.

2. Webster, Harriet. *Family Secrets: How Telling and Not Telling Affects Our Children, Our Relationships and Our Lives* (Reading, MA: Addison-Wesley Publishing, 1991), 11.

3. Ibid., 202.

4. Ibid.

5. Mask, Michael, Julie Mask, Jeanne Hensley, and Steven Craig. *Family Secrets* (Nashville, TN: Thomas Nelson, 1995), 10.

6. Ibid., 9–11.

7. Black, Evan Imber. "The Power of Secrets." *Psychology Time* (April 26, 2013). Adapted from a book by that same title. www.psychologytoday.com/em/25442

8. Schooler, 105–6.

9. Lifton, Betty Jean. *Journey of the Adopted Self: A Quest for Wholeness* (New York, NY: Basic Books, 1993), 22.

10. Riley, Helen J. "Listening to Late Discovery Adoption and Donor Offspring Stories: Adoption, Ethics and Implications for Contemporary Donor Insemination Practices." In Ceridwen Spark and Denise Cuthbert (Eds.), *Other People's Children: Adoption in Australia* (Australian Scholarly Publishing, Melbourne, Victoria), 145–60

11. Ibid.

12. Weinrob, M., and B. C. Murphy. "The Birth Mother: A Feminist Perspective for the Helping Professional." *Woman and Therapy* 7, no. 1 (1988): 30.

13. Mask et al., 11.

14. Ibid., 12.

15. Gritter, James. *The Spirit of Open Adoption* (Washington, DC: CWLA Press, 1998), 73.

16. Black, Evan Imber. "The Power of Secrets" *Psychology Time* (April 26, 2013). Adapted from a book by that same title. www.psychologytoday.com/em/25442

17. Schooler, Jayne E., and Betsie L. Norris. *Journeys After Adoption: Understanding Lifelong Issues* (Westport, CT: Bergin & Garvey, 2002), 82.

18. Reitz, Miriam, and Kenneth W. Watson. *Adoption and the Family System* (New York, NY: Guilford Press, 1993), 3.

19. Ibid., 4

20. Quoted in Schooler, 41.

21. Ibid.

22. McRoy, R. G., H. D. Grotevant, and L. A. Zucher. *Openness in Adoption: New Practices, New Issues* (New York, NY: Praeger, 1988), 14.

23 Adapted from "Openness in Adoption," from the National Adoption Clearinghouse, www.calib.com/naic.

24. Brodzinsky, David, and Marshall Schecter. *The Psychology of Adoption* (New York, NY: Oxford University Press, 1990).

25. Adapted from *Openness in Adoption.*

26. Gritter, 12.

27. Livingston Smith, Susan. Researcher for the Evan B. Donaldson Institute and author of several books in the field of adoption and child welfare. Personal interview (July 15, 2014.)

28. Livingston Smith, Susan. Personal interview (July 15, 2014); Debbie Siegel and Susan Livingston Smith. *Openness in Adoption: From Secrecy and Stigmas to Knowledge and Openness* (New York, NY: Evan B. Donaldson Institute, 2013), 14.

29. Siegel, Debbie, and Susan Livingston Smith. *Openness in Adoption: From Secrecy and Stigmas to Knowledge and Openness* (New York, NY: Evan B. Donaldson Institute, 2013), 14.

CHAPTER 2

1. Kirk, H. David. *Shared Fate: A Theory and Method of Adoptive Relationships* (revised) (Port Angeles, WA: Ben Simon Publications, 1984), 73.

2. Stein, L. M., and J. L. Hoopes. *Identity Formation in the Adopted Adolescent: The Delaware Family Study* (New York: The Child Welfare League of America, 1985); C. Schoenberg. "On Adoption and Identity." *Child Welfare, 53*(9), (1974): 549.

3. Wrobel, Gretchen Miller, Julie K. Kohler, Harold D. Grotevant, and Ruth G. McRoy. "The Family Adoption Communication (FAC) Model: Identifying Pathways of Adoption-Related Communication." *Adoption Quarterly,* Vol. 7(2). The Haworth Press, Inc. (2003): 56.

4. Pearl, Lynn. Post Adoption Resource Centre. Presentation for the Tasmanian Adoption Conference (May 2000).

5. Pearl, L., and S. Markham. *Why Wasn't I Told?: Making Sense of the Late Discovery of Adoption* (Post Adoption Resource Centre, 1999).

6. Brodzinsky, David. *Psychological Issues in Adoption* (Westport, CT: Bergin & Garvey, 2005), 151.

7. Watkins, Mary, and Susan Fisher. *Talking with Young Children about Adoption* (New Haven, Conn.: Yale University Press, 1993), 217–18.

8. Neufeld, Dr. Gorden. *The Art and Science of Transplanting Children* (Vancouver, British Columbia: Neufeld Institute, a training curriculum, http://seattleneufeldcommunity.org/what-we-offer/transplanting-children/).

9. Hechtman, L. "Families of Children with Attention Deficit Hyperactivity Disorder: A Review." *Canadian Journal of Psychiatry* 41 (August 1996): 350–60.

10. Schooler, Jayne, and Betsie Norris. *Journeys After Adoption: Understanding Lifelong Issues* (Westport, CT: Bergin & Garvey, 2002), 18.

CHAPTER 3

1. Singer, Ellen, and Marilyn Schoettle. *Adoption and Adolescence* (Burtonsville, MD: Center for Adoption Support and Education [CASE], 2002).

2. Pavao, Joyce Maguire, quoted in Jayne Elizabeth Schooler, *Searching for a Past* (Colorado Springs, CO: Pinon Press, 1995), Page 165.

3. Schooler, Jayne. *The Whole Life Adoption Book* (Colorado Springs, CO: NavPress, 2008), 20–29.

4. O'Shaughnessy, T. *Adoption, Social Work and Social Theory: Making the Connections* (Brookfield, VT: Ashgate Publishing, 1994), 119.

5. Lifton, Betty Jean. *Journey of the Adopted Self* (New York, NY: Basic Books, 1995), 144. *Adoption Survivor.* https://adoptionsurvivor.wordpress.com/2008/10/14/adoption-pros-and-cons/

6. Powell, John Young. "Adults Who Were Adopted as Older Children." (PhD dissertation, University of North Carolina, 1983).

7. Wrobel, G. M. et al. "Factors Related to Patterns of Information Exchange Between Adoptive Parents and Children in Mediated Adoptions." *Journal of Applied Developmental Psychology, 19,* (1998): 641–57.

8. Brodzinsky, David, and E. Pinderhughes. "Parenting and Child Development in Adoptive Families," *Handbook of Parenting: Vol. I. Status and Social Conditions of Parenting* (2nd ed.) (Hillsdale, NJ: Erlbaum, 2002), 289.

CHAPTER 4

1. Livingston Smith, Susan. Personal interview, July 15, 2014.

2. Singerland, William H. *Child-Placing in Families: A Manual for Students and Social Workers* (New York, NY: Russell Sage Foundation, 1919).

3. Carp, Walter. *Family Matters: Secrecy and Disclosure in the History of Adoption* (Cambridge, MA: Harvard University Press, 1998), 217–39.

4. Child Welfare League of America. *Standards of Adoption Practice* (Washington, DC: Child Welfare League of America, 1932).

5. Freundlich, Madelyn, and Lisa Peterson. *Wrongful Adoption: Law, Policy and Practice* (Washington, DC: Child Welfare League of America and The Evan B. Donaldson Adoption Institute, 1998), 2.

6. Kohstaat, B., and A. M. Johnson. "Some Suggestions for Practice in Infant Adoptions," *Social Casework* 35 (1954): 91–99.

7. Carp as quoted in Freundlich and Peterson, 3.

8. Ibid.

9. Ibid.

10. Child Welfare League of America. *Standards of Adoption Practice* (Washington, D.C.: Child Welfare League of America, 1959).

11. Freundlich and Peterson, 4.

12. Ibid.

13. *Gathering and Documenting Background Information,* a training curriculum developed by the Institute for Human Services (Columbus, OH, 2010). [Contact Kelley Gruber, kgruber@ihs-trainet.com, 614 -251-6000]

14. Livingston Smith, Susan. Personal interview, July 15, 2014.

15. Livingston Smith, Susan. "Keeping the Promise" (Evan B. Donaldson Institute: 2010).

16. *Infant Safe Haven Laws.* (2013) Child Welfare Information Gateway. Children's Bureau/ACYF/ACF/HHS. https://www.childwelfare.gov/systemwide/laws_policies/statutes/safehaven.pdf#Page=1&view=XYZ.

17. Cook, Alexandra, PhD, et al. Complex Trauma in Children and Adolescents, National Child Traumatic Stress Network, www.NCTSNet.org, 2003

18. Adapted from *Trust-Based Parenting* DVD, www.child.tcu.edu.

19. This tool was developed by the Chadwick Center for Children and Families in partnership with the National Center for Child Traumatic Stress and is free for use. To obtain permission to use the Child Welfare Trauma Referral Tool, please contact Lisa Conradi, at lconradi@rchsd.org or 858-576-1700, ext. 6008.

20. Personal interview, January 25, 2015

21. Putnam, Frank W. "The Impact of Trauma on Child Development," *Juvenile and Family Court Journal* Vol. 57, Issue 1 (January 2006): 1–11.

22. Child Development and Trauma http://www.dhs.vic.gov.au/for-service-providers/children,-youth-and-families/child-protection/specialist-practice-resources-for-child-protection-workers/child-development-and-trauma-specialist-practice-resource

23. http://adoptuskids.org/meet-the-children/state-photolists

24. http://adoption.com/adoptable-kids/

25. http://www.holtinternational.org/waitingchild/photolisting

26. Ibid.

27. Freundlich and Peterson, 70.

CHAPTER 5

1. Child Welfare Information Gateway. *Parenting Your Adopted Preschooler* (Washington, DC: U.S. Department of Health and Human Services, 2009).
2. Ibid.
3. Child Welfare Information Gateway. *Parenting Your Adopted School-Age Child* (Washington, DC: U.S. Department of Health and Human Services, 2009).
4. Ibid.
5. Ibid.

CHAPTER 6

1. *Caring for Children Who Have Experienced Trauma: A Workshop for Resource Parents* (2010). These resources are available from the National Children Traumatic Stress Network. www.nctsn.org
2. Beckett, Celia, Jenny Castle, et al. "The Experience of Adoption: The Association Between Communicative Openness and Self-Esteem in Adoption." *Adoption and Fostering*, Vol. 32, Number I (2008): 29.
3. Ibid., 36.
4. Wrobel, G., J. Kohler, H. Grotevant, and R. McRoy. "The Family Communication (FAC) Model: Identifying Pathways of Adoption-Related Communication." *Adoption Quarterly*, Vol. 7(2) (2003): 77.
5. Ibid., 34.
6. Ibid., 35.
7. Ibid., 35.
8. Gritter, James. *The Spirit of Open Adoption* (Washington, DC: Child Welfare League of America, 1997)
9. Brodzinsky, David. *Psychological Issues in Adoption* (Santa Barbara, CA: Praeger, 2005), 149.
10. Kaplan Roszia, Sharon, and Deborah Silverstein. "The Seven Core Issues of Adoption," workshop presented at the American Adoption Congress conference, April, 1988.
11. Bourguignon, Jean Pierre, and Ken Watson. *After Adoption* (Illinois Department of Children and Family Services, 1987).
12. Anderson, Robert. *Second Choices: Growing Up Adopted* (Chesterfield, MO: Badger Press, 1993).
13. Fossum, Merle quoted in Lewis B. Smede, *Shame and Grace: Healing the Shame We Don't Deserve* (San Francisco, CA: Harper and Row, 1993), 4.
14. Kaufman, Gershen quoted in Fossum and Smede, 7.
15. Kirk, H. D. *Looking Back, Looking Forward: An Adoptive Father's Sociological Testament* (Indianapolis, IN: Perspectives Press, 1995), 11–12.
16. Paddock, Dee. *Affirmations for Conscious Living as Adoptive Families* (Highlands Ranch, CO: Families with a Difference, 1998). www. adopting.org.

17. Quoted in David Brodzinsky and Marshall Schechter, *The Psychology of Adoption* (New York, NY: Oxford University Press, 1990), 19.

18. Ibid.

19. Brodzinsky, David quoted in Jayne Schooler, *The Whole Life Adoption Book* (Colorado Springs, CO: Pinon Press, 2006), 26.

20. Ibid.

21. Ibid.

22. Ibid.

23. The assessment questionnaire is adapted from the work of Dr. H. David Kirk and Dr. Hal Grotevant. Available from On Demand Service, Authors Guild, New York, NY 10036.

CHAPTER 7

1. Adapted from website: Holt International Children's Services, last accessed January 12, 2015, http://www.holtinternational.org/media/language.shtml (2014).

2. Severson, Randolph. "Talking to Your Adopted Adolescent about Adoption." In *A Collection of the Best Articles on Talking with Kids About Adoption: Best of PACT Press* (San Francisco, CA: PACT Press, 1998), 33.

3. van Gulden, Holly. "Talking with Children About Difficult Birth History." In *A Collection of the Best Articles on Talking with Kids About Adoption: Best of PACT Press* (San Francisco, CA: PACT Press, 1998), 36–37.

4. Wrobel, Gretchen, et al. "The Family Adoption Communication (FAC) Model: Identifying Pathways of Adoption-Related Communication." *Adoption Quarterly,* Vol. 7(2) (2003): 59.

5. Hall, Beth. "Grief." In *A Collection of the Best Articles on Talking with Kids About Adoption: Best of PACT Press* (San Francisco, CA: PACT Press, 1998), 20–22.

CHAPTER 8

1. Severson, Randolph. *To Bless Him Unaware: The Adopted Child Conceived by Rape* (Dallas, TX: House of Tomorrow, 1992), 4.

2. Schooler, Dr. David, from Becoming a Trauma Competent Healing Caregiver, an international training curriculum, 2015.

3. Keck, Greg. "Affirming the Hurt Adoptee's Reality." *Jewel among Jewell Adoption News*, Spring 1999.

4. Keck, Greg. Personal interview, May 12, 1999.

5. Ibid.

6. Neufeld, Dr. Gordon. "The Adaptive Process," Intensive I, 2013, www.neufeldinstitute.org.

7. Neurobehavioral Concepts, last accessed January 12, 2015, http://www.neurobx.com/your-tears-are-toxic-chemical-leaks/.

8. Paddock, Dee. Personal interview, May 29, 1999.

9. Ibid.

10. Schooler, Jayne. *Searching for a Past* (Colorado Springs, CO: Pinon Press, 1995), 91.

11. Keck, Greg. Personal interview, May 29, 1999.

12. Paddock, Dee. Personal interview, May 29, 1999.

13. Severson, Randolph. *To Bless Him Unaware: The Adopted Child Conceived by Rape* (Dallas, TX: House of Tomorrow, 1992), 4.

14. Fahlberg, Vera. E-mail correspondence, July 15, 1999.

15. Pelleg, Sue. Phone interview, July 21, 1999.

16. Severson, 11-12.

17. Ibid. For a more complete treatment of the subject, contact House of Tomorrow, 4209 McKinney Ave., Dallas, TX 75205.

18. Adapted from Psalm 139, *The Life Application Bible* (Wheaton, IL: Tyndale House Publishers, 1991).

CHAPTER 9

1. Rose, Richard. Life Story Therapy with Traumatized Children, Foreword, http://www.jkp.com/blog/2012/06/foreword-to-life-story-therapy-with-traumatized-children-by-bruce-perry/.

2. http://www.jkp.com/blog/2012/02/interview-vera-fahlberg-a-childs-journey-through-placement/

3. Goodman, Denise. "Seven Reasons Why Children Need a Lifebook." In Jayne Schooler and Betsy Keefer, *Mystery History: Helping Adopted Children Understand the Past.* A training curriculum for foster and adopted parents. (Columbus, OH: Institute for Human Services, 1998).

4. Schooler and Keefer (Smalley).

5. http://www.adoptionlifebooks.com/.

6. Rycus, Judith, and Ronald Hughes. *Field Guide to Child Welfare* (Washington: DC: CWLA Press, Columbus, OH: Institute for Human Services, 1998).

7. Adapted with permission, from Fahlberg, *A Child's Journey Through Placement* (Indianapolis, IN: Perspectives Press, 1991), 341–42.

8. Rycus and Hughes, 978.

9. Ibid.

10. Schooler, Jayne, and Tom Atwood. *The Whole Life Adoption Book* (Colorado Springs, CO: Navpress, 2008), 188.

11. Fahlberg, Vera. Phone interview, July 13, 1999.

12. Fahlberg. *Child's Journey*, 356.

13. Ibid.

14. Ibid.

15. Fahlberg. *Child's Journey*, 356.

16. Brohl, Kathryn. *Working with Traumatized Children* (Washington, DC: CWLA Press, 1996).

17. The story is taken entirely from Fahlberg, *Child's Journey*, and is used with permission of the author.

18. Anthony, Beth. "A Place for Mike." *Guideposts Magazine*, July 1999. Used with permission.

19. Sue Pelleg, LISW, MSSA, has had extensive experience working with children, first as an elementary school teacher then as a caseworker and therapist.

20. As cited in Fahlberg, *Child's Journey*, 46.

21. Ibid. The questions and the cards were adapted from Dr. Anthony's suggested list. Some additions were made.

CHAPTER 10

1. Goodman, Denise, and Dan Houston. *Cultural Issues in Permanency Planning* (Created by the Institute for Human Services for the Ohio Child Welfare Training Program, 2011), 13.

2. Vandivere, Sharon, Karin Malm, and Amy McKlindon. "Adoption USA: Summary and Highlights of a Charbook on the National Survey of Adoptive Parents." *Adoption Advocate*, No. 22. National Council for Adoption: March 2010.

3. US DHHS, (2000).

4. Silverman, A., and D. Weitzman. "Non-Relative Adoption in the United States." In R. A. C. Hocksbergen, *Adoption in Worldwide Perspective: A Review of Programs, Policies, and Legislation in 14 Countries.* (Lisse: Swets & Zeitlinger; Berwyn Swets North America, 1986).

5. McRoy, R. G., L. Zurcher, M. Lauderdale, and R. Anderson. "Self-Esteem and Racial Identity in Transracial and Inracial Adoptees." *Social Work*, 27 (1982): 522–26.

6. Brodzinsky, David, and Marshall Schechter. *The Psychology of Adoption* (New York, NY: Oxford University Press, 1998), 197–98.

7. Bartholet, Elizabeth. "Race Matching in Adoption: An American Perspective." In *Culture, Identity, and Transracial Adoption*, edited by I. Gaber and J. Aldridge. (London: Free Association Books, 1994), 151–87.

8. Jennings, Patricia. "The Trouble with the Multiethnic Placement Act: An Empirical Look at Transracial Adoption." *Sociological Perspectives*, Vol. 49, Issue 4, ISSN 0731-1214, electronic ISSN 1533-8673 (Winter 2006): 559–81.

9. Weil, R. H. "International Adoption: The Quiet Migration." *International Migration Review*, 18, (1984): 280–81.

10. Ibid.

11. Bureau of Consular Affairs. U.S. Department of State. www.adoption.state.gov.

12. Ibid.

13. Goodman and Houston, 29.

14. Ibid., 30.

15. Cross, William. *Boys No More* (Beverly Hills, CA: Glencoe Press, 1971).

16. Steinberg, Gail, and Beth Hall. *An Insider's Guide to Transracial Adoption* (San Francisco, CA: Pact Press, 1998), 28.

17. Hofmann, Kevin. Personal interview, July 23, 2014.

18. Hofmann.
19. Goodman and Houston. 34.
20. Ibid.
21. Ibid.
22. Steinberg and Hall. 52.
23. Ibid., 51–52.
24. Ibid., 99.
25. Ibid., 100.
26. Child Welfare Information Gateway. *Transracial and Transcultural Adoption* (2014). https://www.childwelfare.gov/pubs/f_trans.cfm.
27. Andersen, M., H. Taylor, and K. Logio. *Sociology: The Essentials*, 8th ed. (Cengage Learning, Independence, KY, 2014), 424.
28. McIntosh, Peggy. *White Privilege: Unpacking the Invisible Backpack* (1989). https://www.isr.umich.edu/home/diversity/resources/white-privilege.pdf.
29. Steinberg and Hall, 393.
30. Hofmann.

CHAPTER 11

1. Irma Herrera, director of Multicultural Education and Training Advocacy, Inc., in the San Francisco area.
2. Census Bureau. Table CH-1, Living arrangements of children under 18 years old: 1960 to the present. From http://www.census.gov/population/socdemo/hh-fm/ch1.xls.
3. Hamilton, L., S. Cheng, and B. Powell. "Adoptive Parents, Adaptive Parents: Evaluating the Importance of Biological Ties for Parental Investment." *American Sociological Review*, 72 (2007): 95–116.
4. Kreider, Rose M., and Renee Ellis. "Living Arrangements of Children: 2009." *Current Population Reports,* U.S. Census Bureau, Washington, DC (2011): 70–126.
5. Ibid.
6. U.S. Department of Health and Human Services. "National Study of Protective, Preventive and Reunification Services Delivered to Children and their Families." U.S. Government Printing Office, Washington, DC (1997).
7. "Keeping the Family Tree Intact Through Kinship Care." National Adoption Information Clearinghouse, Washington, DC (1999).
8. Ibid.
9. Ibid.
10. Maza, Penelope. "Patterns of Relative Adoption." *Roundtable,* Volume 20, Number 1. National Child Welfare Resource Center for Adoption, 2006.
11. Child Welfare Information Gateway. "Major Federal Legislation Concerned with Child Protection, Child Welfare, and Adoption." U.S. Department of Health and Human Services, Children's Bureau, Washington, DC (2012).

12. Child Welfare Information Gateway. "Placement of Children with Relatives." U.S. Department of Health and Human Services, Children's Bureau, Washington, DC (2013).

13. Maza, Penelope. "Patterns of Relative Adoption." *Roundtable,* Volume 20, Number 1. National Child Welfare Resource Center for Adoption: 2006.

14. "Keeping the Family Tree Intact," 2.

15. Hamilton, L., S. Cheng, and B. Powell. Adoptive Parents, Adaptive Parents: Evaluating the Importance of Biological Ties for Parental Investment. *American Sociological Review*, 72 (2007): 95–116.

16. Ibid., 3.

17. "Relative Adoption." http://relative.adoption.com (2014).

18. Brindo, Beth, Bellefaire Jewish Children's Bureau. Personal interview, July 23, 1999.

19. Kaplan Roszia, Sharon. *The Open Adoption Experience* (New York, NY: Harper Collins Publishers, 2010).

20. Child Welfare Information Gateway. "Placement of Children with Relatives." U.S. Department of Health and Human Services, Children's Bureau, Washington, DC (2013).

CHAPTER 12

1. Child Welfare Information Gateway. *Parenting Your Adopted Teenager.* U.S. Department of Health and Human Services, Children's Bureau (October 2009). https://www.childwelfare.gov/pubs/factsheets/parent_teenager/index.cfm.

2. University of Massachusetts Amherst. "Outcomes for Adopted Children and Adolescents." www.psych.umass.edu/adoption/key_findings/outcomes_for_adopted_children_and_adolescents/ (2008).

3. Neufeld, Dr. Gordon. *Making Sense of Kids* course, Neufeld Institute, Vancouver, BC.

4. Ibid.

5. Escobar, María Josefina, Ximena Pereira, and María Pía Santelices. "Behavior problems and attachment in adopted and non-adopted adolescents." *Children and Youth Services Review* 42 (2014) 59–66.

6. Benson, P. L., A. R. Sharma, and E. C. Roehlkepartain. *Growing Up Adopted: A Portrait of Adolescents and Their Families* (Minneapolis, MN: Search Institute, 1994).

7. Rhodes, J. Lynn. *Dysfunctional Behavior in Adopted Children* (1993), as quoted on www.lrhodes.com/adoption2.html.

8. Smith, S. L., and J. A. Howard. "The Impact of Previous Sexual Abuse on Children's Adjustment in Adoptive Placement." *Social Work* 39, no. 5 (September 1994).

9. Brodzinsky, David, Ann Brodzinsky, and Daniel Smith. *Children's Adjustment to Adoption: Developmental and Clinical Issues* (London: Thousand Oaks, 1998), 35–36.

10. Interview with Victor Groza, editor of *Clinical and Practice Issues in Adoption,* 1998.

11. Siegel, Dr. Daniel. *Brainstorm: The Power and Purpose of the Adolescent Brain* (New York, NY: Jeremy P. Tarcher/Penguin, 2013), 2.

12. Ibid., 8.

13. Ibid., 11.

14. Clark, Deborah. *Teen Talk.* www.parentingteens.com/commun.html.

15. Ginott, Haim. *Between Parent and Teenager* (New York, NY: Macmillan, 1969), 25.

16. Siegel, 11.

17. Dr. Karyn Purvis, at a training seminary, TCU, Fort Worth Texas, January, 3, 2014.

18. Illustration attributed to Ruby Johnson, MSW, presented in workshop Building Trauma Competent Healing Caregivers, February 19, 2014, Dayton, Ohio.

19. Dr. Joeph Nielson, Olivet Nazarene University, Masters in Counseling Program.

20. Siegal, 17.

21. Ibid., 33.

22. Ibid., 38.

23. Reza, Frances. "Are You an Approachable Parent?" *Parenting Today's Teen.* www.parentingteens.com/commun5.html. Kayena Communications (5/25/9).

24. Child Welfare Information Gateway. *Parenting Your Adopted Teenager.* U.S. Department of Health and Human Services, Children's Bureau (October 2009). https://www.childwelfare.gov/pubs/facSsheets/parent_teenager/index.cfm.

CHAPTER 13

1. Child Welfare Information Gateway. *Openness in Adoption: Building Relationships Between Adoptive and Birth Families* (Washington, DC: U.S. Department of Health and Human Services, Children's Bureau, 2013), 3.

2. Grand, Michael, http://adoptionconstellation.blogspot.com/p/excerpt.html.

3. Gritter, James. *The Spirit of Open Adoption* (Washington, DC: Child Welfare League of America, 1997), 19.

4. Child Welfare Information Gateway. *Openness in a Adoption: Building Relationships Between Adoptive and Birth Families* (Washington, DC: U.S. Department of Health and Human Services, Children's Bureau, 2013), 3.

5. Ibid., 6.

6. James, Gritter. *The Spirit of Open Adoption* (Washington, DC: Child Welfare League of America, 1997).

7. Brodzinsky, David. *Psychological Issues in Adoption* (Westport, CN: Bergin & Garvey, 2005).

8. Child Welfare Information Gateway. *Openness in Adoption: Building Relationships Between Adoptive and Birth Families* (Washington, DC: U.S. Department of Health and Human Services, Children's Bureau, 2013), 8.

9. Ibid.
10. Kaplan Roszia, Sharon. Phone interview, July 7, 1999.
11. Ibid.
12. Ibid.
13. Ibid.
14. The points were adapted from Lois Melina and Sharon Kaplan Roszia, *The Open Adoption Experience* (New York: HarperCollins, 1993), 332.
15. Ibid.
16. Soonkeum Cox, Susan. "Search and Reunion in International Search." Available through Holt International Children's Services, P.O. Cox 2880 (1195 City View), Eugene, Oregon, 97402; Phone: (541) 687-2202 and phone interview.
17. Child Welfare Information Gateway. *Openness in Adoption: Building Relationships Between Adoptive and Birth Families* (Washington, DC: U.S. Department of Health and Human Services, Children's Bureau, 2013), 9.
18. Interview with Martha Nabor, International Adoption Services Center, Gardiner, Maine, June 1999.

CHAPTER 14

1. Grand, Michael. http://adoptionconstellation.blogspot.com/p/excerpt.html.
2. Schooler, Jayne E., and Thomas Atwood. *The Whole Life Adoption Book* (Colorado Springs, CO: Navpress, 2008), 112.
3. Freidman-Kessler, L. "The Measurement of Teachers' Attitudes Toward Adopted Children." PhD dissertation. Fielding Institute, Santa Barbara, California, 1987.
4. "Adoption and School Issues." National Adoption Information Clearing house. Website: www.calib.com/naic/factsheet/school.htrnl. Updated 1999.
5. Irwin Johnston, Patricia. "Teaching about Adoption." *Adoptive Families Magazine,* May/June 1999: 56–57.
6. Vandivere, Sharon, Karin Malm, and Amy McKlindon. "Adoption USA: Summary and Highlights of a Chartbook on the National Survey of Adoptive Parents." *Adoption Advocate.* National Council for Adoption. No. 22, March 2010: 1.
7. Kreider, Rose M. and Daphne A. Lofquist. "Adopted Children and Stepchildren: 2010." U.S. Census Bureau, April 2014. http://www.census.gov/prod/2014pubs/p20-572.pdf.
8. Adoption Place. 2014. adoptionplace.org/adoption-statistics-in-the-us http://website-box.net/site/adoptionplace.org.
9. Annie E. Casey Foundation. Data Center. "Children in Foster Care." Updated July 2014. www.datacenter.kidscount.org/data/tables/ 6243-children-in-foster-care#detailed/1/any/false/868,867,133,38,35/any/12987.
10. McCurdy, Deborah. "Answering a Stranger's Questions about Adoption." July 2007. http://www.adopting.org/question.html.

Index

Abandonment, 6, 35, 36, 41, 42, 57, 73, 74, 77, 114, 124, 127, 203, 206, 207
Abby, 217–20
Abuse, 35, 44, 53, 60, 72, 82, 85, 101, 116, 117, 118–19, 135, 146, 151, 159
Acquaintances, 54, 108
ADHD (attention deficit hyperactivity disorder), 246
Adolescence, 24, 68, 69, 70, 102, 191, 192, 193, 195, 197, 199, 200, 201, 202–3, 206–9; early, 61, 69, 70, 73, 103, 196
Adolescent brain, 192, 195, 196
Adolescents, 16, 17, 21, 42, 73, 102, 103, 153, 193, 194, 196, 197, 203, 207, 208; adopted, 72, 193, 194, 195, 203, 205
Adopt-a-Child in New York City and minority adoption recruitment, 156
Adopted child, 16, 89, 92, 94, 99–100, 181, 183, 225, 226, 234, 236, 248, 249, 250; older, 234
Adopted children overreact, 77
Adopted persons, 11, 12, 17, 30, 36, 70, 73, 84, 102, 157, 193, 237, 244; adult, 24, 30, 34, 65, 88
Adoptees, 10, 11, 16, 17, 24, 32, 33, 36, 38, 49, 195, 207, 211, 225, 233
Adoption, 9–10, 12, 18, 21–27, 42, 61, 62–67, 78–86, 89–95, 211, 214–25, 228–31, 238–45, 247, 249–50; children's, 148; child's, 30, 236, 243; child's perception of, 80; confidential, 34, 76; domestic infant, 49, 211; formal, 179; older child, 53, 223; open, 17, 84, 88, 182, 188, 212, 214, 215, 217, 230; parent, 56; subject of, 26, 67, 103, 244; topic of, 61, 98, 183
Adoption adjustment, 82, 83
Adoption Advocate, 247
Adoption agencies, 10, 43, 91, 211, 231, 246
Adoption and Safe Families Act, 179
Adoption awareness in school assignments, 246
Adoption caseworker, 135, 136
Adoption communication, 12, 82, 83, 84, 88, 94, 104, 106, 107, 185, 214–15, 234, 236, 237, 247
Adoption communication research, 83
Adoption decisions, 43, 48, 114

Adoption disclosure, 26, 45, 46, 47
Adoption experience, 59, 84, 115, 147, 215
Adoption expert, 9, 89, 182
Adoption history, 82, 173, 183, 238; child's, 250
Adoption information, 135, 136, 137, 238, 239
Adoption practice, 9, 10, 34, 44, 45, 46, 56, 188
Adoption practitioners, 10
Adoption process, 48, 234
Adoption professionals, 47, 56, 127
Adoption-related issues, 16, 34, 67, 83, 88
Adoption secret, 183
Adoption story, 40, 62, 63, 64, 65, 66, 91, 106, 149
Adoption subsidies, 186
Adoption triad, 84, 99, 148, 211
Adoption worker, 46, 50, 56, 92, 234
Adoptive child, 18, 84; prospective, 53; well-adjusted, 216
Adoptive Families Magazine, 244
Adoptive Families of America, 144
Adoptive family, 19, 34, 40, 56, 57, 66, 67, 74, 79, 99–100, 189, 193, 212, 213, 237; healthy, 13, 121; prospective, 157, 234
Adoptive family life, 26, 34, 66
Adoptive family members, 84, 189, 215
Adoptive family relationship, 94
Adoptive father, 35, 83, 163, 173
Adoptive grandparents, 234
Adoptive home, 35, 37, 75, 130, 191, 217, 223, 224; white, 156
Adoptive mother, 19, 20, 34–35, 41, 59, 83, 106, 144, 183, 187, 189, 218, 248, 249; horrified, 79
Adoptive mother gifts, 35
Adoptive mother's decision, 249
Adoptive parents, 19, 21, 22, 26, 45–49, 55, 56, 64, 77, 82, 86–88, 180–87, 206, 223, 230; angry, 92; labeled prospective, 46; new, 234; prospective, 44, 55, 56; shocked, 29; supportive, 191; wise, 72, 206, 207
Adoptive parent support groups, 187, 237, 246
Adoptive parent support organizations, 183
Adoptive parent training, 228
Adoptive placement, 17, 34, 54, 57, 62, 114, 124, 137, 149, 151, 156, 157, 195
Adoptive relationships, 211, 212
Adoptive status, 4, 16, 92
Adult adoptees, 23, 65
Adult children, 181, 208
Adulthood, 8, 34, 37, 38, 50, 69, 75, 197
Adults, 15, 17, 23, 29, 30, 68, 99–100, 102, 146–47, 151–53, 159, 160, 183, 184, 198
Affection, 27, 191, 194
African American, 15, 39, 41, 109, 110, 147, 156, 157, 163, 165, 166–67, 170, 174, 179, 180
Age, 20, 21, 37, 59, 60, 62–66, 69, 72, 73, 80, 108, 122, 167, 195, 219; child's, 49, 148
Agency, 39, 40, 43, 44, 45, 46, 47, 49, 50, 56–57, 61, 119, 121, 178–79, 213
Alcoholism, 17, 18, 21, 124, 125
Allison, 87, 218, 219–20
American adoptive parents, 159
American families, 11, 156, 158, 159
Anger, 40, 41, 70, 71, 75, 76, 77, 78, 118, 129, 189, 191, 192, 206, 246; children's, 71, 206
Anne, 39, 40, 41, 42, 71
Anniversaries, 76, 93, 98, 106
Answers, 8, 11, 12, 38, 64, 203, 205, 216, 217, 219, 220, 221, 225, 226, 230
Arrangements, informal caregiving, 180
Assignments, 40, 78, 237, 239, 240, 241, 242

Assistance, 39, 40, 45, 78, 175, 192, 204, 205
Atmosphere, 89, 90, 91, 218
Attachment, 16, 19, 25, 27, 30, 35, 59, 68, 113, 174, 193, 194, 224, 242
Attention deficit hyperactivity disorder (ADHD), 246
Aunt, 20, 152, 178, 179, 182, 183, 188, 189
Awards, 136, 137

Baby, 39–41, 46, 49, 63, 92, 109, 117, 128, 146, 169, 187, 188, 225, 227, 248
Background: child's, 46, 82; cultural, 156, 159, 219, 220
Background information, 46, 47, 48, 50, 58
Behaviors, 21, 42, 60, 62, 63, 66, 67, 68, 122, 156, 193, 194, 196, 197, 200; distancing, 71, 200
Beliefs, 23, 26, 31, 32, 74, 86, 156, 160, 161, 162, 167, 204, 241
Benefits, 48, 49, 107, 148, 174, 177, 180, 186, 203, 216, 219, 245
Beth, 218, 219
Birth, 9, 33, 34, 50, 51, 55, 114, 134, 135, 154, 165, 186, 189, 217, 223
Birth child, 67, 78, 86, 90, 94, 99, 188
Birth children, 15, 87, 173, 182, 194
Birth country, child's, 225
Birth culture, 32, 170; child's, 175
Birth dad, 123, 184, 215, 216
Birthday, 1, 21, 67, 75, 76, 98, 133, 154, 218; children's, 75
Birth family, 18, 19, 30, 49, 57, 66, 67–73, 75, 98, 99–100, 104–5, 107, 115, 132, 204
Birth family contacts, 223, 228, 229, 230, 231
Birth family histories, 24, 48, 103
Birth family members, 17, 54, 56, 69, 73, 99–100, 101, 110, 131, 192, 203, 207, 215, 216, 229
Birth father, 15, 31, 108, 110, 121, 123, 128, 129, 130, 181, 183, 184, 218, 220, 222–23
Birth grandmother, 188, 235
Birth grandparents, 189, 215, 216, 236
Birth history, 25, 39, 53, 54
Birth information, 134, 136
Birth mother, 8, 19, 21, 22, 35, 37, 76, 106, 120–21, 144–45, 183, 188–89, 218–20, 222, 227
Birth parents, 10, 21, 33–34, 38, 63, 65, 69, 104, 115, 123–24, 126, 181, 185–86, 191–95, 221; adoptive, 228; child's, 93, 99–100, 214
Birth parents share, 222
Birth relatives, child's, 184
Boundaries, 129, 182, 184, 189, 190, 200
Boys, 26, 34, 44, 64, 138, 153, 155, 165, 166, 168, 174, 193, 207
Briana, 235, 236
Brodzinsky, David, 84, 90, 91, 214
Brothers, 22, 53, 54, 64, 111, 124, 138, 140, 174, 220, 236, 248, 249
Building relationships, 214

Cameron, 107–8
Cards, 19, 35, 76, 98, 136, 137, 149, 151, 152, 199
Care, 20, 21, 34, 37, 114, 116, 120, 122, 125, 145, 177, 178, 179, 180, 248; interim, 146, 147; kinship, 178, 180, 186; relative, 178, 186
Caregivers, 51, 60, 74, 134, 135, 136, 178, 225
Care of children, 123, 179
Carrie, 191, 192
Case record, 134, 135, 136
Caseworkers, 46, 48, 55, 133, 134, 135, 136, 139, 146, 151, 152; child's, 53
Cassie, 120, 121, 213
Caucasian parents, 165, 244
Cause, 30, 33, 62, 86, 121, 123, 125, 181, 235

Certificates, 89, 136, 137
Chantel, 74–75
Characters, 41, 148, 245
Child, 16, 18–27, 34, 42–43, 45–58, 61–65, 85–95, 99, 101, 102, 128–32, 169–75, 214, 223, 238–41; local, 120, 121, 186, 187; middle school, 21; older, 53, 85, 107, 226, 234, 248; school-age, 102; small, 116; unborn, 43, 187; waiting, 54, 99; young, 34, 51, 144, 148, 165
Child abuse, 18, 213
Child age, 82, 156
Child development, 50, 52, 75, 79, 80, 132, 246; normal, 52, 159
Child following losses and transitions, 206
Childhood, 30, 36, 72, 102, 112, 184, 197; middle, 65, 103
Child maltreatment, 50, 246
Child neglect, 99–100, 116
Child relationship, 99–100, 223
Child remembers, 103, 122
Children, 20–27, 30–31, 34–39, 60, 62–72, 76–80, 101–9, 133, 137–45, 149, 158, 178, 179, 180, 240–48; adopted black, 157; helping, 244; language of, 68, 197; maltreated, 145, 152; non-adopted, 206, 235; older, 22, 37, 45, 48, 68, 72, 85, 110, 113, 122, 129, 132, 150, 153; problem, 238, 242; separated, 30; small, 21; time, 65, 240; waiting, 54, 156, 157; young, 33, 60, 61, 63, 65, 77, 102, 106, 124, 144, 151, 203, 243; younger, 55, 76, 103, 140, 149, 238
Children's feelings, 76, 107
Children's perception of adoption, 60, 62, 70, 73
Children's understanding, 182, 247
Child's ability, 24, 101
Child's birth family, 175, 214, 216
Child's culture, 170, 174
Child's description, 55
Child's developmental characteristics and tasks impacted, 59, 62, 65, 69
Child's eyes, 59, 61, 63, 65, 67, 69, 71, 73, 75, 77, 79
Child's feelings, 24, 121
Child's history, 44, 45, 47, 53, 56, 58, 61, 99–100, 107, 110, 145, 148, 233, 236, 240
Child's life, 34, 50, 53, 62, 82, 111, 127, 152, 214, 217, 235
Child's love, 19, 90
Child's prenatal care, 53, 54
Child's questions, 64, 93
Child's relationship, 10, 223
Child's story, 50, 82, 114, 130, 145
Child's trauma experiences, 51
Child Welfare Information Gateway, 18, 243
Child Welfare League of America (CWLA), 45, 180
Child welfare system, 180
Chosen child story, 65
Classrooms, 117, 166, 237, 242, 243
Closed adoption, 12, 88, 203, 212, 214, 217, 218, 221, 222, 224, 225, 229, 230, 231
Close friends, 4, 234, 235, 236, 244, 245
Cognitive ability, 63, 64
College, 74, 75, 79, 187, 207
Color, 41, 107, 156, 158, 159, 160, 161, 169, 172, 173, 175, 218; child of, 164, 166, 167, 175; children of, 157, 165, 167, 170, 171, 172; family of, 172, 173, 175
Communication, 16, 23, 24, 25, 82, 83, 94, 185, 196, 197, 202, 212, 214, 225, 235; adoptive father/child, 83; level of, 82, 83; open, 12, 16, 22, 91, 139, 207, 215, 217
Communication plans, 185
Community, 159, 164, 165, 166, 167, 172, 177, 187, 193, 237, 238, 241, 246, 247, 250

Community newspapers, 136, 137
Complex developmental trauma, 50, 51
Complexities, 22, 97, 202
Concepts, 34, 60, 62–63, 66, 67, 101, 103, 129, 139, 161, 178, 236–37
Confidentiality, 5, 13, 45, 234
Conflict, 34, 35, 73, 92, 158, 160, 179, 198, 206, 223, 242, 243; parent-child, 92
Consequences, 13, 15, 16, 17, 19, 21, 23, 24, 25, 27, 72, 74, 166, 168, 202
Constellation, term adoption, 211, 233
Contact, 53, 54, 119, 140, 182, 185, 186, 187, 188, 211, 212–18, 222, 223, 235, 236; level of, 161, 223, 224, 236
Context, historical, 119
Control, 3, 4, 37, 41, 70, 71, 73, 75, 78, 79, 80, 125, 129, 166, 206
Conversation, 88, 90, 97, 98, 104, 106, 110, 115, 143, 173, 196, 220, 228, 230, 234
Co-parenting, 184
Coping styles, 88, 94, 95
Counselors, post-adoption, 24, 203
Country, 44, 47, 49, 57, 78, 114, 115, 158, 178, 203, 205, 225, 226, 227; child's, 115
Courts, 121, 133, 149, 151, 178, 179, 212, 233
Cousin, 1, 23, 38, 89, 182, 183
Crisis, 16, 35, 37, 49, 92, 94, 106
Critical incidents, 161–62, 167, 168, 174, 237, 250
Cultural issues, 155, 158, 159, 173
Cultures, 32, 34, 36, 156, 160, 161, 162, 169, 170–71, 174, 177, 179, 180, 225, 226
CWLA. *See* Child Welfare League of America

Daddy, 116, 118, 120, 121, 145, 151; first, 122, 123
Danger, 51, 166
Darlene, 183, 184
David, 3, 44, 216, 234, 235
Decisions, 37, 38, 44, 45, 71, 114, 115, 166, 187, 188, 189, 238, 239, 241, 247
Department of Health and Human Services, 134
Depression, 17, 34, 74, 123, 124, 243
Development, 9, 10, 85, 89, 92, 132, 133, 135, 136, 162, 167, 168, 170, 171, 195–96; child's, 47, 52, 75, 84; neurodevelopment, 52, 145; psychosocial, 52
Developmental checklist, 51, 52
Developmental history, child's, 53
Developmental level, child's, 102
Developmental stage, 59, 61, 63, 64, 65, 67, 69, 70, 71, 73, 75, 77, 79
Developmental tasks, 79, 80
Differences, 82, 88, 89, 90, 91, 92, 94, 157, 160, 161, 162, 167, 193, 219, 223
Disclosure, 3, 10, 44, 47, 56, 112
Disconnectedness, 36, 38, 92
Discrimination, 17, 155, 160, 161, 164, 167, 168, 172, 173, 175, 244
Disloyal, 19, 26, 30, 67, 68, 73, 76, 98
Distort information, 20, 183, 190
Dominant culture, 162
Drugs, 20, 25, 113, 116–17, 124, 125, 182; history of, 53, 54
Dysfunctional behavior, 21, 194, 199

Early adolescents, 69, 70
Educational Information, 136, 137
Educators, 237, 239, 240, 242, 246, 247
Elizabeth, 216, 217
Emancipation, 63, 72, 73, 79, 193, 207
Emotions, 7, 25, 34, 118, 149, 150, 151, 202, 214, 225, 228; adoption-related, 84, 215
Empathy, 91, 94, 202
Ethnicity, 23, 32, 33, 41, 69, 156, 169, 180, 193

European children, 158
Evening, 43, 44, 79, 126, 170
Events, 3, 5, 33, 43, 89, 107, 112, 114, 143, 218, 219
Exercise control, 71, 206
Expectations, child's, 222, 226, 231; realistic, 48
Experience, child's, 86, 171; first, 73
Extended family, 39, 53, 54, 77, 179, 180, 182, 183, 186, 187, 188, 190, 231, 234, 235
Extended family members, 99–100, 108, 177, 215, 234, 235

Facebook, 17, 203, 227, 228, 229
Fact-finding mission, 43, 45, 47, 49, 51, 53, 55, 57
Fahlberg, Vera, 127, 129, 132, 143, 144
Fairness, 66, 67
Families: biological, 10, 11, 53, 142–43, 194, 242; child's, 45, 132; foster/adoptive, 175; lost, 77, 193; minority, 155, 175; mother's, 184; multiple, 40, 242; multi-racial, 163, 164; non-traditional, 242, 245; nurturing, 186; white, 163, 168, 175
Families raising children, 187
Family home, adoptive, 193
Family members, 2, 3, 7, 25, 26, 92, 181, 182, 185, 186, 217, 234, 235, 236, 244
Family problems, 92, 94, 118, 119
Family secrets, 2, 5, 6, 7, 13, 89, 183
Family style, insistence upon difference, 92
Family tree, 40, 78, 131, 142, 189, 240
Fantasies, 6, 8, 11, 30, 31, 36, 41, 70, 71, 91, 98, 133, 135, 148, 192; unrealistic, 30, 31, 41, 42, 185
Father, 1, 2, 3, 6, 23, 26, 34, 92, 93, 121, 128, 129, 130, 163, 222
Fear of telling children information, 20
Films, 41, 78, 79, 98, 143
Finalization, 56, 135, 136, 137, 221
Foster/adoptive families of persons of difference, 167
Foster child: adopted, 74; building self-esteem, 160; facts, 128; family, 124; function, 130; helping, 82; identity confusion, 32; loss, 144; preschool, 118
Foster child adoption, 12, 242
Foster child issues, 80
Foster child race, 180
Foster child rules, 72
Freundlich, Madelyn, 46, 55
Functions, 9–10, 160, 180, 186, 202, 230

Girls, 70, 110, 191, 193, 207, 227; adopted preschool-aged, 62
Goodman, Denise, 132, 143
Grandchildren, grandparents raising, 187
Grandmother, 138, 146, 152, 164, 166, 179; adoptive, 235
Grandparents, 21, 35, 57, 74, 77, 166, 178, 181, 182, 212, 234, 235, 240; child's, 235; maternal, 87, 164
Great debate, truth or consequences, 15, 17, 19, 21, 23, 25, 27
Greg, 26, 78, 236, 237
Grief, child's, 106, 195
Gritter, James, 214–15
Groups, 129, 137, 156, 160, 162, 166, 169, 172, 205, 233, 243, 244, 247
Guidance counselors, 241, 242, 246, 247
Guilt, 67-68

Hair, 33, 69, 71, 80, 85, 165, 166, 217
Hair care, 166
Heredity, child's, 43, 45
High school graduation, 74, 75
Histories, 20, 22, 30–31, 40, 63, 64, 70, 99–100, 102, 105, 108, 204, 239, 240, 241; adoptive, 239; children's, 68, 70, 109, 138, 149; fantasy, 16–17; medical, 11, 24, 38, 44,

46, 135; personal, 26, 243; social/medical, 53, 54, 55
History of kinship adoption, 178
Holidays, 76–77, 98, 133
Holt International Children's Services, 99
Home, 34, 35, 39, 40, 61, 63, 75, 92, 121, 127, 134, 135, 138, 140, 170; new, 35, 36, 60; white, 157
Homeland, 225, 226
Homeland tour, 115, 225, 226
Homework, 123, 136, 137, 153, 198
Honesty, 12, 19, 23, 24, 26, 44, 82, 99–100, 185
House, 8, 9, 31, 81, 87, 91, 138, 218, 220, 227
Hurt, 11, 15, 19, 23, 98, 107, 113, 118, 146, 147, 151, 205, 245

Identifying school information, 56
Identity, 11, 21, 30, 32, 33, 69, 71, 160, 162, 164, 188, 192–94, 204, 206, 208; bicultural, 160
Identity confusion, 41, 42, 157, 160, 192, 195, 239
Identity development, 91, 133, 160, 171, 220, 246; adoptive, 193
Identity formation, 16, 24, 32, 41, 69, 159, 160, 161, 162, 192, 203
Image, 4–5, 17, 20, 130, 167, 222; body, 168–69; public, 4, 5
Impact of trauma on child development, 50
Incest, 6, 127, 129, 130
Incidents, 64, 151, 159, 168, 249
Independence, 21, 63, 69–70, 72, 74, 75
Individuals, 3, 6, 10, 23, 45, 74, 161, 162, 172, 173, 174, 183, 235, 236, 242; adopted, 127
Individual's contact information, 248
Infancy, 59–61
Infant adoptions, 53
Infants, 21, 45, 47, 54, 59, 60, 61, 66, 132, 134, 135, 194, 226, 234, 236
Infertility, 10, 43, 85, 86, 89
Information, 15–18, 24, 27, 29, 38–51, 55–58, 61, 68–70, 105, 107, 109, 119, 133, 204, 208–9
Information search, 203, 204
Information-sharing meetings, 53, 55
Insistence, 66, 92, 94, 95
Institute for Human Services, 160
Institutionalization, experienced, 60
Interactions, 140, 152, 247, 249
International adoptions, 35, 47, 49, 138, 158, 211
Interview, 22, 105, 203
Intimacy, 6, 9, 32, 73, 74, 99–100, 207
Intrinsic trust, 6, 7
Involuntary termination of parental rights, 104
Iowa Foster and Adoptive Parents Association, 247

Jail, 31, 126, 130, 151, 236
Jennifer, 3, 9, 15
Jessica, 187, 188–89
Jewish, 23, 99–100
John, 34–35, 83, 107, 119, 213
Jordan, 109–10
Journey, 80, 86, 111, 196, 218
Judy, 88, 89, 184
Justin, 87–88

Katherine, 83, 92, 151
Keck, Greg, 113
Kenneth, 117, 182, 213
Kevin, 163–64, 173, 174
Kids, 19, 113, 121, 133, 155, 166, 174, 199, 205, 227, 243
Kinship, 149, 179, 181, 183, 185, 186–87, 190
Kinship adoptions, 34, 178, 180–85, 189, 190
Kinship families, 9, 143, 149, 179, 237; informal adoptive, 179
Kinship foster care and adoption, 177, 179, 181, 183, 185, 187, 189
Kinship placements, informal, 178–79

Knowledge, 11, 18, 36, 38, 42, 43, 46, 64, 66, 79, 114, 166, 183, 212, 230
Korea, 64, 78, 108, 115, 158, 226, 227, 248
Korean children, 57, 158

Label, 11, 154, 200, 201
Language, appropriate, 60, 241, 242
Late Discovery Adoptee (LDA), 17–18
Laurie, 1, 2
Laws, 49, 56, 126, 158, 244
Layer, 15, 21, 159, 192, 221
LET'S, 144, 145
Letters, 19, 40, 79, 91, 135, 153, 154, 213, 214, 224, 229
Lifebook development, 134
Lifebook/Life Story Box, 131–32
Lifebooks, 38, 67, 128, 129, 130, 132, 133, 134, 135, 136, 137, 154; school-age child's, 135
Life experiences, 43, 121, 122, 131, 143, 145, 153, 205, 223
Life Map, 76, 131, 137–38, 149
Life story, 16, 21, 116, 131, 145
Listening, reflective, 121, 201, 202
Listing, 55; photo, 54, 55
Local adoptive parent association, 242
Loss, 25, 50, 59, 66, 72, 74, 76, 77, 84, 85, 86, 90, 143–44, 182, 217; experienced permanent parental, 63; small, 77
Loss history, 48, 193
Love, 3, 4, 19, 20, 34, 35, 67–68, 73, 105, 106, 126–29, 204, 207, 224, 244
Loyalty, 19, 27, 67, 224
Lutheran Social Services of Illinois. *See* LSSI

Majority culture, 157, 160, 161
Male children care, 158
Managing communication, 211, 213, 214, 215, 217, 219, 221, 223, 225, 227, 229, 231
MARCH (Minority Adoption Recruitment of Children's Homes), 156
Martin, 122, 235, 236
Mary, 36, 170
Mask, Michael, 5, 7
Matt, 184, 244–45
Media, social, 203, 207, 214, 227, 228, 231
Medical information, 58, 135
Medicine, 11, 123, 125
Members, 10, 84, 87, 101, 170, 174, 175, 212, 215, 221, 230, 233, 235, 237, 244
Mementos, 57, 62, 136, 137
Memories, 7, 111, 112, 115, 116, 118, 119, 120, 121, 122, 124, 131, 132, 134, 135
Mental health problems, 31, 123
Mental illness, 17, 18, 20, 122, 123, 223; history of, 53, 54
MEPA (Multiethnic Placement Act), 157
Michael, 5
Minority Adoption Recruitment of Children's Homes (MARCH), 156
Misbehavior, 72, 113, 243
Misinformation, 16, 20, 56
Mom, adoptive, 31, 48, 83, 111, 145, 153, 155, 220, 228
Mommy, 116, 118, 145, 146, 151; first, 116, 122, 123, 125
Money, 116, 117, 125, 126, 177, 241
Mother, 1–3, 6, 7, 20, 24, 31, 87, 89, 106, 108, 116–17, 124, 128, 165, 249; single, 115; stepparent's, 244
Mother's care, 146, 147
Mother's Day, 19, 35, 76, 98
Movie, 36, 41, 98, 220
Moving, 77
Multiethnic Placement Act (MEPA), 157
Myths, 10, 18, 19, 22

Names, 40, 41, 106, 109, 120, 134, 135, 136, 137, 160, 162, 228, 229, 242, 244
National Child Traumatic Stress Network, 51
National Council for Adoption, 247
National Survey of Adoptive Parents, 156
Native American, 39, 41, 71
Natural parent, 36, 99, 248
Negative information, 46, 103, 104, 105, 133
Neglect, 18, 19, 20, 44, 48, 49, 50, 51, 52, 68, 72, 82, 85, 194, 195
Neighbors, 23, 40, 71, 108, 116, 117, 122, 146
Norma, 39, 40
Norms, 12, 160, 162, 242
North American Council for Adoptable Children, 243, 246
Number, 9, 30, 45, 47, 51, 92, 98, 138, 148, 151, 156–59, 178, 180, 222, 228

Ohio, 39, 40, 128, 155, 160, 182, 186, 228
Older school-age children, 147
Older teens, 73, 74, 75, 153
Open adoption experience, 184, 218, 223
Open adoption relationships, 17, 76, 182, 221, 230
Openness, 44, 203, 211, 212, 213, 214–19, 221, 223, 224, 225, 229, 230, 231, 235, 236; communicative, 12, 84; complete, 216, 236; level of, 17, 54, 193, 217, 218, 219, 220, 222, 223, 231
Openness adoption relationship, healthy, 212
Openness arrangements, 84, 216
Openness relationships, 211, 212

Paddock, Dee, 114, 115, 121
Pain, 1, 3, 16, 36, 42, 77, 78, 85, 90, 103, 105, 106, 113, 201, 202; child's, 128, 231
Pain of adoption, 110, 220
PAMY (Parents to Adopt Minority Youngsters), 156
Parental rights, 73, 104, 124, 133, 183
Parental support, 16, 17, 20, 75, 168, 204
Parent/child communication, 131, 133, 135, 137, 139, 141, 143, 145, 147, 149, 151, 153
Parent/child relationships, 6, 60, 91
Parenthood, 19, 21, 86; adoptive, 89
Parenting, 6, 43, 47, 55, 86, 94, 104, 115, 159, 170, 181, 202; adoptive, 88, 97
Parenting children, 187
Parenting strategies, 80, 205
Parenting styles, 82, 140
Parenting teens, 208
Parents, 2, 21–27, 42–43, 47–56, 60–72, 82, 84–92, 98, 99–110, 117–31, 148–49, 171, 197, 200–203, 239–49; adopted, 22; biological, 85, 182, 242, 245; child's, 170, 182; first, 121, 126; foster/adoptive, 101; kinship, 178, 180; lost, 63, 77; new, 138, 140; prospective, 45, 55, 157; real, 61, 64, 248; single, 55, 240; unknown, 11; white, 157; wise, 199, 200
Parents change, 120, 215
Parent's eyes, 81, 83, 85, 87, 89, 91, 93, 95
Parents/families, 192
Parents focus, foster/adoptive, 104
Parents matter, 191, 193, 195, 196–97, 199, 201, 203, 205, 207, 209
Parents to Adopt Minority Youngsters (PAMY), 156
Participation, 107, 169
Parties, 84, 105, 183, 184, 185, 212, 215, 217, 218, 221
Patient, 15, 16, 23
Peers, 54, 64, 73, 75, 165, 167, 196, 197, 244, 245, 247; non-adopted, 192, 193–94

Perceptions, 10, 25, 59, 107, 113, 146, 148, 153, 171; child's, 65, 79, 149, 171
Persons of difference, 160, 167
Pets, 77, 78, 134, 135, 138
Photos, 132, 133, 136, 137
Pictures, 22, 23, 38, 40, 61, 62, 133, 134, 135, 136, 137, 138, 143, 144, 229
Placement, 35, 39, 40, 45, 92, 98, 133, 134, 135, 139, 149, 152, 156, 164, 179
Placement history, child's, 138
Placement information, 134, 135, 136
Placement of children, 156
Post-adoption specialists, 105, 183
Power of secrets on family relationships, 1, 3, 5, 7, 9, 11, 13
Pregnancy, 2, 9, 10, 33, 101, 157, 165, 187
Prejudice, 160, 161
Preoccupation, 8, 66, 193, 246
Preschool, 40, 62, 114, 116, 121, 122, 125, 126, 148
Preschoolers, 21, 62, 65, 70, 102, 143, 167
Presentation, 244
Prison, 8, 206
Privacy, 5, 184, 200, 201, 229
Privilege, white, 172
Problems, 2, 7, 8, 20, 21, 92, 111, 113, 123, 168, 173, 194, 195, 200, 201
Professionals, 53, 55, 56, 130, 195, 197, 246
Programs, 78–79, 98, 186, 241, 246
Projects, special, 136, 137
Prostitution, 20, 24, 102, 116
Protective services agency, 40, 120, 121, 179, 186, 187, 191
Providers, child care, 53
Puppets, 118, 144, 148, 151

Race, 69, 155, 156, 158, 161, 166, 167, 170, 171, 172, 173, 175, 193, 238; child's, 169, 170, 172
Rachel, 3, 83, 99–100
Racial identity, 161, 162, 175, 219; positive, 155, 170, 175
Racial identity formation, 161, 164, 175
Racial issues, 165, 173
Racism, 158, 162, 163, 164, 171, 172
Rage, 19, 20, 23, 160, 202, 206
Raising children, 186
Rape, 15, 20, 107, 108, 127, 128, 129, 130
Realities, 17, 18, 30
Rejection, 11, 12, 59, 87, 88, 89, 90, 91, 200, 201, 203, 207, 219, 220, 221; managing adoption communication, 89
Relationships, 7, 9, 73, 74, 85, 99–100, 181, 184, 197–98, 207, 212, 214, 216, 221, 234; parent-child, 85, 87; romantic, 73, 74, 207
Relative adoption, 177
Relatives, 6, 18, 30, 57, 108, 178, 179, 180, 181, 186, 212, 221, 234, 236, 250
Research, 6, 12, 16, 84, 114, 180, 193, 195, 214, 238; international adoptive parents, 57
Resources, 43, 47, 48, 132, 134, 187, 225, 237, 238, 243, 245, 246
Return, 44, 56, 87, 115, 116, 123, 193, 225, 226
Right time, 107, 109, 128, 129
Risk factors, 50–51
Robert, 3, 81
Robin, 164–68
Role models, 32, 169
Roots, 11, 29, 40, 41, 49, 66, 69, 88, 142–43, 182, 204, 240
Routine, 4, 65, 166, 185
Rules, 66, 97, 102, 126, 148, 170, 184, 197–98, 205, 229
Russia, 158, 159

Samples of homework, 136, 137
School, 63, 76, 77, 117, 122, 136, 140, 171, 205, 237, 238, 239–40, 244,